IN SCORING POSITION

40 Years of a Baseball Love Affair

Bob Ryan and Bill Chuck

TRIUMPH
BOOKS

Library of Congress Cataloging in Publication Data available upon request.

This book is available in quantity at special discounts for your group or organization. For further information, contact:

Triumph Books LLC
814 North Franklin Street
Chicago, Illinois 60610
(312) 337-0747
www.triumphbooks.com

Printed in U.S.A.
ISBN: 978-1-62937-945-6
Design by Patricia Frey

This book is dedicated to the memory of my dad, Bill Ryan.
My baseball DNA comes directly from him.

—Bob Ryan

This book is lovingly dedicated to my wife, Maxie; our
children, Elizabeth (and Lucien) and Jen (and Hannah);
and to our grandchildren, Alexa and Archer. May they
always find something to be passionate about (even if it's
not baseball). And to my pup dog, Casey, who was either by
my side or insisting on a game of catch with me throughout
my writing of this book. He committed no errors.

—Bill Chuck

CONTENTS

FOREWORD

All over my house, I've got these big, thick, spiral-bound books. They're piled one on top of another, stuffed into any spare shelf space I can push aside to make room for them. They're known as "scorebooks." And there's a reason I've hung onto every darned one of them, much to my wife's dismay: They're among my most sacred possessions.

To members of the human race who have never called themselves sportswriters, those books look more like a collection of illegible graffiti than books full of memories and treasures. But to people like me and Bob Ryan, well, we know the truth. The secret meaning of these books is buried deep inside our souls.

We have spent our lives attending games people play, and we can't just sit and watch. We write stuff down. We record it in our personal scorebooks, and it is there forever, any time we need to reach back in time and recall: "Hey, what was the count again when Big Papi hit that walk-off in the middle of the night against Paul Quantrill?" (Correct answer: 2-and-1.)

Every page in those scorebooks tells a story, and I can't believe it took all these years for two guys as brilliant and creative as Bob Ryan and Bill Chuck to recognize there's an awesome book in all those stories. As I devoured this collection of tales and nuggets, I kept asking myself: "Why didn't I think of this? It's brilliant." I hung on every remembrance, on every page, on every scorebook snippet. You will, too.

I've known Bob now for more than 40 years. I met him at Fenway Park when I was just a kid trying to learn how to be a real sportswriter and he was already one of the most towering and important figures in his profession. He and Peter Gammons were my sportswriting heroes. Even before I ever joined them in any press box, I didn't just read them in the *Boston Globe*, I studied them. Every epic game story. Every voluminous Sunday notes column. Every cultural reference. Every tiny attention to mind-blowing detail that jumped off the page. Every smart, funny, incisive quote.

Then Peter left the *Globe* for *Sports Illustrated*, and (does anyone else remember this?) he bequeathed the Red Sox beat (temporarily) to Bob. It turned out that Bob Ryan loved baseball every bit as much as he loved hoops at "The Gahden." He exuded that love every day, with every word he wrote. So any time my first employer, the *Providence Journal*, assigned me to a day covering the Red Sox, I recognized how fortunate I was to watch the legendary Bob Ryan work his beat. I hope he didn't notice me following him around the clubhouse. Not to stalk him or steal his best quotes. To learn how it was done. To hear how the great ones asked a question. To pick his brain on what mattered, what it meant, what it reminded him of.

Our paths crossed at many a hoop game, too—including an unforgettable drive one March evening from Indianapolis to French Lick, Indiana, where Bob would lay eyes on Larry Bird for the first time in person… and got so energized, he had to talk his way out of a speeding ticket on the way back to Indy. Throughout my years in the business, those days when Bob Ryan walked into a ballpark I was at became my favorite days of the week. As this book reminds us, there is truly nobody like him.

And then there's my friend Bill Chuck. Long before I ever met him, I felt like I knew we were kindred spirits, through the work of our mutual pal, Nick Cafardo. Reading Nick's Sunday columns, I'll admit there were many weeks I started at the bottom of that column instead of the top—because that was the place Nick reserved for the Bill Chuck tidbits of the week.

What Bill saw in the special numbers of baseball was something not many people see. The truths they reveal. The generations they connect. The comparisons they allow us to make. The "no way" revelations they deliver. His genius has been way too underappreciated—but not by me, lover of those magical numbers that I am.

So we should all be grateful that he and Bob were struck by the same lightning bolt that turned this fantastic idea into a book to remember. It will occupy a proud place on my bookshelves for years to come— right alongside those big, thick, spiral-bound books that nobody in my house understands except me.

—Jayson Stark

PREFACE

"Are you a scout?"

I could be anywhere. I could be in my seat in Fenway Park. I could be at the wonderfully named Epicenter in Rancho Cucamonga, California. I could be in Wrigley Field. I could be in Hickory, North Carolina. I could be anywhere watching a baseball game with my official Baseball Writers Association of America (BBWAA) scorebook in hand, and I am an anomaly. I am very likely the only person not in the press box keeping score, and this confuses people. The only conclusion anyone can come to is that I must be a scout. First of all, scouts do not keep score. People don't know that. All they know is that this guy is keeping score, so he must be a scout because *nobody* keeps score in the 21st century anymore. That went out with the knuckleball and the two-hour game.

Remember the phrase, "You can't tell the players without a scorecard?" Well, guess what? Ballclubs don't even bother to sell scorecards any longer. There is no demand. It's just not part of the deal.

I don't need a scorecard. I have my scorebook. It's conveniently compact at approximately 8½ inches wide and 6 inches long. It's very easy to pack, and pack it I do. For the past 40-plus years, I have never left on a trip without it once the season starts, because you never know when a baseball game is going to break out, and I would feel, well, the equivalent of being undressed were I to attend a baseball game and not be able to keep score. I did get caught with my metaphorical pants down once in Atlanta during a Final Four, but I scored that Braves game on a scorecard—this was a while back, such things were still available—and later copied the game into my scorebook. One slipup in 44 years ain't too bad.

Why do I keep score? Number one, it keeps me in the game. It keeps me focused on the action. If you're scoring the game, you need to pay close attention. You want to know if it's a single to left or a single to center. You want to know if it's a routine fly, a line drive, or perhaps a hump-backed liner, which I call an "SL," for a soft liner. You need to know if a defensive play is worthy of distinction and thus gets a star or two. You need to identify a ground-rule double. You need to know if the caught stealing is a 2-4 or a 2-6. And there's always the central issue of a "K" or a caught-looking backward "K."

Beyond that, when you score a game, you have a keepsake. In my case, I have lots and lots of them.

What it comes down to is that baseball is in my blood. Yes, I have a deep personal and professional association with basketball. It's the one sport I was able to play at a scholastic level. The NBA and the Boston Celtics were my journalistic springboard. I am deeply honored to have received the Curt Gowdy Award from the Naismith Basketball Hall of Fame. I would never say a bad word about basketball (other than the fact that I despise the three-point shot).

But to paraphrase Duke Ellington, "Baseball is my mistress."

Now I was a pretty good Little League baseball first baseman, but given the dual handicap of being slow and in possession of, to be polite, a rag arm, I could not make a successful transfer to the 90-foot diamond. This effectively ended my baseball playing career, except for prep school intramurals. Not being able to play baseball was disappointing, but that didn't diminish my love for the game, and it certainly enhanced my appreciation for its practitioners.

This book reflects the baseball experience of one person who, during a period that began with the Boston Red Sox 1977 spring training and continues through the 2021 season, has witnessed over 1,500 games. During that time, I scored games in 53 major league parks, 15 spring training parks, and 44 minor league parks. I've seen games in 35 states. It does not include games I witnessed in 18 minor league parks prior to acquiring my first BBWAA book. My baseball (and softball) experience during this period also includes three Olympics and one extraordinary college game between Arizona State and North Carolina.

I attended many of these games as part of my job at the *Boston Globe*. But I also attended many, many of these games as a labor of love. I built vacation getaways around baseball. (What? Doesn't everybody?)

There are oddities and historical events of interest recorded in this book that will be appreciated by a good baseball fan. It commemorates the deeds of both Hall of Famers such as Reggie Jackson and historical footnotes such as Bobby Kielty.

Baseball stands apart from our other popular team games because it does not involve a clock. No timekeeper determines the length of a baseball game. It's not over until the winning team records that 27th out (okay, sometimes it's the 21st). But the things that make baseball interesting go way beyond not having a clock. It's a game of 420-foot outs and 15-foot RBI singles. A man could throw a perfect game with 27 line-drive outs. The pitcher-batter confrontation is a complete game-within-a-game. Each defensive position is very well defined and can be minutely analyzed. I have long maintained that baseball produces more conversational fodder than football, basketball, and hockey put together.

There would be no book were it not for Bill Chuck. It was his idea. We were talking over the phone one day early in the pandemic when the subject of my nine scorebooks came up. He said, "I think they can be the basis of a book." I was initially skeptical, but his intuition was correct.

There would also be no book without his astonishing input. Nobody researches baseball better. I think we make for a nice journalistic double-play combo.

These nine scorebooks represent one baseball fan's specific experience. The beauty of baseball is that someone could have gone to 1,500 different games over that same period of time and come out with an entirely different book. I truly believe that.

Oh, one more thing. You really want to know why I feel compelled to keep score?

Because it's fun; that's why. You should try it.

—Bob Ryan
Hingham, Massachusetts
August 2021

INTRODUCTION

When I was born, my parents were much older than me. Okay, I admit that is a joke, but forty-something new parents in mid-20th century America are much different than parents in their forties today. While I was loving Lennon and McCartney, they were into Rodgers and Hammerstein (or Hart). So we didn't have a whole lot in common as I grew up, except for baseball. My mom wasn't much of a fan (she did love Joe DiMaggio), but my father was a real fan. I remember asking him who his favorite player was, and his answer was always Mel Ott. Even when I asked him on his deathbed, he insisted Ott was the greatest player he ever saw.

My dad had no baseball connections, and we were lower-middle class, which meant my dad would take me to just a few games a year, which was okay since I didn't expect more, and our black-and-white television and AM radio worked fine. He taught me to read the newspapers each day, read the great columnists, and pay attention to box scores.

He also taught me how to score a game.

- 1 is the pitcher
- 2 is the catcher
- 3 is the first baseman
- 4 is the second baseman
- 5 is the third baseman
- 6 is the shortstop
- 7 is the left fielder
- 8 is the center fielder
- 9 is the right fielder

If you learn that and then some of the symbols for scoring, you can honestly state that you are bilingual, because anyone who watches a game anywhere in the world will understand your scorecard.

There was a time when men would defensively claim that they bought *Playboy* "for the articles." I can honestly tell you that I bought scorecards throughout my life as a fan, not just to score a game, but I read the articles too.

Sometimes the articles were good, but they could never compare to the sportswriters of the *New York Times*, my childhood (and adult) bible, and the *Boston Globe* baseball writers, where I spent most of the middle of my life.

Over the years, thanks to my wonderful wife, Max, I have been able to turn my baseball passion into a poorly paid profession. But as they say on *Letterkenny*, "If you do what you love, you'll never work a day in your life." That's how I feel, and that's why in the late 1990s, I started Billy-Ball.com, a daily blog about baseball stories, history, and stats. And I would look for interesting things to send to members of the baseball media in the hope of finding work. And I did. But the most important work I did was to provide the Bill Chuck Files for Nick Cafardo's "Sunday Baseball Notes," which was then the most important, must-read weekly baseball column. I can tell you Nick was one of the finest people I have known. Through Nick, I met the greats of the *Globe* baseball team: Peter Gammons, Dan Shaughnessy, and Bob Ryan. That's the Fab Four, each in a Hall of Fame. There's Mount Rushmore.

Billy-Ball gave me not just professional opportunities, but I met some of the best people as a result. One evening, thanks to the generosity of one of those people, Alex Bok, I was attending a game at Fenway with him and another one of the greats, John McSheffrey. Alex told me that a few rows back was where Bob Ryan sat... and there he was. Bob and I had communicated via email, but I had never met him, and I was not going to miss the opportunity.

Scorecard in hand, I went up and introduced myself to Bob. I'm not going to lie, for me, it was very exciting. Bob noticed my scorecard and asked if I kept score and when I replied in the affirmative, I could tell I reached a new level in the Ryan world. Mid-game, I heard my name being called from above. It was Bob, "Bill, how'd you score that play?" Well, for me, that was as if Aretha Franklin had asked, "Bill, what are the letters after R-E-S-P-E…?" That was at least a half-dozen years ago, and Bob and I would run into each other and stay in touch electronically.

In March 2020, I caught COVID and was very sick. It wasn't until the end of May that I had the strength to return to my computer, and when I went to Twitter, there was Bob tweeting about that day's game from 1977, the year Bob was the Sox beat writer. Each day, in place of our missing MLB action, Bob would write a highlight from the corresponding date from 1977. It was great, and it occurred to me that this would be a great read for all baseball fans.

I will tell you that I had been fascinated with Bob's scorebooks for years, and I knew a book about the games that he scored would be a unique memoir. Now, here's where Bob and I differ in our recollection. I called Bob, and he was immediately enthusiastic, so much so that I pulled back and said, "Let's just think about this a little bit, and you can run it by some people." That day, Bob had lunch with Dan Shaughnessy, and that afternoon Bob called me back and said we should do it. Dan had agreed it would be great.

Bob and I spent hours on Zoom going over his games, and it was amazing. His insights, his vision, his humor, his appreciation for the game is unparalleled. Max said that she could always tell when I had spoken to Bob that day because I was in such a good mood.

One of the joys of doing this book with Bob has been finding the buried gems amongst the games he has seen. Bob is not Zelig, he was not there for every great moment and every great game, but some of the games he has seen and memorialized through his scorecards have been historical in nature. Bob knew when he had seen history in the making, and my job has been to polish the gem.

Max, a longtime editor, has been invaluable in the process. We would walk our dog, Casey (who's been very patient with me throughout), and talk and talk about the book. She guided me and kept me focused. Alex, John, Steve Markos, and Peter Meisel read parts of the book, and their encouragement was vital. There are two people who would have loved the process and loved the book. One is my dad, and the other is Max's dad, Jack Effenson, whose funeral I attended right before my COVID illness. Jack loved baseball, and he loved great writing. He was a big Bob Ryan fan. I am too, more than ever.

—Bill Chuck
Sleepy Hollow, New York
August 2021

chapter 1

THE

1970s

BOB RYAN

When the 1970s began I was a full-time *Boston Globe* beat man for the Boston Celtics, as well as an all-around jack-of-all-tradesman whose responsibilities included covering high school football and baseball, college basketball, and, yes, some major league baseball. I had become firmly associated with basketball, but those who knew me well understood that first in my heart was baseball.

I had covered random games in 1970, '71, '72, '73, and '74, but my first big exposure to covering major league baseball came when I was sent to cover the 1975 NLCS between the Reds and the Pirates. I loved every second of it, and I remember saying to myself, "Hey, I belong here."

I got myself a Scoremaster scorebook before the World Series began. It was a very different method than the one you will see in this book. The highlight of my Scoremaster book is the 1975 World Series. I scored Games 1, 2, 6, and 7 live in Fenway Park. I scored Games 3, 4, and 5 from television. Game 4 was Luis Tiant's epic 161-pitch complete-game, 5–4 victory over the Reds. I got Looie to sign it a few years ago.

I was there for the famous Carlton Fisk Game 6 homer. My job was to do the visitors' locker room, and so I was among those talking to losing pitcher Pat Darcy, who, as I recall, was polite and gracious in this toughest of moments. I next used this scorebook to cover a pivotal August of 1976 Phillies-Reds series in Cincinnati.

My world changed in 1976. I had gotten off the Celtics beat after seven years and was prepared to live a life of feature writing, some college basketball, and writing occasional columns as a backup.

But in August of that year, my friend Peter Gammons—we had met on June 10, 1968, as summer interns—announced that he was leaving the *Globe* to go to *Sports Illustrated*. Had my ship come in? I told sports editor Ernie Roberts that I was very interested in the Red Sox beat. I spent the months of August and September sharing the job with the late Larry Whiteside and was given the assignment for the 1977 season, my first big task being to cover the 1976 Winter Meetings in Los Angeles.

My beat man career officially began with my first spring training game on March 14, 1977. I now had an official Baseball Writers Association scorebook, and I would score every exhibition game completely that season, something I would never do again. I was just so darn excited. I wanted to dot every "i" and cross every "t" involved with the job.

So that's how it began. Exhibition games aside, I have scored every game, at every level, that I have attended since the Opening Day of the 1977 American League season.

That first season was fruitful. The Red Sox were a wild up-and-down team that hit 213 homers and remained in the AL East race until the final weekend, finishing 2½ games behind the eventual World Series champion Yankees. The culmination of that season was, of course, the historic "Reggie! Reggie! Reggie!' bombardment in Game 6 of the World Series.

My stint as a beat man was short-lived, however. Peter Gammons returned to the *Globe* and reclaimed his rightful place as the Red Sox beat man. I would return to covering the Celtics. But I would still have some occasional baseball assignments, and I instituted a practice that remains to this day. Once the season starts, I never—*never*—leave home on a trip without taking my scorebook because you never know when a baseball game will break out.

The 1978 highlight had to be the famed one-game playoff for the AL pennant on October 2, 1978. I went strictly as a fan.

My favorite moment of 1979 came when I happened to be in Detroit when Sparky Anderson assumed control of the Tigers and signed my book after his first game.

STANLEY'S FIRST SHUTOUT

BOSTON 3 CALIFORNIA 0 | FENWAY PARK, BOSTON, MA
TIME: 2:16 • MAY 7, 1977

BOB RYAN

Yes, 22-year-old right-hander Bob Stanley was on the 1977 Red Sox spring roster, but his 15 wins in 1976 had been with Bristol in the Eastern League, so he was flying under the journalistic radar. Manager Don Zimmer took a liking to him, or, more specifically, to his bowling ball of a sinker. And after a so-so outing (four hits and two runs in 3.0 IP) in Orlando against the Twins, the entire entourage made the 42-mile trek back to the Red Sox base at Winter Haven, where Zimmer called the press around him to announce that Stanley had made the big-league club. He also asked us not to tell Stanley until he did so himself. Of course, being good fellows, we complied.

"I doubt if I'll sleep much tonight," Stanley said after getting the official news. "I know there is always a chance if you get to spring training to make the club. I just wanted to make a good showing."

There was a hierarchy surrounding nighttime activity in Winter Haven. The established people frequented a fine bar/restaurant called "Christy's." The scrubeenies and minor leaguers gravitated to another "earthier bar," whose name I cannot recall. That night I was in that bar with my friend George Kimball of the rival *Boston Herald*. Who do we see having a beer across the bar from his but the newest member of the Boston Red Sox, young Mr. Stanley? George and I amble over to buy the lad a celebratory beer.

A grateful Bob Stanley had a query for us. "What am I going to do with $20,000?" he said.

Swear to God.

Fast-forward to Stanley's May 7 start against the California Angels. I guess I was impressed. Did I really write this the following morning in the *Boston Globe*? "Ah, but the purist, the fan who thinks that right after God gave us trees and grass, he came up with baseball, had something special to savor in the form of a pitching job that might not be duplicated at Fenway Park all season." My goodness, what manner of moundsmanship could possibly merit such gushing approbation?

It was a six-hit, 3–0 shutout victory over the Angels. Seventeen of the first 19 at-bats ended with infield groundouts. From the 3rd through the 6th, this 22-year-old rookie only needed 35 pitches. There were people named Remy, Grich, Rudi, Baylor, Chalk, Bonds (Bobby, the *père*), and Jackson (Ron, not the Other Guy in New York) in the Angels' lineup. Manager Zimmer did feel the need to pay Stanley a mound visit in the 7th with men on second and third and one out in what was then a 2–0 game. Not to worry. Bruce Bochte hit into a 4-6-3 double play.

Stanley was on his way to earning that $20,000.

BILL CHUCK

How can you not love a player whose nickname is "Steamer?"

Bob Stanley pitched for the Red Sox from 1977 to 1989. He was a lifer. He was drafted by Boston in the first round of the 1974 January secondary draft and spent his entire big-league career with the team.

Nobody has ever appeared in more games on the mound for the Sox.

He appeared in 637 games, starting 85, finishing 377. He threw 21 complete games, seven shutouts, and accrued 132 saves. He had a career 3.64 ERA and 1.364 WHIP. He batted twice in the regular season and once in the postseason without a hit.

While he was no Pedro or Roger, he did make two All-Star teams, he twice finished seventh in Cy Young Award voting, and three times he finished in the top 25 in MVP tallies. But for some reason—maybe his frequent appearances, his salary, or maybe just because fans have their biases—Stanley wasn't always a fan favorite. Will Anderson, in his SABR biography of Stanley, wrote this, "As he joked to his teammates at one point: 'Maybe I should change to Lou Stanley.' That way, he reasoned, when the fans began to boo, he could just say they were calling his name… Lou."

In five appearances, totaling 6.1 IP, in the 1986 World Series, Steamer didn't allow a run. While Red Sox fans remember the look of terror in the eyes of Calvin Schiraldi in Game 6 of the 1986 World Series, it was Stanley who threw the wild pitch with Mookie Wilson at the plate, in relief of Schiraldi, that allowed Kevin Mitchell to score from third base in the bottom of the 10th with the run that tied the score. Mookie then hit that roller to first.

By the year 2000, all was forgiven (I think it may have actually taken that long), as Stanley was inducted into the Red Sox Hall of Fame.

I bet Steamer figured out how to spend that $20,000.

And as wonderful as Steamer's shutout must have been, I'm sure it was nowhere near as impressive as the question, "My goodness, what manner of moundsmanship could possibly merit such gushing approbation?"

This was the first of Stanley's seven shutouts. He blanked the Royals and Mariners twice each and the Angels, Blue Jays, and Yankees once apiece.

One of the two Royals blankings was a 10.0 IP job in which he held KC to four hits while the Sox numbered just three hits. Boston scored four in the 10th on one hit, four walks, and one big error.

His second Royals shutout was on April 22, 1987, just about 10 years after this first shutout against the Angels. Steamer was a Red Sox for a long time. Stanley made two All-Star teams in between those shutouts, once won 15 games and once won 16 games, and once saved 33 games.

While I didn't gush, that was my approbation.

One more thing...

You may have noticed on Bob's scorecard that Dave Coleman was Boston's starting center fielder. This was one of the only two games he started in the majors and the only one he played in front of the hometown faithful. I mention Dave because I appreciate any ballplayer good enough to make the bigs, and even though Coleman went 0–3 in this game and 0–12 in his career, he reached The Show.

WELCOME BACK, FREDDY

BOSTON 7 SEATTLE 5 | KINGDOME, SEATTLE, WA
TIME: 2:33 • MAY 13, 1977

BOB RYAN

Fred Lynn had missed the first 27 games of the 1977 season after sustaining an ankle injury in a spring training game against the Pirates. Wasting not a nanosecond in his season's debut, he hit the first pitch thrown by Seattle right-hander (and former Red Sox) Dick Pole into the Kingdome's right-field stands. Leading off the 3rd, he took two balls before hitting the fourth pitch he had seen of the 1977 season even farther into the right-field stands. As season debuts go, this would be hard to top, wouldn't you say?

The injury had occurred on March 24 in Bradenton. Lynn was aboard via a leadoff pinch-hit single in the 6th. After Steve Dillard reached via an infield single, Doug Griffin hit one to left. Al Oliver

7

snared it and fired to second, doubling off Lynn, who made an undignified approach to the bag. "It wasn't really a slide," Lynn explained. "I just wanted the ground to give way a little bit. My spikes caught in the dirt." He would be gone for eight weeks.

Lynn had apparently put the fear of God into Seattle manager Darrell Johnson. When Lynn came up in the 7th with a man on second, two away, and Seattle holding a 5–4 lead, Johnson intentionally walked him. Left fielder Jim Rice flied to center, and manager Johnson exhaled, I'm sure.

Freddy had actually talked his way into the lineup that day. He wasn't expected back for three more days, and Zimmer had even given coach Eddie Yost a lineup without his name. "He came to me and begged to play," Zim explained.

BILL CHUCK

Rookie of the Year, All-Star, Most Valuable Player, Gold Glover… and that was just 1975 for Fred Lynn.

Freddy was one of the primary reasons that the Red Sox finished first in 1975. It took the Big Red Machine of Cincinnati seven games to beat them in one of the most remarkable World Series of all time. You might recall that Carlton Fisk homered in Game 6.

Another reason the Sox made it to the World Series was Lynn's fellow outfielder and fellow rookie Jim Rice. They were labeled "The Gold Dust Twins."

But that veneer did not bring the gold championship ring that the team and its legion of fans so desperately sought. Despite teams that had eventual Hall of Famers Rice, Yaz, Carlton Fisk (Pudge), and Fergie Jenkins, and Hall of Very Good players like Dwight Evans, Luis Tiant, Tim McCarver, Cecil Cooper, Rico Petrocelli, Rick Burleson, and Fred, the 1975 season was Lynn's only visit to the World Series. He did make it one more time to the postseason. Playing for the Angels in 1982, Lynn was the MVP of the ALCS when he hit .611 in a losing cause to the Brewers.

On October 22, 1975, the Reds beat the Red Sox, 4–3, to win the World Series, 4–3; but it was not that game that would spell the ultimate demise for the career of Freddy Lynn with the Red Sox. It was a ruling made by arbitrator Peter Seitz on December 23, 1975, that ultimately ended the Lynn/Boston relationship. Commonly known as The Messersmith Ruling, players became free agents upon playing one year for their team without a contract, killing off the "reserve clause" which broadly stated that if you played for a team, you must play for that team the next season, and the next season after that, and the next season after that, in perpetuity.

In August 1976, Lynn, Burleson, and Fisk signed five-year contracts after a contentious spring training holdout. The new Basic Agreement was in place, and all would be fine as long as everyone simply followed the new rules, in which a team sends a contract to a player and the player signs it and goes nowhere. But the rules must be followed. They weren't. The Red Sox failed to send Fisk and Lynn their contracts by December 20, 1980, the free-agency deadline as established by baseball's Basic Agreement. Whether it was through sheer incompetence, a misunderstanding of the contract language, arrogance, or massive stupidity, the contracts were instead mailed on December 22 and the Sox were in deep trouble.

As Boston awaited the news by now-arbitrator Raymond Goetz, the Sox traded Lynn to the Angels basically for Frank Tanana. The feeling around Fenway was that this was a terrible trade, but what could they do? It was better than nothing. Ray Fitzgerald wrote in the *Boston Globe* the next day, "Excuse me while I go to the blackboard and write 500 times: 'It's better than nothing. It's better than nothing. It's better than nothing. It's better....'"

Fred Lynn, a batter made for Fenway Park (he ended his Red Sox career hitting .350 there with a 1.031 OPS), was gone. On February 12, 1981, Fisk was declared a free agent and signed with the White Sox. Two days late and two players who could have changed baseball history by remaining with the Red Sox were both gone.

Peter Gammons wrote, "Fred Lynn is a frontrunner. But you don't win with 25 muckers—you have muckers and great players, and he is a great player, perhaps the greatest Fenway player of modern times."

As a member of the Sox, Lynn had a dozen multi-homer games. This was his third and his first of two in Seattle.

A little trip down a rabbit hole

It was a huge day back on the field for Lynn in this May game when Bob watched Fred Lynn face his first manager, Darrell Johnson. Johnson, despite the Sox success in 1975, was fired midseason in 1976 and third-base coach Don Zimmer took over the reins (bringing a whole new host of problems). In September 1976, Johnson was hired to become the first manager of the expansion Seattle Mariners by their first GM, Lou Gorman. Gorman was GM in name only when Johnson was fired midseason 1980. On October 1, 1980, Zimmer was fired as manager of the Red Sox. Zimmer became manager of the Texas Rangers to start the 1981 season and then hired as his third-base coach… Darrell Johnson. Zimmer was fired as the Texas manager in July 1982, and his replacement for the rest of the season was, you guessed it, Darrell Johnson.

TWINS HAVE 24 HITS

MINNESOTA 13 BOSTON 5 | FENWAY PARK, BOSTON, MA
TIME: 3:15 • MAY 25, 1977

BOB RYAN

The Twins had two hits in every inning but the 5th en route to a staggering total of 24. And the only reason they didn't have that second one in the 5th was because second baseman Denny Doyle made a highway robbery play on a Glenn Adams smash that merited a star in my scorebook.

But the Twins' fun was just beginning. This was Game 1 of a twilight-night doubleheader. They won the second game, as well, 9–4, but were "held" to 11 hits.

The Sox pitchers were having a bit of a problem.

Game 2 was the culmination of a frightening six-game stretch in which rival batters: scored 62 runs, knocked out 95 base hits, rapped

11

21 doubles, scorched three triples, walloped 13 homers, and enjoyed one 23-inning stretch in which Red Sox pitchers failed to register a 1-2-3 inning.

In case you're wondering, that was the nadir for the 1977 season. Things did get better.

BILL CHUCK

There were 12 different Twins who picked up a hit in this game. For several years that was a Minnesota team record (for a nine-inning game) and tied many times until May 20, 1994, when 13 Twins accumulated 22 hits, again against the Red Sox, in a 21–2 win. The only Twins batter who did not get a hit that game was their DH, Hall of Famer Dave Winfield. But I digress.

The first thing that struck me about this Minnesota barrage was how few runs they scored. If you think 24 hits with just 13 runs is not a lot, you would be right. Only five times in a nine-inning game has a team picked up at least 24 hits and scored these few runs. In each case, it was 13 runs, and in only one case did a team have more than 24 hits. In August 1980, the Orioles' 26 hits against the Angels resulted in a 13–8 victory.

Gimme five

Rod Carew had five hits, and Larry Hisle had five RBI. The HOFer Carew had seven five-hit games in his career; this was the fifth. Larry Hisle had four five-RBI games in his career. This was his second and the first of two he would have in a month.

For starters

Both starters pitched poorly in this game.

Dave Goltz earned the win despite just going 5.1 innings, allowing 10 hits and four runs.

Bob Stanley took the loss, going 5.2 innings, allowing 12 hits and five runs.

Some relief

For the Twins

In the bottom of the 6th, this was still a 5–2 game. After allowing a run to make it 5–3, there was one out and runners on first and second when Ron Schueler replaced Goltz. Schueler immediately allowed a Rick Burleson double, making it 5–4 with runners on second and third. In came Tom Burgmeier for the Twins. Burgmeier easily retired Fred Lynn and Jim Rice and the side. It's no wonder the Sox would sign Burgmeier, the free agent, the following season. Burgmeier went the rest of the game, pitching 3.2 innings of one hit and one run relief and earning a save. A save in a game with an eight-run differential is not something seen every day.

For the Sox

This is a good moment to talk about the inequity accorded to pitchers because of inherited runners. Tom House relieved Stanley with two down in the top of the 6th. House, who you might recall, became a renowned pitching coach and was the guy who caught Hank Aaron's 715th home run in the Braves bullpen, proceeded to allow one of Bob Stanley's runners to score and make it a 5–2 game. In the top of the 7th, it was now a 5–4 game. With two outs and the bases loaded, Tom Murphy became the third Tom to pitch in this game and promptly gave up a grand slam homer to Larry Hisle and made the game a blowout. Three runs were charged to House and just one to Murphy, who Boston acquired in 1976 in exchange for Bernie Carbo. After Reggie Cleveland retired the side, Rick Wise, ordinarily a starter, came in and pitched poorly in relief. Wise had been with the Sox since 1974, when he came from the Cardinals with Bernie Carbo.

So, in summary: a lot of hits, a lot of Toms, and a lot of Bernie Carbo trades.

78 PITCHES

BOSTON 5 MINNESOTA 2 | FENWAY PARK, BOSTON, MA
TIME: 2:12 • JUNE 4, 1977

BOB RYAN

In case you're wondering what breakfast fuel prepares a man to throw a 78-pitch, complete-game victory in a bona fide major league baseball game that very afternoon, the answer was provided by William Francis (Bill) Lee: "Two eggs, an order of toast, a cup of coffee, and go get 'em."

When Bill Lee was on his game, the three-time 17-game-winning southpaw was a mound maestro who undoubtedly never touched 90 mph. As they say nowadays, he "pitched to contact." Hence, in a game like this, in which he struck out one (Butch Wynegar), walked none, and had no three-ball counts, he certainly impressed Twins' old school skipper Gene Mauch, who labeled it a "stylish game."

He made one mistake, and Larry Hisle hit it out in the 4th. Danny Ford hit one out too, in the 8th. But center fielder Fred Lynn brought it back. "He reached down in there, and it was just like somebody stuck a ball in his glove," said first baseman George Scott.

Some loony Twins baserunning resulted in a bizarre 6-2-5-3-6 double play in the 2nd, and, no, I didn't manage to get that one down properly in my scorebook.

TIME: 2:12. Folks hit the cocktail hour early that Saturday afternoon.

BILL CHUCK

Bill Lee pitched this game in a New York minute: 2:12 (Manhattan's area code is 212). This is one of 59 complete games that Lee threw that lasted 2:30 hours or less. Ten of those complete games were shutouts. In contrast, the Sox had a pitcher by the name of Daisuke Matsuzaka (2007–2012), who seemed to spend about 150 minutes in an inning.

Now granted, you need the other team and opposing pitcher to play along, but when you have at least one pitcher who is determined to prevent pace-of-play from becoming an issue, you are almost assured of seeing a better baseball game.

In today's baseball, the three true outcomes are home run, strikeout, and walk. For Bill Lee, the three true outcomes were: one out, two outs, and three outs. Please don't let me give you the impression that Bill was a Hall of Famer—or even a near Hall of Fame-level pitcher—because he wasn't. In his 14 seasons in the bigs, he had a record of 119–90 with an ERA of 3.62 and a WHIP of 1.364.

From 1973 to 1975, he won 17 games each season, his career high. The concept of "pitching to contact" sounds so unique today, and while it has its advantages, it also has its downsides. In those three 17-win seasons, Lee surrendered 275 hits, a league-leading 320 hits, and then another 274 hits. You're never going to confuse Bill Lee for Jacob deGrom.

The pitchers who allowed 800-plus hits from 1973 to 1975 are something you and your friends can marvel at because of the great names on this brief list. .

Rk	Player	H	GS	CG	SHO	W	L	W-L%	IP	ERA
1	Wilbur Wood	995	133	57	7	60	59	.504	971.0	3.70
2	Mickey Lolich	885	115	63	7	44	54	.449	857.1	3.93
3	**Bill Lee**	**869**	**104**	**51**	**6**	**51**	**35**	**.593**	**827.0**	**3.38**
4	Carl Morton	849	114	28	7	48	38	.558	808.2	3.35
5	Jim Kaat	834	115	37	7	56	40	.583	805.1	3.40
6	Gaylord Perry	822	115	82	16	58	49	.542	972.0	3.05
7	Fergie Jenkins	814	116	58	12	56	46	.549	869.1	3.50

Provided by Stathead.com

Our man Bill Lee had the highest winning pct. and the third-lowest ERA, despite all the hits he surrendered. And, while it's not on the chart, he's the only one of these guys who picked up a save as well.

During that time frame, the win column was held in greater esteem than it is today. So, when I tell you that Bill Lee had 51 wins, while Bert Blyleven, Jim Palmer, and Tom Seaver, all Hall of Famers, each had 52 wins, I hope you can appreciate Lee a tad more.

Lee was known as "The Spaceman." Not only could he pitch a good game, he could get you home quickly enough to enjoy the rest of your life.

BILLY VS. REGGIE

BOSTON 10 NEW YORK 4 | FENWAY PARK, BOSTON, MA
TIME: 2:38 • JUNE 18, 1977

BOB RYAN

Here is what *Boston Globe* readers got on this one. "Not since Shirley Temple has there been such scene stealing. Leave it to Billy Martin to upstage, in their own park, a Red Sox team that hit five homers and pounded 16 hits to send an enraptured crown of 34,603 away cheering an authoritative 10–4 victory over his Yankees."

The Red Sox were leading, 7–4, in the 6th. Jim Rice hit an "Excuse me" blooper to right and somehow wound up with a gift double. A seething Martin, whose growing exasperation with Reggie Jackson was well-known and an open secret in the Yankee community, thought Jackson had nonchalanted the ball. Martin sent Paul Blair out to remove Reggie from the game. When Reggie reached the dugout, he expressed his,

17

um, objection, to all this. And then things got physical between the two, with coach Yogi Berra actually tackling Martin to keep him from reaching Jackson. Needless to say, all this did not go unnoticed by the New York media.

The Red Sox were especially rude to future teammate Mike Torrez, knocking him around for 13 hits and 7 earned runs in 5.2 IP. Yaz and Bernie Carbo hit two homers each. George Scott added Boston's 11th homer in two games to the total with a 7th inning solo shot off former teammate Sparky Lyle.

A classic Yankee postscript: Both owner George Steinbrenner and GM Gabe Paul were in attendance. The next day, Steinbrenner announced, "The ballclub is not under control. To me, it didn't look on television that Reggie was dogging it." Can't you see the smoke coming out of Billy's ears right now?

BILL CHUCK

Let's start by saying it was more than the New York media who was watching; this game was a Saturday afternoon nationally televised contest. And after the brouhaha, a seething Billy Martin pointed to the television camera by the dugout and shouted, "Throw a towel over that thing." Phil Pepe in his *Daily News* article continued, "Later, Martin had his say: 'I only ask one thing of my players. Hustle. If said they hustle for me, they can play for me. I told them in spring training. I had a meeting. I told them you play only one way, to win. You play hard and give your 100 percent best. If you don't hustle, I don't accept it. If a player shows up the club, I show up the player.'"

The Red Sox had won 9–4 on Friday night. The Yankees lost on Sunday in Boston as well, 11–1, as Reggie went 0–3 and every player to come to bat for Boston had at least one hit. This meant that the Yankees had been outscored 30–9 in the sweep. Boston had out-hit them 44–28. And as a result, the first-place Yankees coming into this series left Boston in third place trailing the first-place Red Sox 2½ games creating incredible fodder for the sports pages.

Of course, it was only June. And by the time all was said and done, Billy Martin had his only World Series championship as a manager and Reggie Jackson had the nickname, "Mr. October."

FIRST FOUR PALMER

BOSTON 7 BALTIMORE 3 | FENWAY PARK, BOSTON, MA
TIME: 2:46 • JUNE 9, 1977

BOB RYAN

It was *Jim Palmer*, okay? Baseball royalty. You don't hit four home runs in one game off Jim Palmer. But Jim Rice (with two), Fred Lynn, and Carlton Fisk all went deep off the Exalted One.

But there was still a game at stake in the 8th, and the Sox lead was down to 4–3. Bill Campbell was on in relief of Bill Lee, who had departed after 5.0 IP (six hits, two earned runs). "The Szechuan scallops got me," he explained in classic Lee fashion. There were men on first and third with two out. The ever-menacing Lee May hit one high and deep to left.

Here's how I saw it: "Lee May crushed a Campbell sidearm curve in the general direction of Kennebunkport." That's me in the morning

Boston Globe. There but for a gusting wind, well, you know. A three-run jack. Except...

"I thought it was a home run," said Don Zimmer. "Then I saw (left fielder) Bernie Carbo looking at the wall, and I thought it was off the wall. Then I looked up and saw Carbo was catching the ball."

That's a lot of "looking ups," by the way. That ball was waaaay up there, I tell you.

BILL CHUCK

The first time I met Jim Palmer, I went up to him in a naïf-like fashion and said that I had just been speaking of him and had told my friends that he had never permitted a grand slam homer. Palmer was more than a tad dismissive in his response. In the half-dozen or so times I met him after that, he could not have been more gracious. He has probably tired of hearing the grand-slam oddity after the 213th time (he faced 213 batters with the sacks filled). I mention that simply if you have the thrill or honor to meet Jim Palmer, don't start with that. Come to think of it, don't start with this game either (or the next one Bob recounts).

Jim Palmer pitched in 558 games and allowed homers in just 231 of them, which is pretty damn good and good for him because he wouldn't be a Hall of Famer if he allowed more homers. I don't say that for the apparent reason of runs allowed and his ERA, I say that because of the results of the homers. In those 231 games in which he allowed at least one homer, Jim's record was 83–83. In the 327 games in which he allowed no homers, Jim's record was 185–69. In the 58 games in which he allowed multiple homers, Jim's record was 15–26.

Jim Rice (who, as Bob said, went deep twice in this game) and Graig Nettles each went long on Palmer nine times, the most homers he allowed to any of the 173 batters who homered off him. Carlton Fisk (who, again, also homered in this game) was next on his dingers list, ringing the bell seven times. In fact, the Red Sox hit 43 homers off Jim, the most of any team in his career. Despite that, in 59 games, including 57 starts, Palmer's record against the Sox was 22–16 (the Sox homered in nine of those games), shutting them out five times and having an ERA of 2.98. The Sox were one of 11 teams that Palmer defeated at least 20 times.

Jim Palmer had never given up four homers in a game before this one, and he blamed Fenway for his performance. Just go to the next page, Jim.

FIRST FIVE PALMER

BOSTON 7 BALTIMORE 4 | MEMORIAL STADIUM, BALTIMORE, MD
TIME: 2:22 • JUNE 22, 1977

BOB RYAN

Who's writing these Red Sox scripts? They pummel the Yankees, and now they hit five more homers off Hall of Famer Jim Palmer? They've now won six in a row, 12 of 13 and 15 of 17? *What?*

Palmer has a 4–1 lead and is sitting on a one-hitter through six, the only hit a George Scott solo homer in the 2nd. And then... pow!

Rice and Fisk go deep in the 7th. But it's still 4–3 Orioles entering the 9th. Rice doubles, Fisk hits one to left, and left fielder Pat Kelly tips it over the fence for an oopsie two-run homer, 5–4, Sox.

With two away, Bernie Carbo walks, and Butch Hobson homers. Final tally for Palmer: 9.0 IP, 7 hits, 5 homers, 7 earned runs. That makes nine homers off him in his last two starts vs. the Sox.

"No cheapies, either" marvels Orioles shortstop (and Pittsfield, Massachusetts, native) Mark Belanger. "I'm getting whiplash looking over my shoulder."

"Oh my God almighty," wails O's skipper Earl Weaver. "What a sight that was."

P.S. Weaver hears Kelly, an ordained minister, say that he "walks with the Lord." Grunts Earl, "I'd rather he walk with the bases loaded."

Lord, do we miss Earl.

BILL CHUCK

Jim Palmer was truly one of the greatest pitchers I have ever seen. But, oh my goodness.

Jim Palmer pitched in 558 games. In those games, he allowed:

- One homer in 173 games
- Two homers in 47 games
- Three homers in nine games
- Four homers once
- Five homers once

In 1977, Palmer had a record of 20–11, his third straight 20-plus win season. He had an ERA of 2.91, which turned out to be worse than his career ERA of 2.86. He started 39 games. He completed 22 games (most pitchers today are pleased if they can start 22 games). He tossed a career high 319.0 IP. From 1976 to 1978, Palmer made 117 starts and threw 930 innings(!). He permitted 63 homers.

For a sense of perspective, Michael Wacha, who pitched for the Cardinals and Mets from 2013 to 2020 and appeared in 173 games, making 158 starts, totaled 901.2 IP in that span. He allowed 106 homers.

Palmer won three Cy Young Awards, in 1973, 1975, and 1976. In 1977, the year of this game, he finished second in the voting. Starting in 1972 and ending in 1978, Palmer finished in the top five in Cy Young voting six times and in the top three five times.

And, on top of that, he looked great in Jockey underwear.

SEASON TURNS AROUND

NEW YORK 6 BOSTON 5 | YANKEE STADIUM, THE BRONX, NY
TIME: 2:50 • JUNE 24, 1977

BOB RYAN

Yankee Stadium, 9th inning. Sox led, 5–3. Two away, none on. Bill Campbell is wrapping up his fourth inning of shutout relief. I am standing with my friend Chaz Scoggins of the *Lowell Sun* in the back of the Yankee Stadium press box, waiting to head down to the clubhouse level. Willie Randolph hits one toward the left-field line. Yaz territory. I say, "Captain's got it." Chaz says, "Not this one." Indeed, the nonpareil left fielder had overrun the ball, which flew over his left shoulder. Randolph pulled into third with a triple. Roy White hit Campbell's first pitch into the right-field upper deck. Game tied.

We go into the 11th. Campbell has gone five full innings and manager Zimmer brings in itinerant southpaw Ramon Hernandez. I will remember the sequence for as long as I live: Graig Nettles walks. Hernandez balks him to second. Mickey Rivers is walked intentionally. Reggie Jackson singles to right. Game over. Walk, balk, walk, single. I'll never forget.

The season would never be the same.

The Red Sox would lose nine in a row, including a score-settling three-game Fenway sweep by the Orioles. The Red Sox would not win again until July 4, when they were fortunate enough to encounter the expansion Blue Jays.

BILL CHUCK

From 1965 to 1979, Hall of Fame pitcher Ferguson Jenkins led the majors, allowing 410 homers in 549 games, 3812.0 IP (0.746 homers per game). Second on the list was Hall of Fame pitcher Catfish Hunter, who permitted 374 homers in 500 games, 3449.1 IP (0.748 homers per game). I mention this because in back-to-back starts against the Red Sox on June 17 and June 24, Hunter allowed seven homers in 9.1 IP (0.769 homers per inning).

In this game, all the Sox runs came across as a result of three homers. That gave them a record 33 homers in 10 games.

A very quick Reggie Jackson story: Did you notice he wasn't in the starting lineup for this game? The day before, Jackson had an eye examination and complained to trainer Gene Monahan that his eyes were still blurry from the drops he had received. Monahan walked into Billy Martin's office and told the manager that Reggie couldn't read the numbers on the wall in the trainer's office. So, Martin, dropped Reggie from the starting lineup. Reggie seemed to be shocked. Once the game started, Yankees team president Gabe Paul spoke to Dr. Maurice Cowen, the team physician (and an orthopedic surgeon), who declared that Reggie's eyes were okay. Paul called Martin in the dugout and told him that Reggie was fit to play. Postgame, Martin said, "So when I got the opportunity, I put him in." Reggie was an unsuccessful pinch-hitter in the 9th but got the game-winning hit in the 11th.

This game ended a Red Sox winning streak at seven games. They had won 13 of 14 and 16 of 18. As I wrote it before, it was only June, and the Sox still had a four-game lead over the second-place Yankees. No sweat, right?

In case you are curious…

There were 15 occasions in Bill Campbell's career that he pitched at least five innings in relief, this was the first of three times he did it for Boston.

Also, that day…

The Milwaukee Brewers signed their first pick in the free-agent draft, University of Minnesota shortstop Paul Molitor.

AASE THE AACE

BOSTON 4 MILWAUKEE 3 | FENWAY PARK, BOSTON, MA
TIME: 2:15 • JULY 26, 1977

BOB RYAN

A major league debut is stressful enough, but consider making a mid-season pitching debut in the middle of a pennant race at a time when your team has lost three straight, and the manager says the squad is in need of a pick-me-up. So, offer a belated salute to rookie Don Aase, who breaks into the bigs with a complete-game, 11-strikeout victory over the Milwaukee Brewers.

The 22-year-old right-hander had spent five years working his way through the Red Sox system. The pitcher those Milwaukee batters faced was offering up fastballs, curves, sliders, and a tantalizing changeup that accounted for a large portion of those 11 Ks.

"I don't know how good he'll be," said Brewers' cleanup man Sal Bando, who had gone 0-for-4 with a strikeout and a fly to right I labeled as "long" in my scorebook. "After all," he continued, "he beat the Milwaukee Brewers, not the Yankees. But I'll tell you this: what I really liked was his poise. I've seen guys with a lot more stuff with half his poise."

BILL CHUCK

- Don Aase never struck out as many as 11 batters ever again.
- Don Aase never struck out as many as 10 batters ever again.
- And no, Don Aase never struck out as many as nine batters ever again.
- Aase never struck out more than eight in any of his remaining 447 appearances, including 90 starts.

While Aase had a really good first appearance in the majors, it was certainly not one of the greats. It doesn't compare to Juan Marichal's debut on July 19, 1960, when he pitched a one-hitter for the Giants, striking out 12 and shutting out the Phillies. Or to Luis Tiant's debut for Cleveland on July 19, 1964, when he shut out the Yankees, who were on their way to the pennant, allowing four hits and striking out 11 while defeating Whitey Ford. But the Red Sox fans were starved for a home-grown pitcher who could get them to the promised land and Aase appeared to be the main course.

Charles Scoggins, the next day in the *Lowell Sun*, used this word-play in describing the performance, "Aase showed he might be the aace the Red Sox are desperately searching for...."

After Aase's debut victory, the Sox were in second place, one game behind the Orioles. After his next start, a 1–0 complete-game blanking of California, the Sox were tied for first. After his third start, a Sox win over Oakland in which Aase pitched seven innings of one-run ball, the Sox were in first place, up by 2.5 games.

The team went 34–21 the rest of the way and finished tied for second place with the Orioles, 2.5 games behind the Yankees. But you can't blame Aase, who did his share in 13 starts. He finished 6–2 with a 3.12 ERA and 49 strikeouts in 92.1 IP.

Perhaps his greatest contribution to Boston occurred on December 8, 1977, when Aase (born in Anaheim) was dealt to the Angels (along with a newly signed Rick Miller) in exchange for their team captain, a second baseman from Somerset, Massachusetts, by the name of Jerry Remy, who played seven seasons with the team before becoming beloved by Red Sox Nation as their announcer from 1988 to 2021, when he passed away.

As for the potential impact of the trade, on December 11, 1974, in the *Boston Globe*, the headline of the baseball column read, "Remy for Aase? A brilliant trade." The writer, at one point, wrote, "So let's have no adverse post-mortems in a few years if Aase wins 20, the other kids are in the minors and Remy is hitting .220. This deal makes perfect sense now." Of course, it is obvious that the writer was Bob Ryan.

The Jerry "Rem Dawg" Remy was inducted into the Boston Red Sox Hall of Fame in 2006, while Don Aase lasted in the majors for 13 seasons pitching for five teams, retiring following the 1990 season with a lifetime 66–60 record and a 3.80 ERA.

In case you weren't sure...

Aase still holds the record for most strikeouts for a Red Sox pitcher in his first game.

TED COX 4-FOR-4 DEBUT

BOSTON 10 BALTIMORE 4 | MEMORIAL STADIUM, BALTIMORE, MD
TIME: 2:58 • SEPTEMBER 18, 1977

BOB RYAN

51,798 Oriole faithful had come on this sweltering Sunday afternoon to salute the beloved Brooks Robinson, who was retiring after 23 years manning the Baltimore hot corner. They didn't see much of a show from their lads, but at least they went home having seen a little history made.

The story of the day was a 22-year-old Red Sox rookie third baseman named Ted Cox, fresh from knocking in 81 runs in 95 games as the International League MVP. Batting second in his major league debut, he singled to left off Mike Flanagan in the 1st, walked and scored in the 3rd, reached on an infield single (and also scored) off Flanagan in the

5th, singled to center off Scott McGregor for his first career RBI in the 6th (and also scored), and doubled and scored off McGregor in the 9th.

He was 4-for-4 with three runs scored and a ribbie in his MLB debut. He was the seventh man to break in with four hits. "Four hits," he sighed. "I was just hoping to get one."

He wasn't through. Batting second against Yankee righty Ed Figueroa the following evening at home, he singled in the 1st and singled and scored in the 3rd. He rolled out to first baseman Chris Chambliss for his first major league out in the 5th.

BILL CHUCK

It was deemed "Thanks Brooks Day" at Memorial Stadium, and the tears were flowing. Not from Brooks, but from more than 50,000 adoring fans who were saluting the magnificent third baseman who debuted on September 17, 1955, 237 days after Ted Cox was born. Bob Maisel, the sports editor of the *Baltimore Sun*, wrote the next day, "There were some misty eyes in the stands, on the field, among the supporting cast, even in the press box where you almost never see misty eyes under any circumstances." But you can ask Bob about that.

Ted Cox is one of six players to ever go 4–4 in his first MLB game. Mike Mitchell did it in 1907. He had nine games with at least four hits in his career. The great Casey Stengel did it in 1912 and ended with 10 career four-hit games. Casey is in the Hall of Fame as a manager, not a player. Russ Van Atta did it in 1933. It was the only four-hit game of Van Atta's career, but we need some special love here because not only did Russ get four hits, but he also pitched a five-hit, complete-game shutout. Willie McCovey, who is in the Hall as a player, did it in 1959 (and he hit two triples). Stretch McCovey had a dozen four-hit games. And Derrick Gibson did it in 1998. It was the only four-hit game of Derrick Gibson's 17-game (14 hit) career.

Ted Cox had two four-hit games in his career, this one for Boston and one for Toronto.

Brooks Robinson went 2–4 in his MLB debut and was not in the lineup on his day of gratitude. Since mid-August, Brooks had been a coach for the team. Brooksie not only had 26 games with at least four hits in his career; but I'm confident that he also had at least that many games in which he took four hits away from the opposition with his magnificent glove. This is how he got the nickname, "The Human Vacuum Cleaner." He was a 16-time Gold Glover at third.

The crowd was the Orioles' largest for a regular-season game in their 24 years in Baltimore, which makes sense since it's not every day that you can thank a player of Brooks Robinson's magnitude.

ANOTHER LEE GEM

BOSTON 5 DETROIT 1 | TIGER STADIUM, DETROIT, MI
TIME: 2:11 • SEPTEMBER 23, 1977

A handwritten baseball scorebook sheet for the Detroit Tigers lineup with columns for positions and innings 1 through 12, at-bats, runs, hits, and RBIs. Listed players include LeFlore (.315), Fuentes (.305), Staub (.276), Kemp (.259), Thompson (.269), Parrish (.269), Ogilvie (.259), Rodriguez (.224), Trammell (.211)/Stanley (9), and Sykes. Umpires: Denkinger, McCoy, Ford, Merrill. Time of Game 2:11. Attendance 11,344. Pitcher Lee (9-4). 79 P 60 strikes. LOB: 0-0-0-0-0-0-0-0-0= 0. HR Parrish.

BOB RYAN

My scorebook says 79 pitches, 60 strikes. But my *Globe* game story says 80 pitches, 61 strikes. As Joe E. Brown says at the end of *Some Like It Hot*, "Nobody's perfect."

What's true is that Bill Lee said this was his best performance of the season, even better than his 78-pitch gem against the Twins on June 4. As in that game, he fanned just one (Jason Thompson) and walked none. He gave up four hits, but he faced only 28 men, thanks to three double plays.

His only regret was a "hanging slider" Lance Parrish hit out in the 8th. Primary run support came from Butch Hobson, whose three hits included a double and three-run homer, his 29th. Some of the 11,344

33

on hand at Tiger Stadium saved on babysitting dough since the TOG was 2:11.

BILL CHUCK

The folks at Retrosheet.org state that Bill Lee threw 79 pitches and 60 strikes, so one way or another, Bob was correct.

Bill Lee had authentic moments of greatness, and this was one of them. On April 21, 2004, Tim Redding of the Astros started against the Cardinals. Like Bill Lee, he threw 79 pitches, and he even threw 61 strikes, one more than Bill.

However, data like that is like when our current Statcast experts tweet that a player hit a ball 101.5 mph, 25 degrees off a 93.9 mph 4-seam fastball. We need some context. Context like this: Redding pitched a total of 3.2 innings, allowing eight earned runs on nine hits.

No more is needed here. Consider me saving you some dough on your babysitter.

REGGIE CLEVELAND'S 18-HIT CG

BOSTON 12 DETROIT 5 | TIGER STADIUM, DETROIT, MI
TIME: 2:56 • SEPTEMBER 25, 1977

BOB RYAN

Don Zimmer thought that Reggie Cleveland might have had enough. He had a 12–3 lead. He was going to get the W. "I was ready to take him out after the eighth," Zim explained. "But he said, 'I'm all right. I just got my second wind.'"

Hey, the man just wanted to finish what he had started, 14 hits, three runs, and 130-odd pitches ago. Four more hits and two runs later, Reggie Cleveland's 145th pitch was smoked by Phil Mankowski—right into the glove of shortstop Rick Burleson. Reggie Cleveland's complete-game, 18-hit W was in the books.

Reggie Cleveland was an affable native of Swift Current, Saskatchewan, who had his moments of career glory, but not enough of them. He always had good stuff, but he could have been a bit more dedicated to the task. I used to kid he was the only player I ever knew who actually *gained* weight during the season. "If I had applied myself better," he later admitted, "I could have lasted longer and won 200 games…. I had good years, but I could have been a lot better. I look back and say, 'I was a (naughty word) idiot.'"

Carlton Fisk, Butch Hobson, and Yaz (his 30th career Tiger Stadium homer) backed him with homers in a 15-hit attack. Reggie allowed a hit in every inning except the third, but he walked none and only had two three-ball counts. The most notable of those 18 hits was a mammoth Ben Oglivie (a former Red Sox) 6th-inning clout that hit the right-field roof a couple of feet from the top. "They talk about the Reggie Jackson homer in the ('71) All-Star Game," Cleveland joked, "but this one went a *lot* farther."

It was the final Red Sox road game of the season, and the final game Reggie Cleveland would win in a Red Sox uniform. No one can say he didn't work for it.

BILL CHUCK

"In Ashtabula, Aliquippa, and Azusa, there are undoubtedly a great number of box score readers gagging over their cereal this morning. For there, preserved for posterity, is official confirmation of an 18-hit complete game. A winning 18-hit complete game." Bob Ryan, *Boston Globe*, September 26, 1977

Nine to know about Reggie Cleveland and his 18-hitter

1. Reggie Cleveland pitched for St. Louis, Boston, Texas, and Milwaukee. Sadly, he never pitched for Cleveland.
2. Reggie Cleveland pitched in five seasons for the Red Sox. He had a career record of 46–41. This was win No. 46, his final Sox win, and it was his 25th and final complete game for Boston.
3. Seven times since 1950, a pitcher has allowed 18 hits in a game. There have just been three occasions since 1977.
4. In their history, the Red Sox have had two other games in which a pitcher allowed at least 18 hits and won the game. In 1923, Jack Quinn had a complete-game, 7–5 win over the Philadelphia

Athletics, in which he allowed 18 hits. In 1901, Ted Lewis defeated the Philadelphia Athletics, 23–12, and allowed 19 hits.

5. In the bottom of the 1st in this game, Ron LeFlore led off with a double. Tito Fuentes reached on a bunt single. Rusty Staub hit into a DP, scoring LeFlore, and Steve Kemp ended the inning by striking out. It was Detroit's only double play of the game and Cleveland's only strikeout of the game.

6. It remains the only 9-inning game in which the Tigers had at least 18 hits and no more than one strikeout and lost.

7. Seven Tigers had at least two hits, with LeFlore and Fuentes getting three apiece.

8. Future HOFer Alan Trammell was the only Tiger with an at-bat and without a hit, going 0–3. It was Trammell's 13th career game. His first was on September 9, 1977, when he and Lou Whitaker made their major league debuts… against Reggie Cleveland. Both singled in their first at-bats against Cleveland.

9. Reggie Cleveland's first Red Sox start was on April 15, 1974. Against the Tigers. And he pitched a complete game. But this time, he was the losing pitcher, dropping a 1–0 decision. He struck out five, walked none, and allowed only three hits, 15 fewer than in his final Sox win.

1977 NLCS GAME 3

DODGERS LEAD 2–1 IN BEST OF FIVE
LOS ANGELES 6 PHILADELPHIA 5
VETERANS STADIUM, PHILADELPHIA, PA
TIME: 2:59 • OCTOBER 7, 1977

BOB RYAN

What just happened?

That was my reaction. That was the reaction of the 63,719 in attendance at The Vet in South Philly. And I'm sure that was the universal reaction of the Phillies themselves after the endlessly bizarre events of the Dodger 9th inning turned an apparent 5–3 victory in Game 3 of the NLCS into a stunning 6–5 loss. Yes, teams have scored three runs in the 9th inning. But few of those rallies begin with a two-out bunt by a 38-year-old pinch-hitter (Vic Davalillo), followed by a double that should have been caught (why was there no defensive replacement for lumbering Greg Luzinski in left?) by a 39-year-old pinch-hitter (Manny Mota).

Want more? Davalillo was a Mexican League refugee who had last been in the bigs in 1974. Mota? Oh, that was his career pinch-hit number 123.

And the fun was just beginning.

A bad throw to the infield by Luzinski allowed Davalillo to score and moved Mota to third. Davey Lopes hit a shot that ricocheted off third baseman Mike Schmidt. Aha, but shortstop Larry Bowa picked it up and gunned it to Richie Hebner at first in time to end the game. Right?

Ah, no. First base ump Bruce Froemming called Lopes safe, and Hebner will take it to his grave that Lopes was out. So now it was 5–5. Wait, it gets worse.

Phillies reliever Gene Garber, who had retired the first eight men he faced, made a wild pick-off throw, moving Lopes to second. He was moving with the pitch when Bill Russell singled him home with the go-ahead run.

Long forgotten was the raucous crowd that had—gotta say it—"hooted" L.A. starter Burt Hooton off the mound as he walked four consecutive batters in a three-run Philly 2nd. Instead, it was all about the Dodger 9th, and Dodger pitcher Mike Garman summed it up best. "I was happy to concede. I forgot about our Latin connection. Our over-40 bunch killed 'em."

BILL CHUCK

Before you say, "What do you expect? Losing reliever Gene Garber was in his third inning of relief?" Garber had 19 saves during the regular season, and eight of them occurred when Garber pitched at least three innings. On top of that, Garber, on this strange night, had retired the first eight batters he faced before the Davalillo drag bunt. BTW, if you were wondering, from 1974 to '77, Davalillo had been playing in the Mexican League, only to be rediscovered by scout Charlie Metro. And if the name "Gene Garber" sounds familiar, it might be because the guy pitched effectively for 19 seasons in the majors, or it might be because on August 1, 1978, now pitching for the Braves, Garber was deemed the most responsible for stopping Pete Rose's 44-game hitting streak. In that game, he pitched three innings and earned that save in a 16–4 blowout of Pete's Reds.

Talk about being in the right place at the right time. Lance Rautzhan pitched a third of an inning and got the win in this game. Rautzhan had come in with two outs in the bottom of the 8th with Bob Boone on third and got Bake McBride on a grounder. It was his only career postseason decision, and he only had two more wins in the remaining 58 games of his career.

In defense of Greg Luzinski, in the top of the 2nd, Dodger starting pitcher Burt Hooton doubled to left, and Luzinski threw to the cutoff man, Mike Schmidt, who then got Steve Yeager out at the plate. But I agree with Bob in questioning why Luzinski was still out there. During the regular season, the Phils often used Jerry Martin as their defensive outfielder. Martin that season had appeared in 116 games, but only started 49. And he played 47 games in left, but only started four.

Before the bottom of the 2nd was complete, the Phils knocked out Hooton. Well, "knocked out" is a little strong. After a couple of singles, Hooton walked four straight batters with two outs and three runs scored.

And so that is the story as to why if you mention "Black Friday" to any old Phillies fan, they think of this day and not the day after Thanksgiving.

1977 WORLD SERIES GAME 6

YANKEES WIN THE SERIES 4–2
NEW YORK 8 LOS ANGELES 4 | YANKEE STADIUM, THE BRONX, NY
TIME: 2:18 • OCTOBER 18, 1977

BOB RYAN

"REGGIE! REGGIE! REGGIE!"

Most baseball fans know the reference, and every good Yankee fan certainly knows what I am referring to. With this performance, Reggie Jackson capped a season of personal drama unparalleled in Yankee (maybe even in baseball) history. I was there on June 18, 1977, when Billy Martin pulled Jackson from right field for "lackadaisical play" *mid-inning*, which resulted in a Jackson and Martin rumble in the jungle of the Fenway Park visitors' dugout, and I was there again when the season ended with a three-home run barrage in the clinching game of the World Series at Yankee Stadium.

Reggie was only the second person ever to hit three home runs in a World Series game, the other being another guy, also with a candy bar, named Ruth, who did it twice. But that's not the whole story. Reggie's three homers were off three different Dodger pitchers, and each came on the first pitch. One more thing: He had hit a homer in his final at-bat in Game 5 back in L.A. So, Reggie had hit four World Series home runs not just in his final four at-bats but in his final four swings.

For the record, the first homer Reggie hit was a fastball over the plate off Burt Hooton. The next was a fastball high and over the plate off Elias Sosa. And, of course, a knuckleball low and away off Charlie Hough. The third, a bomb to the faraway black seats in distant right-center field, well, let me tell you what I provided the next day for the *Boston Globe* readers: "His eighth inning smash off the knuckleballing (Charlie) Hough was the Baked Alaska, the Double Dutch chocolate cake, the Creme Caramel of the batting banquet."

Dodger first baseman Steve Garvey tipped his metaphorical cap to his rival. "Anybody can appreciate three homers in a championship game," he said. "It's like a hat trick in a Stanley Cup or 40 points in an NBA Final."

Fast forward 26 years. Reggie was traveling with the Yankees during the 2003 Red Sox–Yankees ALCS, and so was I. One night, we're on the field at Fenway. I handed to Reggie the scorebook from 1977 to sign during batting practice. He was startled at the sight of a writer's scorebook. He snatched it from me and scampered to the batting cage. I watched him gesticulate wildly as he proudly showed the book to Yankee manager Joe Torre, who in 1977, was the player/manager for the Mets. He brought the book back to me, signed, as you can see, as only Reggie Jackson could. Reggie, remember, is a man who once pondered aloud about the "magnitude of me." The "Mr. October" is great, but, to me, the *piece de resistance* is the "44" inside the big "J" loop.

BILL CHUCK

Why would anyone think it's surprising that Reggie Jackson is the one who hit three momentous homers in a row? After all, a wise man said, "This team, it all flows from me. I'm the straw that stirs the drink. Maybe I should say me and Munson, but he can only stir it bad." Wait, that wasn't a wise man; that was Reggie, who later claimed he was misquoted.

A wise man said, "There isn't enough mustard in the whole world to cover that hot dog." That was pitcher Darold Knowles talking about Reggie. Reggie is the one who said, "The only reason I don't like playing in the World Series is I can't watch myself play."

It was the wise man who said, "The best thing about being a Yankee is getting to watch Reggie Jackson play every day. The worst thing about being a Yankee? Getting to watch Reggie Jackson play every day." That was wise guy Graig Nettles talking about his teammate.

What Reggie said while playing for the A's in 1973 was, "If I was playing in New York, they'd name a candy bar after me." And it was Reggie's teammate Catfish Hunter who said, "When you unwrap a Reggie bar, it tells you how good it is."

Jackson had 42 multi-homer regular-season games but only had two three-homer games in his career, not including this one. His only other postseason game with as many as two homers was in the 1971 ALCS, when he was on the A's and facing the O's. Reggie had four Series games in which he had three hits and one in which he had four.

In this momentous finale, Reggie's three home runs tied him with Babe Ruth for the most hit in a game. Since that game, Albert Pujols (2011) and Pablo Sandoval (2017) have had three-homer Series games. Honestly, nobody cares. And Reggie's remain the most ever hit consecutively.

His World Series total of five homers was another record tied by Chase Utley (2009) and George Springer (2017). But nobody shouts "Chase! Chase! Chase!" or "George! George! George!" Despite the fact that they are two very likable players.

In that Series, Reggie Jackson broke or tied eight World Series batting records against the Dodgers (and broke the heart of young Dodgers fan Buster Olney). He was amazing. Even now, watch the video and you will see him fill the space as few could ever do.

When Jackson signed his Yankee contract, he said, "I didn't come to New York to become a star, I brought my star here."

He came to New York to become "Mr. October."

And by the way…
There were four homers in this game hit by Reggie, three by Reggie Jackson and one by Reggie Smith.

And one more thing…
This Reggie Jackson performance brought Billy Martin's only World Series championship as a manager.

UNI(QUE) CYCLE

CLEVELAND 13 BOSTON 4 | FENWAY PARK, BOSTON, MA
TIME: 2:52 • APRIL 22, 1978

BOB RYAN

Cleveland opened with five in the top of the 1st and finished with six, shall we say, pad runs, in the 8th. But the real story was cleanup man Andre Thornton, who had a cycle off four different Red Sox pitchers.

The big guy had an infield single off starter Allen Ripley in the 1st, a triple off Bob Stanley in the 2nd, a homer off Jim Wright in the 7th, and a double off Tom Burgmeier in the 8th. At age 28, he was in the prime of a 14-year career with the Cubs, Expos, and Cleveland. He would finish with 33 homers, 105 RBI, and an .893 OPS that year. His victims were two pretty much forgotten right-handers in Ripley (2–5, 5.55 in '78) and Wright (9–4, 3.82 in a two-year Sox career), a long-time Red

Sox stalwart in Stanley, and a reliable lefty reliever for five clubs over a 17-year big-league career in Burgmeier.

It was Jacket Day at Fenway, and a crowd of 36,005 was not just the fourth-highest Fenway crowd ever but also the biggest home turnout since 1956. Cleveland's triumph ended an eight-game Boston winning streak and gave the Sox their first home loss of the season.

Sure, the Sox lost, but I'm wondering if any of those 36,005 in attendance went home realizing what a rare baseball treat Andre Thornton had given them. Well, at least they got a jacket.

BILL CHUCK

Hitting for the cycle is an oddity. It's a fluke. It's meaningless. Yet, watching someone hit for the cycle is fun. Perhaps some of you deeply entrenched in the "Statcast Era" might sometimes forget, but in the words of Mike Veeck, Bill's son, and minor league baseball team owner, "Fun is good."

Cycles are not hit that frequently. In 1933 and 2009, there were eight each, the most for any season. In the pandemic-shortened 2020 season, there were none. There seems to be no reason as to their frequency. For example, in 2015, there were four, and in 2016 there were three. That total of seven equaled the number of cycles hit in 2017.

Andre the Big Guy

Andre Thornton was a big guy, a solid hitter, and someone you would be surprised to find hitting 22 triples in his 14-season career. He was just not that kind of baserunner.

- Andre hit his 22 triples in 22 different games.
- He homered and tripled in five games, including this one.
- He doubled and tripled in five games, including this one.
- He fell shy of a cycle in five games because he didn't triple.
- He never fell a single shy of the cycle.
- He never fell a double shy of the cycle.
- He twice fell a homer shy of the cycle.
- He tripled in four games against the Red Sox.
- Cleveland was ahead 12–10 when he tripled.

In 1977, Thornton hit .404 against Boston with five homers and three triples, and in the first four games against the Sox in 1978, Thornton was 8–14 with three homers. All of which led Boston manager Don Zimmer to tell the A.P., "He'd probably lead the league in everything if he played 162 games against us."

Since this cycle, the Red Sox have allowed had just two cycles (Mark Ellis in 2007 off two pitchers, Bengie Molina in 2010—off three pitchers).

And since we are talking about a rare moment, allow me to present:

Ripley, Believe It or Not
In this game, Sox starter Allen Ripley faced five batters, allowed four hits and a walk, and five earned runs. There have been 11 times that a Sox starter retired no one and allowed at least five earned runs. *There have been none since Ripley.*

Nine to Know—Cleveland hitters who have hit for the cycle

Player	Date	Opp	Result	AB	R	H	RBI	Pitchers faced for the cycle
Jake Bauers	6/14/2019	DET	W	5	2	4	4	3
Rajai Davis	7/2/2016	TOR	L	5	2	4	2	3
Travis Hafner	8/14/2003	MIN	W	5	3	4	2	2
Andre Thornton	**4/22/1978**	**BOS**	**W**	**5**	**2**	**4**	**2**	**4**
Tony Horton	7/2/1970	BAL	W	5	2	4	2	3
Larry Doby	6/4/1952	BOS	L	5	3	4	6	2
Odell Hale	7/12/1938	WSH	L	5	1	4	5	3
Earl Averill	8/17/1933	PHA	W	4	4	4	3	3
Bill Bradley	9/24/1903	WSH	W	5	4	5	3	1

Only Andre Thornton cycled against four different pitchers, and Bob Ryan was our witness. One question remains, did he get a jacket that day?

One Wise thing to know...

Rick Wise won for Cleveland, his first win with the team that acquired him at the end of March from Boston, along with Ted Cox, Bo Diaz, and Mike Paxton, for Dennis Eckersley and Fred Kendall. That season, Wise went 9–19, leading the AL in losses.

PLAYOFF ASSURED

BOSTON 5 TORONTO 0 | FENWAY PARK, BOSTON, MA
TIME: 2:11 • OCTOBER 1, 1978

BOB RYAN

It was 1978. No internet. No smartphones. The good news came via transistor radios.

Luis Tiant was taking care of business on the mound, holding the Blue Jays to two hits. Rick Burleson hit his fifth and Jim Rice, having a monster year, hit his 46th. All this was Part A.

Part B was keeping up with the Bronx Bombers, who were concluding their season against Cleveland. A Red Sox win plus a Yankee loss would force a Monday one-game playoff for the AL East title. A radio station in southeast Massachusetts was carrying the Yankee games that year, and the Fenway bleachers were ground zero in Boston. Cleveland was pounding the Yanks, and Rick Waits was shutting them down. The

49

news traveled through the park via transistor and cheers. Many loud cheers.

Jerry Remy had been a 14-year-old fan sitting in the right-field grandstand when the Red Sox had won the pennant exactly 11 years earlier to the day. Now he was the Red Sox starting second baseman. "I was at second, playing Roy Howell, and I heard that screaming in the bleachers," he explained. "I knew Cleveland had done something. That game flashed across, and my knees started shaking. I can't believe I've gone from the grandstand to second base."

Cleveland won, 9–2. There would be a Red Sox–Yankee game at Fenway the following day.

BILL CHUCK

I always wondered what it must have been like to be a Brooklyn Dodgers fan, particularly on October 3, 1951. Picture waking up and reading the newspaper from that morning and reading the headline, "There Was a Kid From Woonsocket" and the subhead read, "Labine's curved rocket, Goes right in pocket, But Jints cant sock it."

This was not your *Daily Variety*, but the *Brooklyn Eagle*. Harold C. Burr wrote, "The little Rhode Island town of Woonsocket took on bright colors on the map of the United States yesterday, because at the Polo Grounds one of its rising young citizens shut out the Giants, 10 to 0, for the Dodgers to even the playoff for the National League pennant."

There's the story. It was a three-game National League playoff that would come down to one game to be played later that day at the Polo Grounds. As Burr wrote, "But today will write the ending of the story. The lights were turned on yesterday in the sixth and there is sure to be a decision this afternoon—or tonight, unless more rain intervenes to cause a postponement. President Ford Frick says the teams can play all night in case of a prolonged deadlock."

The AP added, "The entire season is wrapped up in today's game for these old flaming baseball antagonists—Brooklyn's redoubtable Dodgers and New York's miracle Giants."

You can change that copy for Bob's game to read: "The entire season is wrapped up in today's game for these old flaming baseball antagonists—Boston's redoubtable Red Sox and New York's miracle Yankees."

Then the games were played.

Bobby Thomson.

Bucky Dent.

There you have it.

1978 AMERICAN LEAGUE PLAYOFF

THE YANKEES WIN THE AMERICAN LEAGUE EAST
NEW YORK 5 BOSTON 4 | FENWAY PARK, BOSTON, MA
TIME: 2:52 • OCTOBER 2, 1978

BOB RYAN

His birth certificate name is Russell Earl Dent. But he is far better known in so-called "Red Sox Nation" as Bucky (Bleeping) Dent. His lazy little fly ball, an out in every other major league ballpark, plopped gently over the cozy left-field wall with two men aboard in the 7th inning to give the Yankees a 3–2 lead en route to a 5–4 triumph in the first one-game playoff for an American League pennant in 30 years. A pitch before, he had fouled a Mike Torrez pitch off his foot. Mickey Rivers took the opportunity during Dent's brief recovery period to change bats. "As he was being treated," Rivers explained, "I grabbed the bat boy and told him to take the bat up and take away the one Bucky had." As for the homer, Dent was as surprised as anyone else by the outcome. "I didn't know it was a home run," he said. "When I hit it, I hoped it would hit the wall, and I just put my head down and kept running. Then when I turned toward second, I saw the umpire circling that it was a home run."

What most people have forgotten is that it was Reggie Jackson's 8th inning leadoff homer off reliever Bob Stanley that made the score 5–2 and created the actual winning run. The Red Sox would score two in the 8th, making it 5–4.

The final drama took place in the 9th. Rick Burleson drew a one-out walk off Rich Gossage. Jerry Remy then hit a shot to right, and Fenway Park right field is the most notorious late afternoon destination in baseball, then and now. Right fielder Lou Piniella appeared clueless as to the location of the ball. After it landed in front of him, he stuck out his left arm, and—Voila!—the ball stuck to his glove. Burleson had been unsure of the ball's trajectory, and he ignored third-base coach Eddie Yost's signal to keep running. Thus, instead of a run-scoring, game-tying triple, or perhaps even an inside-the-park homer (Remy could really run), or men on first and third with one out, it was men on first and second with one out.

Lou Piniella, always a stand-up guy, fessed up. "Remy's ball, I didn't see at all," he said. "I didn't know where it was going to land. Over my head. In front of me. I didn't know if it was going to hit me in the head. I was just fortunate that somehow, I had lined myself up right. So, when the ball bounced in front of me, I had a play."

Jim Rice, in Game 163 of an MVP season, hit a long fly to right. I was in attendance strictly as a fan, both of the Red Sox and baseball history itself. From my vantage point in Row 2 of the press box, I was certain I was looking at a game- and pennant-winning three-run homer. I yelled, quite loudly and unprofessionally, "IT'S OUTTA HERE!" It wasn't. It remains in my scorebook as a "Long 9." If only Burleson had been on third...

The final, final drama brought Captain Carl Yastrzemski to the plate. The baseball gods weren't with him. He went after an unhittable

Gossage heater on the outside corner and fouled meekly to third baseman Graig Nettles. Season over.

The next day, an anonymous *Boston Globe* editorial writer spoke for the multitudes: "Don't blame the Red Sox for the season that ended in the afternoon shadows. In breaking our hearts repeatedly during this unforgettable pennant race, and in their manner of losing yesterday, they were being faithful to their nature and to their destiny and that of their fans."

BILL CHUCK

First of all, it is essential that we distinguish a "playoff game," which this was, and a "postseason game," which this wasn't. A playoff game is still part of the regular season, and all the stats you see on Bob's scorecard counted toward the 1978 stats. That means that winning pitcher Ron Guidry ended 1978 with a record of 25–3, giving him a winning percentage of .893, the highest winning percentage of any pitcher with 20-plus wins other than Al Spalding's .915 when he went 54–5 in 1875, playing in a world of baseball that bears little resemblance to the modern era.

Jim Rice won his only MVP in 1978 (Guidry finished second, but did win the Cy Young Award), leading the league with 163 games played, PA, AB, hits, triples, homers, RBI, and WAR. In 1978, Rice hit 46 homers and 15 triples, the same as Joe DiMaggio in 1937 and Lou Gehrig in 1931.

Bucky's home run was his fifth of the season. He hit 40 homers in his career, four off the Sox and three at Fenway, two of which were off Dennis Eckersley, and this one, off Mike Torrez. Dent was 1–4 with three RBI. It was his first game with three ribbies since August 1977 and his last until August 1980. As Bob mentioned, Dent fouled a ball off his upper ankle on the prior pitch and hobbled about as he was treated by the trainer. Torrez threw no pitches to stay warm during that 1:20 delay, a decision that has haunted him.

Reggie Jackson's homer was his 27th of the season and the only one he ever hit off Bob Stanley.

Mickey Rivers hit his 25th double of the season and stole two bases to give him 25 swipes on the season. He never stole that many again.

Thurman Munson went 1–5 with three whiffs. He would be killed in a plane crash the following August.

Yaz was 39 and on the downslope of his career. In 1977, the Captain had hit .296 with 28 homers and 102 RBI. After this game, his 1978 totals were .277 with 17 homers and 81 RBI. Yaz never reached the postseason after 1975 and retired following the 1983 season.

The key to a playoff or tie-breaker game is that the winner goes on to the postseason, and the loser goes on to making golf dates. At the time of this game, the only other playoff game in American League history took place on October 4, 1948, also at Fenway Park as Boston faced Cleveland. Boston lost that one as well, 8–3. While the AL played a single sudden-death game, the NL would play a best of three. In perhaps, the most famous of all playoff games, the Giants' Bobby Thomson hit "the Shot Heard 'Round the World" in the third game of the 1951 playoffs against the Dodgers.

New York baseball fans in 1978 could only read about this game from out-of-town or make-shift newspapers as the three dailies were in the midst of an 88-day strike.

The Yankees finished the season 100–63, while the Sox finished 99–64. The Curse of the Bambino lived on.

SPARKY'S AL DEBUT

SEATTLE 3 DETROIT 2 | TIGER STADIUM, DETROIT, MI
TIME: 2:36 • JUNE 14, 1979

BOB RYAN

I honestly don't know why I was in Detroit, to begin with. But there I was, front and center, when new Tigers' skipper Sparky Anderson made his AL debut, having replaced Les Moss, who was let go after just 53 games as the Detroit manager. And, yes, that's Sparky's signature at the top of the scorebook page.

His debut was an unusual loss, unusual in that the winning Seattle run came home when a routine Larry Milbourne grounder went through the legs of third baseman Aurelio Rodriguez, who was normally a damn good fielder.

Sparky arrived with a flourish. "If I can't make this ballclub a winner in five years, then I'll walk away and say I've failed," he announced. "And I will have failed. But I don't intend to fail."

The 1984 Tigers would go 104–58 en route to defeating the Padres in the World Series. As they say, do the math. If only I'd gone right to Vegas.

An added bonus for me that day was that a foul ball came right at me in the Tiger Stadium press box. All I had to do was pick it up. I had Sparky sign it. Sadly, the ball was later destroyed when I sustained some water damage in my home office. But I do have his signature on my scorebook.

BILL CHUCK

Expectations can be brutal. The player expected to hit 30 homers or bat over .300 and or drive home a hundred runs. The sportswriter who expects a preseason prediction to be accurate and in-season punditry to be brilliant. The fan who is expected to fill a seat and see the championship banner fly. The owner who expects a return on investment. Expectations do in managers. You can understand why Sparky, also known as Captain Hook, had totally white hair, yet he was only 45 years old.

So, what is the first thing Sparky does as he takes over the Tigers? He sets expectations, a winner in five years.

And then, he met expectations.

Promises made, promises kept

Here are the Tigers of Sparky Anderson, 1979–1984:

Season	Record	Finish	Manager(s)
1979	85–76	5th in AL East	Les Moss
	27–26		Dick Tracewski
	2–0		Sparky Anderson
	56–50		
1980	84–78	4th in AL East	Sparky
1981	60–49	3rd in AL East	Sparky
First Half	31–26	4th in AL East	
Second Half	29–23	2nd in AL East	
1982	83–79	4th in AL East	Sparky
1983	92–70	2nd in AL East	Sparky
1984	104–58	1st in AL East	Sparky
1984 AL Championship Series	3–0 over Kansas City Royals	Won	Sparky
1984 World Series	4–1 over San Diego Padres	Won	Sparky

A little bit more…

The Tigers had won two straight for the fired Les Moss and two more for the interim manager Dick Tracewski before this loss. The loss came on a two-out error in the top of the 9th with a runner on third. Aurelio Rodriguez, the 1976 Gold Glove third baseman, committed the error.

The second out was a strikeout by Mario Mendoza, who has achieved immortality by being attached to the "Mendoza Line," representing hitting ineptitude. At the conclusion of this game, Mendoza was hitting .200 and finished the season hitting .198 in 148 games, the most he would play in his nine MLB seasons. He finished five of those nine seasons, hitting less than .200.

MUNSON DAY AFTER

BALTIMORE 1 NEW YORK 0 | YANKEE STADIUM, THE BRONX, NY
TIME: 2:22 • AUGUST 3, 1979

BOB RYAN

Thurman Munson had died in a crash while piloting his own plane the day before, but the theme of the evening at Yankee Stadium was that The Show Must Go On, no matter what. "After something like this, I just don't feel like playing the game," said Lou Piniella, speaking, I am sure, for many. "You wish you could just get away for a couple of weeks and try to put things in perspective."

The Yankees declined pregame media access. Orioles manager Earl Weaver addressed his own shaken team two hours before game time. Four hours north, Carlton Fisk, Munson's great individual rival, was in disbelief. "As far as everyone made a big thing out of our rivalry, it was entirely in baseball terms, not human terms," he explained. "I just wish we'd been able to know each other off the field."

Terence Cardinal Cooke offered a pregame prayer. Yankee mainstay Robert Merrill sang "America The Beautiful." And then Luis Tiant, who had known Munson far more as a bitter foe than a beloved teammate, took the mound.

Two hours and twenty-two minutes later, a crisp, beautiful, dignified game of baseball was over, and the visiting Orioles had a 1–0 victory, courtesy of a 2nd inning John Lowenstein home run. Tiant was 38, far past his prime, but he had turned the clock back. The trouble is he was matched by Scott McGregor with a little help from Tippy Martinez. The 51,151 Yankee Stadium mourners had been well-served, Yankee victory or no Yankee victory.

BILL CHUCK

Thurman Munson remains the only Yankee who won both the ROY and an MVP. He never led the league in batting average, home runs, RBI, doubles, walks, hits, or extra-base hits. But he was a Rookie of the Year, an MVP, a seven-time All-Star, and a three-time Gold Glover, because that's the kind of player he was.

He was not tall and handsome like Carlton Fisk. One of his nicknames was "Squatty Body."

Munson was a lifetime .292 hitter, and he hit .307 when runners were on base and .302 with runners in scoring position. He hit 113 homers, 57 with the bases empty and 56 with runners on base. He batted over .300 five times and played on three Yankee pennant winners and two world championship teams.

Munson hit .357 in 30 postseason games and .373 in 16 World Series games.

He became the Yankees captain in 1976, the first Yankees captain since Lou Gehrig in 1939.

He was the 13th and last Yankee to wear uniform No. 15.

He loved his family far more than he loved the game. That's why he was in his plane as often as possible, flying to Canton, Ohio, to be with his wife and kids.

Billy Martin, the Yankee manager, said: "For those who never knew him and didn't like him, I feel sorry for them. He was a great man, for his family, friends, and all the people who knew and loved him, my deepest sympathy. We not only lost a great competitor, but a leader and a husband and devoted family man. He was a close friend, I loved him."

BILL CHUCK ON THE 1970s

Leaders (1970–79)

- Hits: Pete Rose (2,045)
- Homers: Willie Stargell (296)
- Wins: Jim Palmer (186)
- Losses: Phil Niekro (151)
- Strikeouts: Nolan Ryan (2,678)
- Team wins: Reds (953)
- Team losses: Padres (942)

1979	4–3	Pittsburgh Pirates (98–64, NL) vs. Baltimore Orioles (102–57, AL)
1978	4–2	New York Yankees (100–63, AL) vs. Los Angeles Dodgers (95–67, NL)
1977	4–2	New York Yankees (100–62, AL) vs. Los Angeles Dodgers (98–64, NL)
1976	4–0	Cincinnati Reds (102–60, NL) vs. New York Yankees (97–62, AL)
1975	4–3	Cincinnati Reds (108–54, NL) vs. Boston Red Sox (95–65, AL)
1974	4–1	Oakland Athletics (90–72, AL) vs. Los Angeles Dodgers (102–60, NL)
1973	4–3	Oakland Athletics (94–68, AL) vs. New York Mets (82–79, NL)
1972	4–3	Oakland Athletics (93–62, AL) vs. Cincinnati Reds (95–59, NL)
1971	4–3	Pittsburgh Pirates (97–65, NL) vs. Baltimore Orioles (101–57, AL)
1970	4–1	Baltimore Orioles (108–54, AL) vs. Cincinnati Reds (102–60, NL)

chapter 2

THE
1980s

BOB RYAN

My 1980s baseball experience started off slowly. I was heavily involved in NBA and college basketball, and I didn't get to Fenway, or any other ballpark, with any regularity in the beginning of the decade. But all that would change.

For one thing, I left the *Boston Globe* to work in local television for a period of 19 months between September of 1982 and April of 1984. But once I returned, things changed for the better.

One personal highlight in the decade was a week-long trip my wife and I made to Chicago to see both Cubs and White Sox games. We stopped off for minor league games along the way, my scorebook in hand.

Though I was primarily a basketball man still, I covered the 1986, 1988, and 1989 NLCS series, as well as the 1989 ALCS. I was worming my way into as much baseball coverage as possible.

Things changed once again in 1989 when the great Leigh Montville left the *Globe* for *Sports Illustrated*. Dan Shaughnessy and I were both named to succeed him, and one thing we share is a love of baseball.

There was going to be a lot of baseball in my future. My scorebooks were going to get a workout.

YAZ'S FINAL AT-BAT

BOSTON 3 CLEVELAND 1 | FENWAY PARK, BOSTON, MA
TIME: 2:38 • OCTOBER 2, 1983

BOB RYAN

There was no confusion over what was in Carl Yastrzemski's mind as he stepped into the batter's box for the 13,992nd and final regular-season plate appearance in a 23-year career. "I was trying to jerk it out," he admitted.

The Cleveland pitchers knew what was up. "We were in the bar with the umpires Friday night and Rich Garcia told us, 'Look, fellows, if he doesn't swing, it's a ball,'" explained Cleveland pitcher Lary Sorensen (yes, that's how Sorenson spelled his first name).

So right-hander Dan Spillner was under no illusions. The score? It was 3–1, Boston (a three-run Jim Rice bomb), but who cared? There were two away and a man on first, but who cared? It was about the drama taking place 60'6" apart, period.

"I could see Spillner was trying to aim the ball," Yaz said. "It was coming in about 80 miles an hour." Plate ump Vic Voltaggio called them balls until it was 3–0 and Spillner "aimed" a pitch that was heading for the bill of Yaz's cap. But there was no way Yaz was ending his career with a stroll to first base. He flailed at ball four and hit a meek pop to second. Jack Perconte thus has the honor of making the last out on Carl Yastrzemski. Let the record show that Chico Walker replaced him in left for the Cleveland 8th.

The day's Yaz highlight had come in the top of the 7th. Yaz had long ago become a regular first baseman, but Red Sox skipper Ralph Houk had the good sense to put him in his old Gold Glove–winning stomping grounds in left field for his final game. Sure enough, Toby Harrah lined one off the wall. Let the *Boston Globe*'s Peter Gammons tell the story: "Yaz didn't play it quite the way he used to, but he stretched for the carom, whirled, and fired in toward second. Harrah stopped 30 feet past the first-base bag, returned, and went back."

You think I wasn't going to ask Yaz to sign my book?

BILL CHUCK

Cleveland's starting pitcher this October day was Bud Anderson, pitching his final major league game. Boston starter Al Nipper won his first major league game. Wade Boggs won his first batting title. Jim Rice won his third and final home run title. All of those events were memorable, but that's not why the tears were flowing at Fenway that day.

Carl Yastrzemski was clearly a Hall of Famer and one of Boston's greats. Let's get that out the way first. However, he was also one of those players who stayed too long at the fair. He didn't have the sharp decline that many players had and that, in some respects, was part of the problem.

From 1975 to 1983, the last nine seasons of Captain Carl's career, Yaz played 1,191 games, so I looked at players who played at least 800 games over those years. Yastrzemski's .792 OPS was equal to John Lowenstein's and good for 52nd in the majors. He hit 149 homers, 36th in the majors. His .272 BA was the same as Dale Murphy's and

Bobby Grich's, all at 78th in the majors. And his WAR (Wins Above Replacement), according to Baseball Reference, was 17.8, the same as Bake McBride, sitting at 86th in the majors.

The overall numbers that Yaz accumulated through talent and longevity were indeed extraordinary. He deservedly collected amongst the highest vote totals when he was elected to the Hall of Fame in his first time on the ballot. The fact that Yastrzemski only reached the postseason twice was certainly not his fault, just like Mike Trout's absence in the postseason is not his fault. Great players can only do so much.

Captain Carl told an emotional crowd at Fenway that final day, "I'll miss you, and I'll never forget you." As Leigh Montville wrote the next day in the *Boston Globe*, Yaz said, "You wanted the opposition to know you're a machine. That nothing could bother you." Montville added, "Well, the machine cried yesterday."

1983 WORLD SERIES GAME 4

ORIOLES LEAD SERIES 3 GAMES TO 1
BALTIMORE 5 PHILADELPHIA 4
VETERANS STADIUM, PHILADELPHIA, PA
TIME: 2:50 • OCTOBER 15, 1983

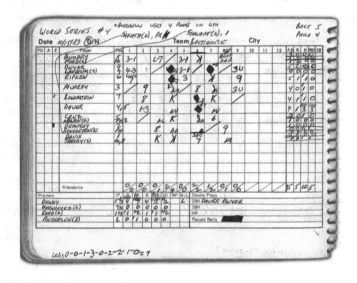

BOB RYAN

It had been an otherwise unremarkable World Series game. The Phillies led the Orioles, 3–2, in the 6th behind John Denny. But now, in the top of the 6th, the Orioles had men on second and third with one out, and the Phillies had no idea they were about to be the vanquished parties of the second part as Orioles' skipper Joe Altobelli prepped to make World Series history.

Ready?

- Due up was the number seven hitter, Todd Cruz, but Joe Nolan pinch-hit for him and was intentionally walked, and now the bags were filled.
- Next up was Rick Dempsey (destined to be the MVP of the Series), but the switch-hitting Ken Singleton pinch-hit for him and was unintentionally walked (on four pitches), and now the game was tied.
- Singleton quickly headed back to the dugout as Lenn Sakata was his pinch-runner.
- Phils' manager Pat Corrales now got into the action and pulled Denny and brought in Willie Hernandez.
- Pitcher Storm Davis was next up, but Altobelli sent up another switch-hitter, John Shelby, whose sac fly drove home the go-ahead run.
- Corrales got into the swing of things and replaced Hernandez with Ron Reed.
- Which didn't bring up Al Bumbry because Altobelli sent up Dan Ford, who took a called third strike, but the damage had been done.

They were the pinch-hitters, four in succession. Never before, or never since, has a World Series manager gone this route. Add to that, a pinch-runner and three pitchers. As a bonus, the Orioles now had a superior defensive team to protect their lead. The Final: Baltimore 5, Philadelphia 4, and a 3–1 Series lead. Five pinch-somethings had toppled the proud Phillies.

BILL CHUCK

The eight pinch-hitters used by both teams is a Series high for a nine-inning game. Joe Durso, in the *New York Times* the next day, quoted the O's manager, "Any time you use four pinch-hitters in one inning, you're going for broke," Altobelli said. "I was going for the pot of gold."

Versus 21 batters, John Denny, who walked Ken Singleton with the sacks filled, did not have a bases-loaded walk during the regular season.

In that memorable inning, the four pinch-hitters went 0–1 with two RBI. During the 1983 regular season, the Orioles were 12th in the majors and second in the A.L. with their pinch-hitters making 225 PA. Their pinch-hitters hit .220, 22nd of the 26 MLB teams and the worst in the American League. On the other hand, their 37 RBI, tied for the fifth best in the majors and second in the A.L.

One last item from the scorecard, Larry Andersen, who finished the game pitching two scoreless for the Phils, is the same Larry Andersen who in 1990 was famously or infamously (depending on your point of view) traded by the Astros to the Red Sox for Jeff Bagwell.

1983 WORLD SERIES GAME 5

ORIOLES WIN SERIES 4–1
BALTIMORE 5 PHILADELPHIA 0
VETERANS STADIUM, PHILADELPHIA, PA
TIME: 2:21 • OCTOBER 16, 1983

BOB RYAN

Scott McGregor's five-hitter took care of the pitching as the Orioles won the Series. But my everlasting takeaway was the slugging of Eddie Murray, particularly the second of his two home runs.

The future Hall of Famer had, well, stunk up the joint in Games 1 through 4. When he stepped to the plate against Charles Hudson to lead off the 2nd inning, he was 2-for-37 with 10 runners left stranded in scoring position for the Series. Murray responded by blasting a homer to right.

But the real fun was his second at-bat. Cal Ripken was on first when Hudson hung a curve. The *Boston Globe*'s Peter Gammons will take you home from there. "The ball carried over the wall, over the black cloth covering against the huge scoreboard in right. At that precise moment, the scoreboard was flashing the American League RBI leaders: 'Cooper 126,' it read. 'Rice 126. Winfield 116. Parrish 114. Murray 111.' The ball landed just above Murray's own name, denting the scoreboard and darkening the bulbs that lit the last letter in Parrish's name. Literally, Eddie Murray knocked the 'H' out of it."

I was in my brief incarnation as a TV man and thus was sitting in the auxiliary press box in the outfield. I can still see this missile off the bat of Eddie Murray heading right at me. Swear to God.

Eddie Murray was the anti-Reggie. Neither a showman nor a braggart was he. "I didn't know my name was out there," he explained. "All I knew was that when I hit it, the ball was good enough to go. After that, I didn't even bother looking at it."

BILL CHUCK

There have been 19 World Series that have ended with a complete-game shutout. Scott McGregor's effort on this night was the 16th and the first since another Orioles pitcher, Dave McNally, finished off the Dodgers in 1966. McGregor whiffed six and walked a pair, and impressively threw 113 pitches, of which 83 were strikes (73.4 percent).

Eddie Murray, thanks to his three hits in this game, ended up the Series hitting .250, significantly better than his HOF teammate and 1983 AL MVP, Cal Ripken Jr., who hit .167 in his only World Series appearance. The Phillies future Hall of Famers struggled as well, Joe Morgan hit .263, Tony Perez hit .200, but no one suffered more than Mike Schmidt, who started 0–13 and finished 1–20 (.050) with a broken-bat single. Not-in-the-HOFer Pete Rose hit .313. There were two 38-year-old HOF pitchers in this Series: Steve Carlton went 1–1 with a 2.70 ERA, and Jim Palmer went 1–0 with a 0.00 ERA in two innings of relief.

Rick Dempsey was the Series MVP, hitting .385 while going 5–13, but I love that of his five hits, four were doubles, and the fifth was a homer. In Game 5, Dempsey homered and doubled, Murray hit two homers and singled in the 9th, which was the only offense the winning O's had: five hits.

One of the many things that I treasure about Bob's scorecards is his diligence in providing us with Time of Game. What you won't see is that this game started at 5:00 PM. Daylight, what a concept.

1984 WILD HOME OPENER

DETROIT 13 BOSTON 9 | FENWAY PARK, BOSTON, MA
TIME: 3:11 • APRIL (FRIDAY) 13, 1984

BOB RYAN

The 1984 Tigers were one of the great one-season teams of all time. The Red Sox got an early glimpse of their greatness when the Tigers scored eight runs off Bruce Hurst and Mike Brown in the 1st inning of the '84 Sox home opener. That was a good idea because the Red Sox answered with five of their own in their first at-bat.

Among the oddities in this game: Detroit catcher Lance Parrish made all three outs in the first with a called third strike and an inning-ending 6-4-3 double play. (Baseball being baseball, he homered in his 3rd at-bat.)

The Red Sox got the leadoff man aboard in seven innings, but four of them were erased by four of the record-tying six double plays induced by Tiger pitchers.

Thirteen combined 1st inning runs? "If you tried to invent a nightmare of an inning, you couldn't invent that one," said Sox catcher Rich Gedman, "You couldn't think of all the things that happened."

The crowd of 35,179 was the largest Sox Opening Day crowd since 1969. Good or bad, they sure had something to talk about.

BILL CHUCK

Eight Quotes to Know About Opening Day

"People ask me what I do in winter when there's no baseball. I'll tell you what I do. I stare out the window and wait for spring."
—Rogers Hornsby

"You always get a special kick on Opening Day, no matter how many you go through. You look forward to it like a birthday party when you're a kid. You think something wonderful is going to happen."
—Joe DiMaggio

"An Opener is not like any other game. There's that little extra excitement, a faster beating of the heart…. You know that when you win the first one, you can't lose 'em all."
—Early Wynn

"Opening Day. All you have to do is say the words, and you feel the shutters thrown wide, the room air out, the light pour in. In baseball, no other day is so pure with possibility. No scores yet, no losses, no blame or disappointment. No hangover, at least until the game's over."
—Mary Schmich

"There is no sports event like Opening Day of baseball, the sense of beating back the forces of darkness, and the National Football League."
—George Vecsey

"There's nothing like Opening Day. There's nothing like the start of a new season. I started playing baseball when I was seven years old and quit playing when I was 40, so it's kind of in my blood."
—George Brett

"If you want to see a bunch of happy Americans, go out to Opening Day at any baseball stadium in the land."
—Ben Fountain

"A home opener is always exciting, no matter if it's home or on the road."
—Yogi Berra

ARIZONA STATE VS. NORTH CAROLINA

ASU 6 NC 4 | PACKARD BASEBALL STADIUM, TEMPE, AZ
TIME: 2:29 • MAY 17, 1984

BOB RYAN

Arizona State and North Carolina were engaged in a little series prep for the upcoming College World Series. I always have my scorebook with me from April to October because you never know when a baseball game will break out. And this was Jackpot City for me.

ASU won, 6–4, before 2,402 on a 92-degree afternoon. What I didn't know at the time was that this game contained nine future major league players and two future major league managers.

Leading the list, of course, was ASU left fielder Barry Bonds. Batting third, he failed to homer. Ah, but he did get an intentional walk! Too good to be true, right? Teammates Oddibe McDowell, Mike

Devereaux, Luis Medina, and Don Wakamatsu also made the Bigs. McDowell, you will note, homered in the 5th.

Check out the 1–2 batters for Carolina. B.J. Surhoff and Walt Weiss combined for 33 years and 4,808 major league games. DH Matt Merullo likewise made it to The Show.

Wakamatsu (Mariners and Rangers) and Weiss (Rockies) would manage in the majors. This is Exhibit A why you should never leave home without your scorebook.

BILL CHUCK

Another Arizona State University alum, Craig Swan pitched for 12 years in the majors, 11 of them for the Mets, leading the league in ERA in 1978. At ASU, Swan won a school-record 47 games.

I mention that because the headline for the Arizona State team in this win over North Carolina was that Kendall Carter won his 47th game, tying him with Swan for the most in school history. A record they share to this day. Carter was with the ASU in 1981 when they won the College World Series (Carter was 19–1 that season) and this team, under coach Jim Brock, would reach the CWS for the third time in Carter's four seasons.

Carter almost didn't get to play in this game because there had been a question of eligibility because the school had ruled that Carter had exceeded normal scholarship aid by about $500 due to government financial aid. Carter and five of his teammates paid the money and by 6:15 that evening were permitted to play. Despite losing their automatic berth in the postseason, the team still managed to reach the College World Series.

Oddibe McDowell slammed his 22nd homer of the season in this win. He led the team with 23 that season. Some dude named Barry Bonds led the team the season before with 11.

Arizona State University

Kendall Carter was drafted by the Texas Rangers in the 14th round of the 1984 MLB June Amateur Draft. He pitched that year for Single A

Burlington in the Midwest League in his only professional season. He eventually became a scout.

- Oddibe McDowell never hit more than 18 homers in a major league season.
- Barry Bonds hit a lot of home runs and drew a lot of intentional walks.
- Mike Devereaux had a 12-year MLB career with five teams.
- Luis Medina played parts of three seasons with Cleveland in the majors.
- Don Wakamatsu had an 18-game big-league career and a 284-game managerial career.
- Doug Henry pitched in the majors for 11 seasons for five teams.

North Carolina
- B.J. Surhoff played 19 major league seasons for three teams.
- Walt Weiss played 14 major league seasons for four teams and managed for four.
- Matt Merullo played in the majors for six seasons for three teams.

"I am Spartacus!"
The last name of the relievers for North Carolina were Kirk and Douglas.

Bob felt at home
At Packard Baseball Stadium, the former home of ASU, in center field is a 30-foot-high batting-eye wall, painted green so that the batter standing at home plate 400 feet away can better see the baseball coming out of the pitcher's hand. Its nickname? "The Green Monster."

VIOLA'S QUICK EXIT

BOSTON 17 MINNESOTA 7 | FENWAY PARK, BOSTON, MA
TIME: 3:16 • MAY 20, 1986

BOB RYAN

Hope Frank Viola's dad made it up to Fenway on time from Long Island, New York. His kid Frank faced six men and didn't get any of them out. Bye, bye, Frank.

Mound foe Roger Clemens, en route to a 24–4 season, wasn't exactly stellar (nine hits and five earned runs in 7.0 IP), but it didn't matter on a night when the Red Sox banged out 20 hits (no homers), five of them by Wade Boggs. It was his first 5-for-5 ever. He spiced it up by scoring from second base in the third when Dave Stapleton's swinging third strike eluded Twins' catcher Mark Salas. Sox catcher Marc Sullivan, son of CEO Haywood, had three hits and scored three runs. That didn't happen very often.

BILL CHUCK

We are not mean people. Sometimes it's important to remind you of that as we often seem to be fascinated with the failures of players. It's just that we like the unusual… like a performance such as this.

Frank Viola made 420 starts in his 15 seasons in the majors. Sweet Music retired at least one batter in 419 of them. This was the exception.

You want some positives?

Try this:

- Wade Boggs, in his career, had three games in which he had a career-high five hits. This was his first and his second was 11 days later and also against Minnesota. His third, against Oakland was in 1991. In 1986, Boggs hit .460 against the Twins (23–50).

- Roger Clemens moved to 7–0 in this game on his way to 14–0 as the Sox won his first 15 starts.

- Marc Sullivan recorded the first three-hit and the first three-run game of his career. Wade Boggs had 224 games with exactly three hits. He was a Hall of Famer. Five days later, Sullivan had his second three-hit game, and in September, he had the third three-hit game and second three-run game, both the last of his career. He retired with a career .186 BA. Marc's father was Heywood Sullivan, also a Red Sox catcher and .226 lifetime hitter. Heywood, at the time Marc was playing, was also one of the owners of the Red Sox. Sigh.

FISCHER BALKS IN THE WINNING RUN

BOSTON 8 CALIFORNIA 7 (12 INNINGS)
FENWAY PARK, BOSTON, MA
TIME: 4:27 • JULY 10, 1986

BOB RYAN

Madness!

The Angels break a 4–4 tie with three runs off the completely ineffective Mike Brown in the top of the 12th. The Red Sox won it with four in their half, capped by the winning run being balked home by a relief pitcher before he even throws a pitch.

Todd Fischer was summoned by Gene Mauch after Rich Gedman's gutsy at-bat (he singled after he fouled off five 1–2 pitches), tied the game, and left men on second and third with two away. Before he even threw a pitch, Fischer made a false move. Umpire Joe Brinkman called a balk and sent Dwight Evans home.

Mauch was predictably upset. "Fischer did balk," he admitted. "And even if he did, the umpire had no business calling it because nobody in the ballpark knew it but him." And, well, you too, Gene.

What had really upset the Angels' skipper was Brinkman's missing what Mauch thought should have been an inning-ending called strike three to Evans earlier in the inning.

Brown had relieved Steve Crawford with two out and no one on in the Angels' 12th, only to give up three hits, two walks, and a wild pitch without retiring a man.

Evans was on base six times in six plate appearances with two hits and four walks. Oh, and Bill Buckner had been 0–25 on 0–2 counts that season before homering in the 6th.

All in all, this wasn't just another night at the ballpark.

BILL CHUCK

I like to think of this night as the "Great American League Balk-Off." Not that there was an in-game balk other than Todd Fischer's, but actually, Oil Can Boyd balked before the game even started.

This was a season in which everything went right for the Sox up until Game 6 of the World Series. At the time of this game, Boston was on top of the AL East by 8.0 games over the Yankees. The Angels were on top of the AL West by 1.5 games over the Rangers.

Before this game, the All-Star team pitchers had been announced. Boston's Roger Clemens (14–2 at the time) was named by Royals manager Dick Howser not just to the team but as the starter in his hometown of Houston. He would face Dwight Gooden of the Mets. Oil Can (11–6) was tied for second in the league in wins with Baltimore's Mike Boddicker. Neither were named to the All-Star squad. Boddicker wasn't happy, but Boyd exploded in rage. He went so bonkers that the clubhouse was cleared of media and visitors for five minutes, as manager John McNamara's team tried to get settled for the game in front of them. Boyd, meanwhile, balked at remaining with the team and stormed off in his car toward his home in Chelsea, where he sat parked atop a hill as the band played on.

As for Fischer's balk, it is the only time in Angels' history that a balk has been committed without facing a batter. I have only found four other occasions in which a pitcher has committed a balk without facing a batter. Only Mike Stanton, pitching for the Nationals against the Brewers, is the only other walk-off balk-off of this nature.

The Angels were up 7–6 with two outs in the bottom of the 12th inning and no one on in this odd game when Don Baylor hit a pop-up that the Angels (and former Red Sox) Rick Burleson, dropped. Burleson, ordinarily a shortstop, was playing third (he only played at third in four games in 1986) and made his only E-5 of the season.

Relatively speaking
- Dick Schofield played in this game for the Angels. Bob also saw his father (also Dick Schofield) play as well.
- Bob Boone played in this game for the Angels. Bob also saw his father (Ray Boone) and his sons, Aaron and Bret, play as well.
- Kevin Romine played in this game for the Sox. Bob also saw his sons, Andrew and Austin, play as well.

About the pitchers
- Mike Brown pitched for Boston and allowed three runs without retiring a batter. That Sunday, in the finale of the series, Brown pitched again (again ineffectively), and that was his finale with the Red Sox as he was soon sent to the Mariners.
- Tim Lollar was the winning pitcher in this game. It was the final decision of his major league career.
- Angels' starter Ron Romanick was making his 17th start of the season. Eleven days later, in his 18th start of the season, he was knocked around once again. He never pitched in the majors again.
- Angels' rookie Chuck Finley made his eighth major league appearance in this game. Finley won 200 games in his MLB career.
- Mike Cook was pitching in only his fourth major league game; he would pitch in five before being sent to the minors until the following season.
- As for the rookie Todd Fischer, it was the first balk of his major league career. It was also his last. He never pitched in another MLB game.

The Sox and the Angels met that season in the ALCS, with Boston coming back from a 3–1 deficit to win in seven games. The key hit was a 9th inning Dave Henderson homer in Game 5 off Donnie Moore, who pitched effectively in this game. Henderson came to the Sox in exchange for Mike Brown and Rey Quinones, who started at short for the Sox in this game.

BACK-TO-BACK PINCH-HIT HOMERS

BOSTON 6 TEXAS 4 | FENWAY PARK, BOSTON, MA
TIME: 3:05 • SEPTEMBER 1, 1986

BOB RYAN

Texas manager Bobby Valentine sure knew which buttons to push. With two out and no one on in the 9th, he sent up Oddibe McDowell to hit for Steve Buechele and Darrell Porter to hit for Toby Harrah. Each man homered off Sox reliever Steve Crawford. Too bad he was losing 6–2.

The game left Bill Buckner scratching his head. He had hit what he thought was a triple in the 1st. But it was belatedly ruled that a fan had touched the ball, and it was thus a ground-rule double. In the 7th, he hit a smash to the 420-foot sign in the famed right-center-field triangle, only to be gunned down by a good 10 feet trying for three via a superb relay from Ruben Sierra to Scott Fletcher to Buechele, 8-6-5 in my scorebook.

"I can't hit a ball better than that," he marveled. "They always tell me that if you hit a ball to the 420-foot sign, it's supposed to be a triple."

BILL CHUCK

This story is about two things that didn't happen. First, the Rangers didn't win this game and not once, but twice Bill Buckner did not triple on two hits that should have been triples. But this is about the back-to-back pinch-hit homers. They are indeed rare.

The Texas Rangers (nee Washington Senators) have been around since 1961, and they had never hit back-to-back pinch-hit homers before and have never done it since. In fact, this was the only game in which they ever hit two pinch-hit homers. The Sox, who have been around since 1901 (before either of us were born), have only had two games in which they hit two pinch-hit homers, and neither of them were back-to-back.

There has only been one game in which a team hit three pinch-hit homers (Cardinals in 2016), and none of them were B2B. And in all of baseball history, there have only been 110 games in which there were two pinch-homers. So even though Valentine's Rangers lost, this was pretty cool.

A Bill Buckner moment

Because of Bill Buckner's oft-injured rickety legs, he was frequently removed for a pinch-runner or for defensive purposes. But, as Bob wrote, the fact that he was "gunned down by a good 10 feet" may have also foreshadowed his egregious error in Game 6 of the World Series that season.

Buckner was a decent baserunner despite not being blessed with great speed. According to Baseball Reference, in his 22-season career, he took the extra base on a hit when possible 45 percent of the time. His lowest rate was 24 percent in 1986. In 1985, that rate had been 41 percent. In the 1986 season, Buckner was on first 14 times when a double was hit, and he didn't score once. He was on second 16 times when a single was hit and scored just 10 times. That fateful season,

Buckner was thrown out at the plate three times and at third three times.

Bob always remembered this game. Sox manager John McNamara should have as well.

TARVER SCORES THE WINNING RUN

BOSTON 4 TEXAS 3 | FENWAY PARK, BOSTON, MA
TIME: 2:42 • SEPTEMBER 3, 1986

BOB RYAN

The old 40-man September roster meant a team could keep a specialist, especially ones who can really run. Say hello to La Schelle Tarver, whose entire big-league career encompassed 13 games and 3-for-25 at the plate. He also scored career three runs, one of which he can tell the grandchildren aided a team in a pennant race.

Called up on this very day, he was sent in to run for Mike Greenwell, who had singled as a pinch-hitter for Marc Sullivan in the 9th inning of a 3–3 game. He was running with the pitch when Wade Boggs hit one to left center. He didn't stop running until he had crossed the plate with the winning run. No other player on the Red Sox roster could have scored that run.

Bob Stanley vultured the 100th win in his career after relieving Tom Seaver after surrendering a game-tying run in the Rangers' 9th.

BILL CHUCK

There have only been 11 pitchers who have won 100 games for the Red Sox, and the fact that Bob Stanley won 115 should not be trivialized. He won 10 more for Boston than Lefty Grove. He won five more for Boston than Jon Lester. Bob Stanley won two fewer games for Boston than Smokey Joe Wood and Pedro Martinez. Let's show a little love for Steamer, who picked up number 100 in this game.

Tarver, on the other hand, appeared in 13 games for Boston and had 26 plate appearances. This represented both Tarver's Boston career and his MLB career. When he was brought up in mid-July in 1986, he said, "I had no idea what Fenway even looked like. So I got in my car in Pawtucket and drove up (Route) 95 to Boston," Tarver recalled. "I got a block away from Fenway out on Yawkey Way and looking for the park. I guess I was looking for a stadium like Dodger Stadium or Candlestick.

"I called the office asking where the park was and whoever answered the phone said, in their Boston accent, 'You see that brick building that looks like a warehouse? Well, that's Fenway Park, just come to that gate,'" Tarver continued with a laugh. "It was a heck of an experience for my first time in Boston."

JOE COWLEY'S NO-HITTER

CHICAGO 7 CALIFORNIA 1 | ANAHEIM STADIUM, ANAHEIM, CA
TIME: 2:42 • SEPTEMBER 19, 1986

BOB RYAN

The 1986 Boston Red Sox and California Angels were each on their way to winning a Division, and the Boston Globe *dispatched me to spend time with the Angels to gather material for feature stories that would appear in our ALCS Playoff Preview.*

It turned out to be an unforgettable week of baseball, starting with this:

Many of my colleagues have seen multiple organized baseball no-hit, no-run games during their careers, but the last no-hitter I've seen in person at any level was thrown by Lawrenceville School right-hander Pete Thurston, when he blanked Delbarton School, 3–0, May of 1963. Oh, I've come close, most notably on September 2, 2001, when

Mike Mussina retired the first 26 Red Sox batters and went to 1–2 on number 27 when Carl Everett singled to left-center. The next-closest I've come, I guess, was this thing.

I mean, a no-hitter in which a guy throws 69 strikes and 69 balls? Meh. What would Greg Maddux say? Joe Cowley fanned eight. Good. He walked seven. Not so good. Three of those walks came in succession during the 6th, prompting a mound visit by skipper Jim Fregosi, who informed him that, no-hitter or no no-hitter, if he walked a fourth, he was coming out. But Brian Downing popped to second. Reggie Jackson followed with a liner to left center that spoiled the shutout but preserved the no-hitter.

California being California, the fans were not particularly interested in seeing any milestone performance, and they left by the thousands after Wally Joyner ended the 8th by lining to short. So, they missed a game-ending 6-4-3 double play, which is an intriguing way to seal a no-hitter.

The losing Angels were more perplexed than embarrassed about being no-hitted. "He did his job," said Joyner. "He got 27 outs. But he wasn't tough at all; he wasn't. We didn't get a hit; that's all that happened. If you guys didn't look up at the scoreboard, you'd think he gave up eight or nine hits…. It wasn't impressive; it wasn't. Not to put Joe Cowley down, but it wasn't impressive."

That evening I was having a few postgame beers with Ed Sherman of the *Chicago Tribune* at the hotel bar. We looked across the bar, and there, sipping a beer all by himself was Rodney Dangerfield, er, Joe Cowley, "Mr. No-Hit" himself. We bought him a congratulatory beer or two, and he graciously signed my scorebook.

Oops, almost buried the lead. That ugly no-hitter was the last game Joe Cowley would ever win in the bigs.

Truly, truly, truly, you absolutely, positively cannot make this stuff up.

For the record, I once made the last out in a Little League no-hitter thrown by a kid named Bobby Czumbil. The catcher was Skip Harlicka, who went on to have a great basketball career at Wake Forest. But you probably don't care.

BILL CHUCK

There have been 22 regular-season no-hitters in which the complete-game pitcher allowed at least seven baserunners. So, based on that alone, Cowley's seven-baserunner no-hitter was one of the worst. But I think we can move Cowley up a bit on this list since in only four of those games, the no-hit pitcher allowed at least one run. Well, at least Cowley won the game as opposed to Matt Young and Andy Hawkins, who won their no-hit bids but lost their no-hit games.

Now, while Cowley would never win another game, it wasn't for lack of trying. He made three more starts in the 1986 season, and he lost two of them, and it's not that he was getting lit up. Although, in his start following the no-hitter, Cowley pitched 6.2 innings and only allowed three hits. The only trouble was that each of the three hits was a homer. In his last four starts, including the no-hitter, Cowley pitched 30.0 innings and only allowed 12 hits and a .126 batting average against. He also struck out 30 batters. But he was wild, walking 24 of the 123 batters he faced.

Cowley never was a control pitcher, and he was often filled with contrasts. Bob's buddy Ed Sherman wrote in the *Chicago Tribune* on May 29, 1986, "First, Joe Cowley made history Wednesday night. Then Texas made history of Joe Cowley." Cowley had struck out the first seven Rangers to face him that night before he allowed six runs in 4.2 innings.

The following March, Cowley was traded to the Phillies. He was just 28 years old and should have been in his prime. But he was done. In four starts in April, Cowley went 0–4, pitching a total of 11.0 innings, allowing 23 runs (17 earned) on 19 hits and 15 walks. He had a 13.91 ERA and .380 BAA. He even allowed six steals in six attempts, including a delayed steal of home. He made one more appearance in May, this time in relief, and fared just as poorly facing six batters, allowing two hits, two walks, three runs in two-thirds of an inning.

The Phils sent Cowley to Old Orchard Beach, Maine, to pitch for the Guides in the International League to get straightened out, but nothing came out straight. In 63.0 IP, he walked 76 batters and hit another 16. In one appearance against Tidewater, Cowley walked 11 in 2.2 innings. On July 21, the Phillies suggested that he take the rest of the summer off.

The following spring, the Phillies invited him to camp and Cowley walked 10 in seven innings, including seven walks and an HBP in his final two innings. On March 18, 1988, he was given his unconditional release.

When Bob first told me this story, I could not shake the image of Cowley sitting alone nursing his drink. I'm glad Bob and Ed got to buy him a beer after the no-hitter on that September night in 1986. It was clear that while Cowley may have won the game, he lost the plate.

PASSED OFF

CALIFORNIA 8 CHICAGO 7 | ANAHEIM STADIUM, ANAHEIM, CA
TIME: 3:12 • SEPTEMBER 20, 1986

BOB RYAN

Managers can scheme, but players must execute. I'm sure that after Wally Joyner had moved to third base in the 9th after a one-out double and a wild pitch and manager Jim Fregosi elected to walk the next two men intentionally, the skipper wasn't planning on Dave Schmidt's pitch eluding catcher Ron Karkovice for a passed ball that would bring in the winning run.

Gene Mauch expressed sympathy for his rival. "There are many ways to do it," he said. "There are so many variables. We could stand here and talk about it till dark."

Karkovice manned up. "I should have caught it," the White Sox catcher said. "I wasn't crossed up. (Schmidt) had good movement on the ball, and I just took my eye off the ball."

By the way, it was a "vulture" win for Donnie Moore, who had blown a save by giving up a game-tying homer to Harold Baines in the 9th.

BILL CHUCK

A passed ball is a bit of an oddity in that according to the definition (which I have abridged) as found on MLB.com, "A catcher is given a passed ball if he cannot hold onto a pitch that—in the official scorer's judgment—he should have, and as a result, at least one runner moves up on the bases. A passed ball is not recorded as an error, but when a run scores as the result of a passed ball, it does not count as an earned run against a pitcher."

So, to quickly recap, it's an error that's not recorded as an error but treated as an error as far as pitchers are concerned. Got it?

This was Ron Karkovice's second passed ball of the game, each resulted in a run. When knuckleballers are not pitching, as is the case in this contest, one passed ball is uncommon, two rare, and when it results in the winning scoring, it gets written about in books.

Karkovice was a rookie who, since his call-up in mid-August, had been the ChiSox regular catcher. This was his 25th game, and these were his fourth and fifth PBs. Now before you start to wonder if he remained a catcher during his 12 years in the majors, I can tell you he did, and he was pretty good. He finished his career with just 50 passed balls in his 776 starts behind the plate. Three times he led the AL in catching runners stealing and was in the top 10 in five different seasons. Hence, the nickname "Officer" that he acquired from White Sox announcer Ken Harrelson, whose nickname is "Hawk," and the reason for that is as plain as the nose on his face.

A couple of final flourishes here.

The night before this game, Karkovice was Joe Cowley's catcher as Cowley tossed a no-hitter and Karko homered.

Finally, oddly enough, this was the second game the Angels had won that season on a passed-ball walk-off. The first had been in June when George Hendrick flailed at a Charlie Hough knuckler and the winning run scored. Orlando Mercado was the unfortunate Texas catcher who allowed two PBs that inning alone. To make that one even more amazing, Wally Joyner, who scored the winning run, had gotten the first Angels hit of that game with one out in the bottom of the 9th. It was their only hit in the 2–1 win.

REGGIE'S BANK SHOT

CALIFORNIA 3 CHICAGO 0 | ANAHEIM STADIUM, ANAHEIM, CA
TIME: 2:14 • SEPTEMBER 21, 1986

BOB RYAN

It was a perfect day for baseball, and a nice day for John Candelaria and Donnie Moore, who combined for a two-hit shutout. It was also a nice day for Reggie Jackson, who hit one out for career wallop number 547.

A game that had started at noon local time was over in a tidy 2:14, which meant there was a lot left in the day. Given that I wasn't writing anything that day, I was perfectly free to accept Reggie's invitation to come to see his famous collection of vintage automobiles down in Contra Costa.

Following him as he weaved through traffic was a challenge. But I got there and enjoyed the visit, though I'm not really a car guy. Now it just so happened that Reggie had a basketball backboard, and I am a basketball guy. He said, "Let's play H-O-R-S-E." Oh boy. We get started, and I'm beating him. That was until Reggie decided he wasn't going to lose to a writer and unveiled his specialty trick shot, a spinning banker. Of course, he came from behind and beat me.

It reminded me of the time I was at Boston Celtics Jo Jo White's house, and we were playing 8-ball on his pool table. I was beating him too, until I wasn't. No way *he* was going to lose to a writer, either.

The moral of the story is that there is Them, and there is Us, and we ain't Them.

BILL CHUCK

In my garage, I have boxes of old photographs, old magazines, old computer equipment, and too much mold. In Reggie's garage in Seaside, California, according to a 2017 *USA Today* feature, Jackson had 17 Corvettes, a 1937 Ford, a 1955 Chevy, a 1969 ZL-1 Chevy Camaro, a 1968 Yenko Chevrolet Camaro, a 1969 Camaro Z28, a 1936 Ford roadster, a 1959 AC Bristol, and memorabilia from his days as a player, including World Series trophies, five World Series rings, a signed picture of Ted Williams and Mickey Mantle, and loads of other very valuable stuff.

Reggie specializes in power cars the way he specialized in power hitting, which is how he hit 563 homers.

In an article from the "Inside Pitch" series for the Hall of Fame, Connor O'Gara included this:

"I'll admit that I've always had trouble in meaningless situations," Jackson wrote in *Reggie*, his 1984 autobiography with Mike Lupica. "Maybe I should have been a better ballplayer than I was, and maybe that was the reason…. But when a game or a season hangs in the balance… I'll do what Cool Hand Luke said: I'll get my mind right. I call those times Reggie Situations."

It's clear that when the thought of losing to Bob in a game of H-O-R-S-E, Reggie quickly got his mind right. It was a Reggie Situation.

SUTTON NUMBER 310

CALIFORNIA 4 CLEVELAND 3 (GAME 1) |
ANAHEIM STADIUM, ANAHEIM, CA
TIME: 2:38 • SEPTEMBER 22, 1986

BOB RYAN

This was career win number 310 for future Hall of Famer Don Sutton, and what made this one interesting was the identity of his batterymate. The 41-year-old Sutton was throwing to 38-year-old Bob Boone. At that moment, Sutton was second on the list of all-time starts with 703, and Boone was seven games away from moving into second place for most games caught. "It's something to reflect on when I'm 50," shrugged Boone. "Don and I don't talk about things like that other than the fact that we're old. And still working."

It was the 12th time Sutton had won at least 15. "Was that Sutton's 15th?" inquired Doug DeCinces. "What can you say? He's 41 years old. Awesome. The mark of consistency, the consummate pro."

BILL CHUCK

From 1966 to 1980, Don Sutton won 15-plus games nine times pitching for the Dodgers. He was a 17-game winner when he pitched for the Astros and Brewers in 1982. He was a 15-game winner when he pitched for the A's and Angels in 1985. And, here in 1986, he finished his final 15-game winning season with the Angels. But those numbers only tell part of the story:

- Don Sutton played 23 seasons in the majors and won 324 games (if that number sounds familiar, it's because Nolan Ryan also had 324 wins). They are tied for 14th all-time.
- Only 24 players have won 300-plus games, and we may never see another join this group.
- Sutton only won 20-plus games once (21 in 1976).
- Sutton won between 15 and 19 games in 11 different seasons (only Greg Maddux beat that record with 16).
- Don Sutton won in double-figures in 21 seasons; no one exceeded that number.
- Sutton won games in 29 different ballparks (he was 0–4 at Yankee Stadium).
- Win number 310 tied him with Old Hoss Radbourn, who pitched in the 19th century.

Like fine wine

In this game:
- The Angels' Don Sutton was 41
- The Angels' Reggie Jackson was 40
- The Angels' Bob Boone was 38
- The Angels' Bobby Grich was 37
- The Angels' George Hendrick was 36
- The Angels' Brian Downing was 35

Also playing in this game for Cleveland was Julio Franco, who was 27. Franco was 48 when he retired in 2007.

With Sutton picking up the win, the Angels had three pitchers with 15-plus wins. Kirk McCaskill and Mike Witt were the other two. In this game, the rookie Chuck Finley earned the first hold of his career. Two other times in Angels' history, they had three pitchers with 15-plus wins. In each case, 1989 and 1991, Finley was one of the three. He learned from one of the best.

When Don Sutton retired in 1988, he was second on the all-time list with 756 starts. Nolan Ryan surpassed him with 773 starts when he retired in 1993.

When Bob Boone retired in 1990, he was tops on the all-time list with 2,094 starts behind the plate. He was Pudged out of first by Carlton Fisk, who had 2,123 starts as a catcher when he retired in 1993, and then by Ivan Rodriguez, who started 2,353 games when he retired in 2011.

FRANCO'S WEIRD K

CLEVELAND 5 CALIFORNIA 2 | ANAHEIM STADIUM, ANAHEIM, CA
TIME: 2:42 • SEPTEMBER 23, 1986

BOB RYAN

Julio Franco struck out 1,341 times in a career that lasted until he was 48 years old. But the one credited to him in this game was unique.

Batting third in the order, he pulled a rib cage muscle while swinging and missing a 1st inning 0–1 offering from Mike Witt. He had to leave and was replaced by rookie Dave Clark, who completed the strikeout. But it went into the books credited to Franco, who was a spry 28 at the time.

You wouldn't believe the postgame raves for Cleveland rookie Greg Swindell, who was the winning pitcher on a complete-game four-hitter. From Bobby Grich: "He's the hardest-throwing left-hander that we have faced this year, except (Dave) Righetti." And this from manager

Gene Mauch: "If that is his normal stuff, you are going to be writing about that boy for a long time. He's as good a young pitching prospect as I've seen in a long time. A *long time*. He has great arm position, classic delivery, and just great stuff. He dominated the game."

I had been stalking Mauch for a sit-down interview all week. He finally gave it to me, and it was worth the wait. All you need to know about winning and losing, comes from Mauch: "If you win 100 games in a year, that's a pretty good year, right?" he said. "You might win a championship. But if you win 100 games, that also means you die 62 times."

And then there's this: "I can handle getting beat," he claimed. "What I can't handle is losing. For example, if I shoot 72 on the golf course—which I've done many times—and the other guy shoots 68, that's getting beat. But if I shoot 76, and the other guy shots 75, I can't handle that, or, I should say, I can't abide that."

BILL CHUCK

Crash Davis to Nuke LaLoosh from the 1988 cult film *Bull Durham*

"Hey. Relax. Don't try to strike everybody out. Strikeouts are boring. Besides that, they're fascist. Throw some ground balls. It's more democratic."

Need proof? Read the official baseball role book.

From the 2019 Official Baseball Rules:

> *9.15 Strikeouts*
>
> *(b) When a batter leaves the game with two strikes against him, and the substitute batter completes a strikeout, the Official Scorer shall charge the strikeout and the time at bat to the first batter. If the substitute batter completes the turn at bat in any other manner, including a base on balls, the Official Scorer shall score the action as having been that of the substitute batter.*

This game features some baseball long-haulers:

Julio Franco played his first game on April 23, 1982 (Age 23-243d), and his final game on September 17, 2007 (Age 49-025d). Playing for Cleveland, Atlanta, Texas, the Mets, Tampa Bay, Philadelphia, the

White Sox, and Milwaukee, Franco finished with a .298 average in his 23 seasons.

Greg Swindell lasted in the bigs for 17 seasons, pitching for Cleveland, Cincinnati, Houston, Minnesota, Boston, and Arizona. He retired with a record of 123–122 and a 3.86 ERA while striking out 1,542.

Mike Witt pitched in the majors for 12 seasons, and like Swindell, finished his career one game over the .500 mark and a very similar ERA. Pitching for the Angels and Yankees, Witt compiled a record of 117–116 with a 3.83 ERA. He faced Julio Franco a total of 56 times, with Julio hitting .354 against him and striking out 10 times, including this bit of fascism.

Dave Clark played 13 MLB seasons and hit .264 for Cleveland, the Cubs, Kansas City, Pittsburgh, the Dodgers, and Houston. And Dave Clark would *never* be able to hit Mike Witt. Clark was 0–10 against Witt in his career, striking out five times. And that doesn't include this non-existent plate appearance in this game.

Bobby Grich was an infielder for the Orioles and Angels for 17 seasons. He had a lifetime .266 BA. Grich played just five more games after this before retiring at the age of 37. This 0–3 with two whiffs was his only time facing Swindell.

Gene Mauch managed for 26 years and 3,942 games, the most of any manager who never reached the World Series. He managed the Phillies, Expos, Twins, and Angels and had a record of 1,902–2,037–3, which meant that he had to abide many losses. He could have used the wisdom of *The Big Lebowski* because as Sam Elliott's Stranger tells us: "The Dude abides. I don't know about you, but I take comfort in that. It's good knowin' he's out there. The Dude. Takin' er easy for all us sinners."

1986 NLCS GAME 1

HOUSTON 1 NEW YORK 0 | ASTRODOME, HOUSTON, TX
TIME: 2:56 • OCTOBER 8, 1986

BOB RYAN

There are very few people in any walk of life who could look you in the eye and say, in all accuracy, "There was a point in time when I was the best in the world at what I did." In September and October of 1986, Mike Scott was one of those people.

Mike Scott had a career record of 124–108. He will never go to the Hall of Fame. But in the second half of the 1986 season in which he would win the NL Cy Young Award, he had developed the single most devastating weapon belonging to any pitcher in baseball. It was a split-finger fastball. It was so good that people quite naturally accused him of doctoring the ball, and indeed that was the charge by some

New York Mets after Scott kicked off the 1986 NLCS with a five-hit, 14-strikeout, 1–0 triumph, the needed run coming via a Glenn Davis 2nd inning winning homer off Dwight Gooden.

Hall of Fame umpire Doug Harvey was behind the plate that day. And he gave Mike Scott the Veteran Plate Ump Seal of Approval. "It's the closest thing to a spitter," he declared. "It goes down left, down right, and sometimes straight down. But believe me, he's doing it legally."

"I always had a pretty good fastball," said Scott, then at 31 and in the eighth year of a career that had begun with—who else?—the Mets. "But I never had anything to go with it."

Among other accomplishments that year, he led the league in ERA (2.22), innings pitched (275.1), and shutouts (five). He capped his 18–10 regular season on September 25 by becoming the only person ever to clinch a pennant by throwing a no-hitter against the Giants (2–0).

I remember one other thing. Doug Harvey also said about that killer pitch: "It's like a fastball with an atom bomb attached to it."

You'll have to take my word for it. But who could forget a line like that?

BILL CHUCK

The 1986 NLCS was a best-of-seven series in which the Astros, in order to beat this Mets team, needed three wins from Mike Scott because somehow, someway, Scott "owned" the Mets.

Scott had only faced the Mets once during the 1986 season, getting a no-decision in a 5–4 win over the Mets in July. But Scott was having himself a season. Prior to the All-Star break, Scott went 9–6 with a 2.29 ERA and did even better after the break going 9–4 with a 2.13 ERA.

There have only been 24 1–0 complete-game shutouts in postseason history. Chris Carpenter pitched the last one in the 2011 NLDS (and one must wonder if it truly was the very last one). Scott's is the only one ever thrown in the NLCS.

There have only been seven 1–0 complete-game shutouts thrown in Game 1 of a postseason series (including three in a row from 1948 to 1950). In just two of these games, a home run made the difference.

- 1918 World Series—Babe Ruth for the Red Sox, who won the Series.
- 1948 World Series—Johnny Sain for Boston Braves, who lost the Series.
- 1949 World Series—Allie Reynolds for the Yankees, who won the Series.
- 1950 World Series—Vic Raschi for the Yankees, who won the Series.
- 1986 NLCS—Mike Scott for the Astros, who lost the series.
- 2001 NLDS—Curt Schilling for the Diamondbacks, who won the series.
- 2010 NLDS—Tim Lincecum for the Giants, who won the series.

ROGER NAILS DOWN CY

BOSTON 4 MILWAUKEE 0 | FENWAY PARK, BOSTON, MA
TIME: 2:32 • OCTOBER 4, 1987

BOB RYAN

It was a dank, dreary, early autumn New England day, good enough for football but providing a daunting circumstance for Brewers' batters standing in the way of Roger Clemens trying to win his 20th and nail down a second straight Cy Young Award.

He gave up two hits. He struck out 12, but it felt like 112. Many a no-hitter has been half as dominating. "The Brewers weren't going to dent Clemens yesterday unless the mound was moved back to second base," I wrote in the next morning's *Boston Globe*.

He walked nobody. Working on three days rest for the third time that season, he threw 115 pitches and only went to three balls three times.

Catcher John Marzano put it this way: "He's hard enough to hit when it's 90 degrees and sunny. A day like today makes it even tougher."

The ever-gracious Paul Molitor took his defeat like a man. "There is no doubt that Roger was on a mission today," he sighed. "We were overmatched."

"That's all I can do," said Clemens of his seventh 1987 shutout. "Put the numbers on the board and leave no doubt in anyone's mind."

BILL CHUCK

The American League 1987 Milwaukee Brewers were a good team. They finished in third place but had a 91-71 record. Over the course of 162 games, they ended up being blanked just five times, by Roger Clemens, Bert Blyleven, Charlie Leibrandt, Mike Witt, and Don Sutton, all solid-to-Hall of Fame-caliber pitchers.

In this game, the Brewers managed only two hits, a double by Mike Felder and a double by Dale Sveum. The only Brewer with a decent game was B.J. Surhoff, who went 0-3 but was the only player who didn't strike out against Clemens. Juan Castillo was 3-for-3—three at-bats, three whiffs.

This was Clemens' ninth double-digit strikeout game of the season. Mark Langston had nine as well, while Nolan Ryan had a dozen. But here's the Clemens difference; he was dominant and successful. Clemens, in the nine games, went 7-1 and struck out 103, and had three shutouts. Langston, in those nine games, recorded 98 strikeouts and went 6-3 with one shutout. Not atypically, Ryan went 4-4 while striking out 135 and didn't even have a complete game.

This was one of three shutouts in 1987 in which Clemens didn't walk anybody. He had 11 such games in his career.

Clemens' seven shutouts that season has only been exceeded three times. In 1988, by Clemens himself and by Orel Hershiser, and in 1989, by Tim Belcher, each with eight shutouts.

Clemens had a rough start in his quest to win his second straight Cy. Through his starts as of June 12, he was just 4-6. Over his last 23 starts, he went 16-3 with a 2.68 ERA as he became the first AL pitcher to have back-to-back 20-win seasons since Tommy John in 1979-1980.

One more thing...

Paul Molitor needed to go 6–6 in this game to overtake Wade Boggs for the AL batting title. The future Hall of Famer, who had had a 39-game hitting streak earlier in the season, went 0–4 against Clemens and finished the season hitting .353. Wade Boggs, who missed this game with a knee injury, won his third consecutive batting title, hitting .363. Clemens said that before the game, he told Boggs, "I told the 'Chicken Man' not to worry, that I was sure I could get (Paul) Molitor at least once in six times at bat, and he would win the batting title." In their careers, Molitor was 33–107 versus Clemens, good for a .308 average.

STEWART GOES 10

OAKLAND 3 CHICAGO 2 | COMISKEY PARK, CHICAGO, IL
TIME: 2:38 • APRIL 23, 1988

BOB RYAN

Dave Stewart was in the midst of a nice little run of four consecutive 20-win seasons when he turned the clock back a bit by throwing a 10-inning complete game. But he needed an assist from Mother Nature in order to avoid a no-decision or perhaps even a loss.

The Oakland 10th began when White Sox reliever John Davis went 3–0 to leadoff man Tony Phillips and then went to his mouth. Oops. That was an automatic ball four. Carney Lansford sacrificed him to second. Jose Canseco was walked intentionally. Mike Gallego hit a fairly routine fly to right. This would be a good spot to point out that the game-time temperature was 44 degrees, and there was a 17-mph wind out of the northwest. Ivan Calderon couldn't corral the ball as the go-ahead run scored on his two-base E-9.

"He just missed the ball," said Chicago skipper Jim Fregosi. "It was a tough wind out there. He slipped. He almost fell down."

The inning wasn't over. Dave Parker was intentionally walked to load the bases. Terry Steinbach hit into an inning-ending 5-2-3 double play. You don't see that too often.

BILL CHUCK

From 1984 to 1990, nobody threw more extra-inning complete games than Dave Stewart's five. Stewart tossed four 10.0 IP games, going 3–1, and one 11.0 inning 1–0 shutout of the Mariners. The fact is that from 1981 through the 2020 season, no pitcher has matched Stewart's five extra-inning games, and I doubt anyone ever will again.

Notice that this 10-inning game took all of two hours and thirty-eight minutes. As the British group Eurythmics, consisting of Annie Lennox and Dave Stewart(!), sang, "Sweet dreams are made of this, who am I to disagree?"

TETTLETON SWITCH-HIT HR

BALTIMORE 6 DETROIT 4 | TIGER STADIUM, DETROIT, MI
TIME: 2:35 • JUNE 13, 1988

BOB RYAN

Eddie Murray hit a 400-foot double off the Tiger Stadium fence in right-center, but he was upstaged by Oriole catcher Mickey Tettleton, who hit a left-handed homer off Walt Terrell in the 7th and a right-handed, game-winning, three-run homer off Willie Hernandez in the 9th.

Mickey Tettleton was a man ahead of his time, not because he was a switch-hitting catcher, but because he was a so-called "Three Outcome" guy before we realized they existed. Get this: 44 percent of Mickey Tettleton's 5,745 plate appearances in a 14-year career resulted in either a strikeout, base on balls, or home run.

His game-winner was only the third three-run homer the Orioles had hit that year. And this was his first career two-homer game.

BILL CHUCK

I suggest we call it "The Wally Schang Award." Each year we should give the Schang Award to the player who has done the most damage from each side of the plate in the same game. Wally was the first player to homer from each side of the plate in the same game when the Philadelphia Athletic went deep against the Yankees on September 8, 1916, at Shibe Park in Philly. Schang was playing left field that day, but he spent most of his 19-season career as a catcher, like Tettleton.

According to Baseball-Almanac.com, the MLB record for career home runs from each side of the plate is 14, held by Mark Teixeira, who had 12 in the American League and two in the National League. Nick Swisher tied Teixeira in 2015, when he hit one in the NL, to go with his AL record 13 instances. Ken Caminiti holds the NL record with 10.

If there were anyone who you would expect to produce the switch-feat in this game, it would be Eddie Murray, who did it 11 times in his career. However, it was Tettleton who pulled it off for the first of three times he did it, and he only had 13 two-homer games in his career. Schang only had two two-homer games as he played primarily in the dead-ball era. Eddie Murray had 31 multiple-homer games. And the most famous of all switch-hitters, Mickey Mantle, had 10 games with homers from each side of the plate and 46 multi-homer games. Babe Ruth holds the record with 72 multi-homer games.

The Orioles were an awful 54–107 that season and ended up hitting just nine three-run homers and one grand slam. This was the only game they won that season when trailing as they entering the 9th.

ROGER'S ONE-HITTER

BOSTON 6 CLEVELAND 0 | FENWAY PARK, BOSTON, MA
TIME: 2:23 • SEPTEMBER 10, 1988

BOB RYAN

Roger wasn't conning anybody. He *knew*.

I don't care who you are or what people say," he explained. "If you get into the seventh or eighth with one, you want it."

Roger never did get that elusive no-hitter, but he gave it a good shot on this September afternoon, carrying a no-hitter into the 8th before Dave Clark dumped a one-out single into center. Roger had to settle for his eighth shutout of the season. Often a no-hitter needs that one key defensive play, and Roger thought he had gotten it when catcher Rick Cerone made a superb play on a Joe Carter nubber down the third-base line, nipping Carter at first.

As for the Clark no-hit spoiler, Roger was philosophical. "I'm not disappointed because of the pitch I threw," he said. "It was a good pitch, a fastball in the right place, not a slider."

This was Roger at his most efficient. He only whiffed five. He threw an economical 86 pitches and had three outs on first pitches and nine on second. "I was going for good pitches," he said. "I threw good pitches ball the way through. (Rick) Cerone called a good game, and people made plays behind me. That's how you get a one-hitter."

BILL CHUCK

There are many great pitchers like Roger Clemens, who never threw a no-hitter. Pedro Martinez never threw a no-no. Steve Carlton never threw one. Neither did Mike Mussina, Don Drysdale, Don Sutton, Ferguson Jenkins, Whitey Ford, Lefty Grove, Early Wynn, or CC Sabathia, just to name a few.

Steve Carlton tossed six one-hitters. Don Sutton threw five one-hitters. Mike Mussina tossed four, Pedro Martinez, Whitey Ford, and Fergie Jenkins threw three apiece, Early Wynn threw two, and Grove, Drysdale, and Sabathia each tossed one, just like Roger Clemens. This was it.

It's not like this wasn't a good day for hitting; the Sox picked up 14 hits. Dwight (Dewey) Evans had four hits falling a homer shy of the cycle. Jody Reed had three hits. But only Dave Clark was deserving of a high five, singling and walking against Clemens.

Just for fun…

I hope you noticed that the pinch-hitter that struck out to end the 8th for Cleveland was Terry Francona.

SELLERS LOSES HIS ONE-HITTER

CLEVELAND 1 BOSTON 0 | CLEVELAND STADIUM, CLEVELAND, OH
TIME: 2:20 • OCTOBER 1, 1988

BOB RYAN

Five times that year, Jeff Sellers lost when his team didn't score a run. No wonder he went 1–7. But nothing could have hurt more than this, when he took a no-hitter into the 8th and lost on the only hit he would surrender, that being a Luis Medina home run.

Sellers tried to stay upbeat afterward. "He used to hit me pretty good in high school too," he joked.

"That's an exaggeration," said Medina.

The winning pitcher was a 14-game winner named John Farrell, whose name should be familiar to baseball fans in both Cleveland and Boston.

The Red Sox had clinched the AL East the day before. While they were losing to Cleveland, the Tigers had beaten the Yankees. Low-key Sox manager Joe Morgan, refused to get overly excited. "I'm going to do the same thing I do every day of my life," he said. "Have a few scotches, eat dinner and go to sleep."

BILL CHUCK

Baseball is a cruel game. You can give up 14 hits and win and permit one hit, albeit a homer, and lose. Not allowing hits was never a Jeff Sellers specialty. In his four years in the majors, in 329.2 IP, he allowed 364 hits, 9.9 hits every nine innings.

Too many hits and not enough wins (13–22 lifetime) were just two of the reasons why this was the last major league game of Sellers' career.

In 1988, eight starters lost 1–0 because they allowed a homer. Sellers was the only one who struck out as many as 10 and the only one who allowed just one hit. There were seven pitchers who allowed just one hit and one homer that season. Sellers was the only one who struck out as many as 10 and the only one who lost. In 1988, Sellers lost 2–0 and 5–0 to the Twins, 3–0 to Oakland and Toronto, and 1–0 to Cleveland.

At least in this game, Sellers held Cleveland's Joe Carter to an 0–3. On June 21 of that season, Carter's line drive fractured Sellers' pitching hand, forcing him on the disabled list for six weeks. Boston scored 10 runs, but Sellers wasn't in the game long enough to get the win. Baseball is a cruel game. Need more proof?

In December of 1988, Sellers was moved in a multi-player trade between Boston and Cincinnati. But before having a chance to pitch for his new team, Sellers tore his rotator cuff and never pitched for the Reds or anyone else ever again.

On this day, Sellers was the losing pitcher, finishing 1–7 with a 4.83 ERA. John Farrell was the winning pitcher for Cleveland, bringing his record to 14–10 with a 4.24 ERA. At this point in his two-season career, Farrell was 25 years of age with a 19–11 record and a 4.03 ERA. But because we know what baseball is (cruel), the rest of Farrell's career was beset with pitching problems and injuries (elbow), and he went 17–35 with a 4.91 ERA from that point forward until his playing career sputtered to an end in 1996. After years as a pitching coach for

Cleveland and Boston, Farrell managed Toronto and then Boston in 2013. In his first season with Boston, the Sox went from worst-to-first and won the world championship. In 2014, the team struggled, and Boston went first-to-worst.

Two days after the 2017 specious Houston Astros knocked the Red Sox out of the ALDS, Farrell was fired. His place was taken by one of Houston's assistants, Alex Cora, who won it all for Boston in 2018, in his first year at the helm. And, you know why that happened to Farrell? Because baseball is… ironic.

1988 NLCS GAME 3

METS LEAD NLCS 2–1

NEW YORK 8 LOS ANGELES 4 | SHEA STADIUM, QUEENS, NY

TIME: 3:44 • OCTOBER 8, 1988

BOB RYAN

For seven innings, it was an ordinary baseball game, tied at 3–3. In fact, the predominant thought of everyone: the players, managers, coaches, umpires, the 44,672 in attendance, and those of us in the press sitting and freezing our tushies off in the auxiliary press arena in left field was, "Please God, let somebody score and get this thing over with." It was 43 degrees at game time that afternoon, and the entire game was being played in a heavy drizzle. Yuck! It was so bad there were 10,897 no-shows. For a playoff game!

But things got interesting in the Mets' 8th. Leadoff batter Kevin McReynolds was at bat with a 3–2 count against Dodgers' reliever Jay Howell, when Davey Johnson came bounding out of the dugout to approach plate umpire Joe West. The two went to visit Howell at the mound and—whoa!—Mr. West ejected him from the game. Jay Howell had just been accused of using pine tar to doctor the baseball. This is illegal.

Long story short. The Mets scored five runs off Howell's three successors. Of course, that was not the primary postgame discussion. Jay Howell was.

He denied nothing. He said, yes, he was using pine tar simply to get a better grip on the ball in those adverse conditions. He maintained that pine tar does not make the ball do um, funny things. It only enables you to grip the ball better.

"Let's face it," he said. "It's illegal. But to me, it's *not* illegal. I don't feel I did anything wrong. If you're scuffing the ball to make it do something abhorrent, that's different." (Extra points for using the word "abhorrent.")

Surprisingly, Mets' star Keith Hernandez agreed. "I don't think that's cheating," he affirmed. "He should not be suspended. It would be very unfair to the Dodgers and Jay Howell. Fans would think he's a cheater, and that's wrong."

Well, originally, he was suspended for three days, but then it was reduced to two. He was available for Games 6 and 7, but went unused. He did appear in two World Series games as the Dodgers defeated the A's.

BILL CHUCK

The use of pine tar is a sticky situation (go ahead, you can groan) for baseball. Baseballs are slippery, and on a 43-degree rainy day, they are hard to grip. There were a combined 13 walks in this game.

In a May 2018 article for Bleacher Report, Scott Miller asked a number of players about the controversy. "I use pine tar on my bat, so the bat doesn't slip out of my hands," Baltimore outfielder Adam Jones told Miller. Miller asked Bryce Harper about the use of pine tar by pitchers. "I'm all in favor of it. If there's a guy out there that needs it,

I'm all for it. I don't want to get hit in the head or the face. So whatever they need out there, I'll let them have it." And this was in 2018, long before the 2021 season of sticky stuff.

Point of record...

In reviewing Retrosheet, Howell's ejection from this game was the only pine tar–related ejection in a postseason game.

1988 NLCS GAME 7

DODGERS WIN NLCS 4–3
LOS ANGELES 6 NEW YORK 0
DODGER STADIUM, LOS ANGELES, CA
TIME: 2:51 • OCTOBER 12, 1988

BOB RYAN

He had started Games 1 and 3. He had saved Game 4. He had warmed up twice in Game 5. But he was Orel Hershiser IV, winner of 23 games in the regular season, a man who had led the league in complete games (15), shutouts (eight), and innings pitched (267). His mates wanted no one else on the mound for Game 7.

So no one in Los Angeles was surprised when Orel Hershiser IV shut the Mets down on five hits in this critical game.

"Several people say Orel was tired, and I'm sure (he was)," said NL MVP Kirk Gibson. "But we call him 'Bulldog' for a reason. It's not like

124

he's a one-pitch pitcher. A one-pitch pitcher gets tired. Orel is as smart as and pitcher run the games. We want him out there."

It was 6–0 after two innings. Manager Tom Lasorda never considered lifting his ace. Orel Hershiser IV threw 130 pitches. Ain't happening today.

BILL CHUCK

It almost seems unfair because whoever faced Orel Hershiser was not going to win, and, on this night, it was never even close.

By the time Orel's Mets' starting counterpart, Ron Darling, had faced 10 batters, six had reached based on hits, and one reached on an error. After 35 pitches, Darling left the game with the bases loaded and no one out in the 2nd inning, trailing 3–0. In came Game 1 and Game 4 starter Dwight Gooden to the mound in relief. By the time the 2nd inning was over, the scoring for this game was over as well, with the Dodgers up 6–0.

Back to Hershiser. Thanks to the Bulldog, the game never became interesting. The Bulldog was relentless.

- In the 1st inning, the Mets reached on a single and a walk.
- In the 2nd inning, the Mets reached on a single.
- In the 3rd inning, the Mets reached on a single.
- In the 4th inning, the Mets reached on a single.
- In the 7th inning, the Mets reached on a double.
- In the 8th inning, the Mets reached on an HBP and a walk.
- In the 9th inning, the Mets reached on an HBP.

Hershiser was the NLCS MVP, appearing in four games, making three starts, and allowing five runs (three earned) in 24.2 IP, worthy of an ERA of 1.09, over a full run better than his regular-season spectacular ERA of 2.26.

One last thing…

In September 1988, Orel Hershiser made six starts and threw 55.0 innings of scoreless baseball. He allowed 30 hits, walked nine, and struck out 34. It was SCORELESS baseball. This means that by the time this NLCS was finished, Hershiser had made nine starts and one relief appearance and had allowed three earned runs in 79.2 innings pitched. That's an ERA of 0.34. And by the time the World Series against Oakland was completed (for which he was the MVP as well), he had allowed five earned runs in 97.2 innings pitched. That's an ERA of 0.46. Bob had been in the presence of brilliance on baseball's highest stage.

KUTCHER HITS FOR RICE

BOSTON 5 CALIFORNIA 2 | ANAHEIM STADIUM, ANAHEIM, CA
TIME: 2:36 • MAY 18, 1989

BOB RYAN

9th inning.

The Sox lead 3–2.

Randy Kutcher is sent up to bunt. But catcher Lance Parrish makes an errant pickoff throw, advancing the runners. Kutcher swings away and hits a single through a drawn-in infield. He gets an RBI and eventually scores when Jody Reed beats out a potential double-play ball.

So, what's the big deal?

He was batting for Jim Rice.

When Joe Morgan had pinch-hit for Rice a year earlier, it was borderline WWIII in the Sox dugout, with Rice drawing a three-game suspension. Not this time. Bliss prevailed.

"It was a situation where he (Morgan) told me, 'If it's first and second, you're up there bunting,'" Kutcher explained. "The guy I pinch-hit for is one of the best hitters in the game, and that includes today. To pinch-hit for him is a privilege."

This time the guy he pinch-hit for had been adequately briefed in advance. "It's passed," Morgan said. "I didn't even think about it. Jimmy was great about it. He wanted me to bunt them over just like everybody else."

And people think managing is always about Xs and Os.

BILL CHUCK

Hey, Bob, it's almost time to bring up Carroll Hardy, right?

But first, Randy Kutcher.

Pinch-hitting is not easy. You sit on the bench all game waiting for your moment of glory, which most of the time is inglorious. Randy Kutcher pinch-hit 26 times in his career. He had one sac bunt to go along with three walks and a mere three hits (one of which you just read about). That's a .136 batting average. He had a total of three RBI (one of which you just read about). His other two ribbies came in his next pinch-hitting PA on June 8, 1989, in Yankee Stadium, when he pinch-hit for catcher Rich Gedman, who had entered the game having pinch-hit the inning before for catcher Rick Cerone. With two down in the 9th, Kutcher hit a pinch double to drive home two off Yankees' closer Dave Righetti and send the game into extras. The fact that the Yanks won in 11 is extraneous to this story.

Hey Bob, it's almost time to bring up Carroll Hardy, right?

But first, Spike Owen.

As Bob mentioned, Jim Rice had been pinch-hit for before. On Wednesday, July 20, 1988. On Thursday, July 21, 1988, he was suspended for three games. July 20 should have been a happy day in Red Sox Nation. A Massachusetts governor became the Democratic nominee for president, interim manager Joe Morgan was given the official go-ahead to be the Boston manager for the rest of the season, and the Sox won their seventh straight (all in Morgan's first seven games), defeating the Twins, 9–7, on a walk-off homer in the 10th.

And yet, it was a stormy night. Roger Clemens blew a 5–0 lead, the bullpen collapsed, and Jim Ed Rice became so enraged at being pinch-hit for that he and Morgan engaged in a shoving match in the runway leading from the dugout to the clubhouse.

Boston held a slim 5–4 lead in the bottom of the 8th as Ellis Burks led off with a walk. Morgan then called Rice, the DH and Sox captain, back from the on-deck circle and sent up Spike Owen to pinch-bunt.

Rice was not a bunter. In 16 years in the bigs, he had five sac hits and hadn't had one since 1980. But he was a future Hall of Famer who expected to be up in situations such as these. Spike Owen was not headed for Cooperstown, but in 13 MLB seasons, he laid down 67 successful bunts. According to Boston's second baseman Marty Barrett, the problem occurred because he never heard Morgan say that Owen would hit (bunt) for Rice if Burks got on base. The brouhaha then took place because of that darned unwritten rules book, as Kevin Paul Dupont wrote the next day in the *Boston Globe*, "That's sort of an unwritten rule, that you don't call guys back like that," said Barrett. "And if Jimmy had understood from the beginning, nothing probably would have happened." And now you know the rest of the story.

Now Carroll Hardy. Carroll Hardy is the only person to ever pinch-hit for Ted Williams. He's also the only one to pinch-hit for Carl Yastrzemski. He also pinch-hit for Roger Maris. Hardy also was the guy who went out to left field and replaced Ted Williams after Ted had homered in his final big-league at-bat. Hardy was 12–63 (.190) as a pinch-hitter in his eight-season career in the majors.

As Bob mentioned, managing and baseball is not an easy psychological exercise. As Yogi Berra famously said, "Baseball is 90 percent mental. The other half is physical."

THE ULTIMATE DOUBLE-SWITCHER

LOS ANGELES 9 CINCINNATI 2
DODGER STADIUM, LOS ANGELES, CA
TIME: 2:23 • JUNE 12, 1989

BOB RYAN

Now it seems to me that if one of your guys enters the game in the 7th inning via a double-switch and in his two at-bats has an RBI suicide squeeze and a two-run homer, he might get a little acknowledgment in your coverage. Nope. Not this time. So, this will have to suffice. Dave Anderson's 2–2–2–3 box score deserves some props.

The juicier L.A. story was that Tom Lasorda had moved Kirk Gibson from third in the order to leadoff, and he had gone 3-for-3 while getting on base five times. Managerial genius, you know?

And then there was this. Earlier that morning, earthquakes registering at 4.5 and 4.3 had taken place 25 minutes apart.

"At 9:56:01, I was laying in bed," said Reds' reliever Norm Charlton. "At 9:56:02, I was holding on to the ceiling like one of those cats… it wasn't very fun. The building isn't supposed to move like that."

BILL CHUCK

Anderson's brief but unusual day began in the top of the 7th with the Reds batting and trailing 4–1. Ricky Horton had come in from the bullpen with the bases loaded and no one out, retired two batters, allowing one run to score. He did his job. Then Lasorda performed the old double-switcheroo (you know, the thing that occurred before the universal DH). Reliever John Wetteland replaced third baseman Tracy Woodson pitching and batting 6th, and Anderson replaced Ricky Horton playing third and batting 9th. Wetteland quickly whiffed Joel Youngblood, and the half inning came to an end.

Enter stage left, the other character in this drama, Norm Charlton, who played a role in the Anderson storyline. With one out, Alfredo Griffin singles. With Anderson at the plate, Charlton attempted to pick off Griffin, throwing wildly. With Griffin now on third, Anderson laid down a squeeze bunt. Reds' manager Pete Rose was none too happy with Charlton's sketchy fielding of said bunt.

Rose was particularly chatty postgame, evaluating Lasorda's decision to have the slumping Kirk Gibson in the leadoff slot. Gibby had led off for the first time in his Dodgers' career in the previous game. Rose said, "He's not a leadoff hitter. He got things going for them tonight, but he'll have to hit some home runs for them to win." Was Rose betting against Gibson? What was that about? Clearly, he didn't understand Lasorda's foresight in having your best hitter leading off, a common practice of today's managers.

Charlton was done after one inning, allowing three runs. Anderson homered off Kent Tekulve in the 8th to close out the scoring. This was game 1,036 of Tekulve's career. About a month later, he pitched in game 1,050, his finale. John Wetteland earned the save, the first of 330 in his career and his only one in three seasons and 59 games with the Dodgers.

Science Section

Charlton's earthquake of 1989
Montebello Earthquake
TIME: June 12, 1989 / 9:57 AM PDT
LOCATION: 34° 1.65' N, 118° 10.78' W Beneath Montebello, near
　East Los Angeles
MAGNITUDE: ML4.9
DEPTH: 15.6 km

The World Series earthquake of 1989
On October 17, 1989, right before the start of Game 3 of the World
Series between the Oakland A's and San Francisco Giants, at 5:04:15,
in Candlestick Park. The Loma Prieta earthquake reached a magnitude
of 6.9 and lasted 17 seconds. It was responsible for 63 deaths, 3,757
injuries, and more than $6 billion in damages.

A "WOW!' GAME

BOSTON 10 BALTIMORE 8 (13 INNINGS)
MEMORIAL STADIUM, BALTIMORE, MD
TIME: 5:23 • AUGUST 12, 1989

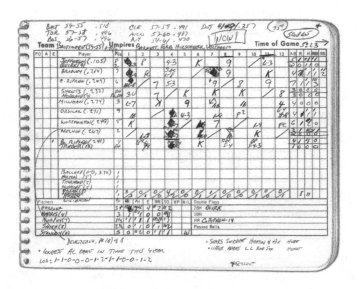

BOB RYAN

"Wow!"

That's what I wrote atop my scorebook page, and why not? We—
which means 50,865 Memorial Stadium fans (the third Orioles' sellout
of the season), the media, and all the participants—had just seen a
month's worth of baseball in a mere five hours and 23 minutes, which
to that point was the AL's longest game in time of the season.

The Red Sox had 20 hits and left 19 men on base, including at least
one in their final 12 at-bats. And the only reason none were left on in
the first was that Ellis Burks hit into an inning-ending 5-4-3 double
play.

There were ejections galore. Ump John Hirschbeck was a busy man. He tossed Orioles coach Al Bumbry on a 2–2 count to Wade Boggs in the 5th. He tossed Sox skipper Joe Morgan for protesting an "out" call on a Boggs inning-ending 5-4-3 in the 11th. Ump Vic Voltaggio ejected Mike Greenwell from the dugout, saying as a player on the Disabled List, he wasn't supposed to be there at all.

Bob Stanley got the win in classic Bob Stanley fashion; namely, a three-inning shutout relief stint.

But the kicker from a Boston viewpoint was that the go-ahead RBI was a resounding ground-rule double by a most unlikely hero, catcher Rich Gedman. It was only Gedman's sixth RBI since May 29.

BILL CHUCK

I hope you appreciate that we don't get a "Wow!" that frequently from the legendary Bob Ryan. If you are familiar with Bob's media appearances, you know exclamation points are part and parcel of his speaking style, but the combination of a "wow" and a "!" on his scorecard means this was a helluva game.

And it was. Not because anything spectacular happened but because lots of little things happened:

- Marty Barrett had his 11th and final four-hit game of his career.
- Nick Esasky had his 13th and final four-RBI game of his career.
- Bob Stanley had his 24th and final 3.0 IP shutout relief appearance of his career. (Steamer won six of those appearances and saved 16 others.)
- Rich Gedman had his 18th and final Red Sox double, which gave the team the lead. (He had one more in his career with St. Louis.)
- Wade Boggs had his first game with eight plate appearances; he went 2–7 with an intentional walk.

At the time, this was the longest 13-inning game ever played. That remained true until 2007.

This battle was part of the war for supremacy in the AL East, meaning this game meant something, even though it was mid-August. The Orioles had been in first place for 74 consecutive games but entered the game with just a 2.5 game lead. Baltimore had a 59-55 record, while Toronto (57–58) and Boston (56–57) were both below sea level yet in second place. The Orioles 7.5 game lead on July 20ᵗʰ was slowly slipping away.

After this game, the lead was at 1.5 games over both Boston and Toronto. Reminder, there were no wild cards. On September 1, the Orioles were in second place. That's where they remained for the remainder of the season. The Blue Jays went 31–15 the rest of the way to win the AL East. The Orioles finished 28–19, and Boston finished third, closing out at 26–22.

Cito Gaston's Jays lost to Tony La Russa's A's in the ALCS. The A's swept the Giants in the famed earthquake World Series that most definitely would have gotten a "Wow!!!" from Bob Ryan.

1989 NLCS GAME 1

SAN FRANCISCO 11 CHICAGO 3 | WRIGLEY FIELD, CHICAGO, IL
TIME: 2:51 • OCTOBER 4, 1989

BOB RYAN

History was being made. It was the first postseason night game ever played at Wrigley Field. Parking was an astronomical $20. The recovery tow for an illegally parked vehicle was $105. It was a big deal, all right.

Beloved Cub third baseman and broadcaster Ron Santo threw out the first pitch. That might have been the evening's highlight for Cubs fans.

Greg Maddux started, and he just didn't have it. The future Hall of Famer was rocked for eight hits and eight earned runs in four innings. His chief assailant was Will Clark, who had six runs batted run thanks to a 1st inning double and then home runs in both the 3rd and 4th. The

136

second homer was a grand slam, and it wasn't just any old grand slam. Forgive me for again quoting myself from the pages of the *Boston Globe*. I said the homer was "stopping at Saturn or Sheffield Avenue, whichever came first." You get the idea.

BILL CHUCK

On October 4, 1989, Graham Chapman, of Monty Python fame, and Secretariat, the great racehorse, both passed away. And for the fans in Wrigley, in this best of seven NLCS, this opening night disaster, with your ace who went a regular-season 19–12 on the mound, this felt nearly as momentous in Chicagoland.

Let's talk for a moment about the less-than-thrilling night that Will "The Thrill" Clark caused for Greg Maddux. It certainly wasn't a love for Wrigley that set off this night. In 44 career regular season games, including 40 starts at Wrigley Field, Clark was a .204 hitter and totaled two homers and 13 RBI in 173 PA.

As you can see on Bob's scorecard, in four at-bats, Clark scored four runs, had four hits (including two homers and a double), and drove home six. This was the worst-pitched game in the magnificent Hall of Fame career of Greg Maddux.

Maddux appeared in 35 postseason games, of which he started 30 of them and pitched 198.0 innings. This was the first of only two postseason games in which Maddux gave up two homers (October 7, 1995, pitching for Atlanta vs. Colorado—to two different players). This was the only postseason game in which he allowed two HR and two doubles.

There were no other postseason games in which Maddux allowed eight earned runs. Maddux allowed eight-plus earned runs in only four regular season games in his 23-season career. He allowed nine runs once, but at least he lasted seven innings. This night in Wrigley, he was gone after four.

Credit this to Will Clark. No one totaled as many postseason RBI *in their career* against Maddux as Clark had in this game.

Check this out:

- In less than four innings, Clark had tied the NLCS record for RBI for an entire series.
- Only 21 players have ever had four hits in an NLCS game.
- Only 21 players have ever had two homers in an NLCS game.
- Only four players have ever had four hits, including two homers, in an NLCS game.
- Only Will Clark has ever had four hits and six RBI in an NLCS game.

1989 ALCS GAME 4

A'S LEAD THE ALCS 3–1

OAKLAND 6 TORONTO 5 | SKYDOME, TORONTO, CANADA

TIME: 3:29 • OCTOBER 7, 1989

BOB RYAN

What people most remember is that Jose Canseco hit one where a baseball had never gone before; namely, the fifth deck of what was then known as "Skydome." What losing pitcher Mike Flanagan most remembers is that Rickey Henderson hit *two* off him, the second KO'ing him in the 5th.

Rickey was feeling pretty good about himself after his first one, which went an estimated 430 feet to dead center. But two batters later, he was rudely one-upped by his teammate. Canseco blasted one that kept going up, up, up, and up, landing in the never-before-visited fifth deck. "I thought I hit the ball pretty good," sighed Henderson. "Then I saw Jose's."

Everyone was impressed except Canseco. "I'd say it only ranks 10th or 11th among those I've hit," he declared. "You know it's only 326 down the line. The ball carried well. But you know, if you get it up, it's going to be a mammoth hit... I went to see the replay to see where the ball was. It was a fastball in, and I haven't seen one of those from a left-hander in a while."

Said left-hander wasn't particularly fazed by either wallop. Flanagan was far more upset with himself about the second Henderson homer, which sneaked inside the left-field foul pole at that 329 mark. "The ball that hurt me was Henderson's second home run," Flanagan explained. "That made it 5–1, not 3–1."

BILL CHUCK

The Skydome was just four months old, but the Canseco blast is still momentous over 30 years later. Ross Newhan in the *Los Angeles Times* shared the reaction of Billy Beane (the Oakland A's reserve first baseman): "That wasn't just a home run. It was a home run of biblical proportion."

The next day, Frank Blackman, in the *San Francisco Examiner*, wrote that Jose Canseco had "a modest proposal to revolutionize the game."... "Home runs should be measured in 100-foot increments," Canseco said, grinning. "If you hit a ball over 500 feet, game's over, A's win." I know there are Statcast aficionados out there today who would find that to be a totally acceptable plan.

But as Bob points out, it was Rickey Henderson who continued to haunt the Blue Jays. Bob Costas doing play-by-play for the national audience, remarked after Rickey Henderson's mammoth first blast, "There aren't many leadoff men who can launch one like that. To dead center field." After the second homer, Costas' broadcast partner Tony Kubek said, "Can you imagine how many ways this guy can beat you? In Games 1 and 2, the great base stealing, a record, and then he does this today."

Here's how Henderson became the MVP of the ALCS.

- In Game 1, Rickey was hitless, except he walked twice, was hit by a pitch, stole two bases, and scored a run. In five plate appearances, he saw 26 pitches.
- In Game 2, Rickey went 2–2, with two walks, four stolen bases (two steals of second, two steals of third), and he scored two runs. In four plate appearances, he saw 16 pitches.
- In Game 3, Rickey went 1–4 (a double), with one walk, a stolen base, and he scored two runs. In five plate appearances, he saw 21 pitches.
- In Game 4, Rickey went 2–4 (a pair of homers), with one walk, he was picked off first, he scored two runs, and he had four RBI. In five plate appearances, he saw 15 pitches.
- In Game 5, Rickey went 1–3 (a triple), with one walk, one stolen base, he scored one run, and he had one RBI. In four plate appearances, he saw 21 pitches.
- In total, Rickey went 6–15 (with an ALCS cycle with two homers), hitting .400, with seven walks, eight stolen bases, he scored eight runs, and he had five RBI. In 23 plate appearances, he saw 99 pitches. He did not strike out even once.

In this game, Dennis Eckersley picked up the save, after pitching 1.2 innings and allowing two hits. He was credited with allowing no runs. However, he did allow each of the two runners he inherited from Rick Honeycutt to score. The second one was a beaut, as with two outs, Mookie Wilson scored from first on a ground ball single to right by Fred McGriff. With two outs in the 9th, Eck gave up a single to Kelly Gruber, which put the tying run on and the winning run coming to the plate. But the Blue Jays pinch-hitter Lee Mazzilli was no Kirk Gibson, and on a 3–2 pitch, he popped to third to end the game.

This save was the sixth of Eck's career in the LCS, which broke a tie with Tug McGraw for the most at the time in League Championship Series history. A brief tie as Eck picked up his seventh the next day. Dennis Eckersley finished his career with 11 LCS saves, second all-time. The all-time leader is Mariano Rivera with 13 LCS saves.

BILL CHUCK ON THE 1980s

Leaders (1980–89)
Hits: Robin Yount (1,731)
Homers: Mike Schmidt (313)
Wins: Jack Morris (162)
Losses: Jim Clancy (126)
Strikeouts: Nolan Ryan (2,167)
Team wins: Yankees (854)
Team losses: Mariners (893)

Season highlights
1980—The Phillies win their first title, George Brett hit .390
1981—The players strike, Fernandomania
1982—Rickey Henderson swipes 130 bases, Rollie Fingers becomes the first to 300 saves, Gaylord Perry gets win No. 300
1983—Dan Quisenberry saves 45 games, Steve Carlton wins his 300th game
1984—The Tigers go wire-to-wire
1985—Umpire Don Denkinger's blown call, Pete Rose becomes the all-time hit king, Tom Seaver and Phil Niekro both win their 300th
1986—Bill Buckner's error, Don Sutton wins No. 300
1987—Mike Schmidt hits No. 500
1988—Kirk Gibson's homer, Cubs play their first night game at Wrigley, Orel Hershiser sets the scoreless inning record, Jose Canseco becomes baseball's first 40/40 player
1989—The World Series earthquake

World Series

1989	4–0	Oakland Athletics (99–63, AL) vs. San Francisco Giants (92–70, NL)
1988	4–1	Los Angeles Dodgers (94–67, NL) vs. Oakland Athletics (104–58, AL)
1987	4–3	Minnesota Twins (85–77, AL) vs. St. Louis Cardinals (95–67, NL)
1986	4–3	New York Mets (108–54, NL) vs. Boston Red Sox (95–66, AL)
1985	4–3	Kansas City Royals (91–71, AL) vs. St. Louis Cardinals (101–61, NL)
1984	4–1	Detroit Tigers (104–58, AL) vs. San Diego Padres (92–70, NL)
1983	4–1	Baltimore Orioles (98–64, AL) vs. Philadelphia Phillies (90–72, NL)
1982	4–3	St. Louis Cardinals (92–70, NL) vs. Milwaukee Brewers (95–67, AL)
1981	4–2	Los Angeles Dodgers (63–47, NL) vs. New York Yankees (59–48, AL)
1980	4–2	Philadelphia Phillies (91–71, NL) vs. Kansas City Royals (97–65, AL)

Four baseball commissioners

Bowie Kuhn

Peter Ueberroth

Bart Giamatti

Fay Vincent

chapter 3

THE
1990s

BOB RYAN

The 1990s gave me an opportunity to attend more games at both Yankee Stadium and Shea Stadium, because I was in New York on many a Saturday in preparation for my Sunday morning appearance on ESPN's *The Sports Reporters*, which then emanated from Manhattan. There were also the requisite number of postseason visits, most notably the first "Division Series" ever, the epic 1995 Yankees-Mariners five-gamer, which may very well be the best ALDS yet waged.

BOGGS' THREE IBB

BOSTON 4 DETROIT 2 | FENWAY PARK, BOSTON, MA
TIME: 2:54 • APRIL 10, 1990

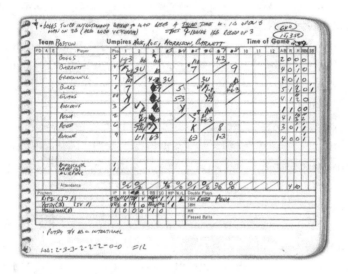

BOB RYAN

I think we can safely say that Sparky Anderson respected Wade Boggs. I mean, he did walk him intentionally three times in this game.

The first time: 2nd inning. No score. Loads the bases.

Second time: 3rd inning. Sox lead, 4–0. First base open.

Third time: 5th inning. Sox lead, 4–2. First base open.

Did it work? Yes. Marty Barrett grounded out, walked, and flied out.

"It's part of the game," Boggs shrugged. "Sparky told me a couple of years ago that if there's a chance of putting me on, he's going to do it. He's doing it… I just go along with the flow. I go to first base and root for Marty. There's no need for me to get upset, glare over there (to the opposing dugout), and throw hats and helmets out there. That's part of the game, and you accept it."

Sparky? He was beaming. "If the situation came up again, he would have set the record," he said. "Every time he was up with a man on base. I was gonna walk him. That's no disrespect to Barrett, who hits .280-something. Boggs hits .340-something. If I hadn't walked him, I guarantee he would have got me. This was my way of keeping it 4–2 instead of 7–2."

Damn right, Wade Boggs knew what was coming. This was Day 2 of the season. On Day 1, he had come up in the 4th with Kevin Romine on second and two away with the Sox ahead, 4–0. Sparky put him on. And Barrett whiffed. Sparky wasn't going to let it become 5–0, no sir.

BILL CHUCK

Hall of Famer Wade Boggs is enshrined in Cooperstown primarily because of his 3,010 hits. He did, however, draw 1,412 walks as well. In the five years from 1985 to 1989, Boggsie drew 538 walks, the most in the majors. His 75 intentional passes during that time were tied with Dale Murphy for fifth.

Today, you intentionally walk a batter because of his home run potential. Over those five years, Boggs hit a total of 48 homers. But then, from 1985 to '89, Boggs hit .357. When you look at those five years, you will see that Kirby Puckett led the majors in hits with 1,078, while Boggs had 1,066. Boggs had 69 more plate appearances, but Kirby was a .328 hitter because he only had 171 walks. That's also why Wade led that half-decade with a .454 on-base percentage.

As a basis for comparison, Hank, Yaz, and Ted only had one game apiece with three intentional walks. Tony Gwynn didn't have one. The Mick had none; same with Willie. And while Boggs had 52 career games of three or more walks, it was Boggs' only career game with three intentionals.

Sparky knew best. Walk the Chicken Man and take your chances with Marty Barrett.

EVANS BRINGS THE SUN

BOSTON 4 BALTIMORE 3 | FENWAY PARK, BOSTON, MA
TIME: 3:19 • JUNE 23, 1990

BOB RYAN

Again, I'm asking you to take my word for it. Trust me when I tell you that it had been a gloomy Saturday afternoon until the very moment Dwight Evans stepped into the batter's box to face Gregg Olson with pinch-runner Randy Kutcher on first and two out in the 10th inning and the Orioles leading, 3–2, courtesy of a Mickey Tettleton home run. But the moment Evans stepped in, the sun suddenly made an appearance.

Olson's first pitch was a checked swing plate umpire Mark Johnson called a strike. Evans wasn't pleased. Olson then wild-pitched Kutcher to second. And then… Evans teed off on Olson's second-best pitch, a fastball (the man had a legendary curveball). Two-run homer. Game over.

But there's more, lots more. What had Evans done in his previous at-bat? He hit a two-out, game-tying homer in the 8th off Mark Williamson. Hang on. The last home run off Olson, then in his prime, was 479 batters ago. And guess who hit it? Nope, you can't make this stuff up: Dwight Evans.

"Somebody told me that," said Evans. "One of the TV or radio guys pointed that out. That's interesting. He's a tough pitcher. I hit a high fastball. He's tough. He's got a great curveball and a tough fastball."

Additional props go to Tom Brunansky, who kept the Sox alive with a two-out single in the 10th.

The sun had come out at just the right dramatic moment. Swear to God.

BILL CHUCK

There are many people who believe that Dwight Evans belongs in the Hall of Fame. I'm just not one of them. Bill James thinks he should be, and he knows way more about baseball than I do. Dewey Evans was a really good player and should be in the Hall of the Very Good, and perhaps with more games like this one, I would have thought of him as a Famer. Now that I've ticked you off, let's move on.

Evans hit 385 homers in his career, hitting 199 of them at Fenway Park, including four walk-offs, three of which were in extra innings.

Dwight Evans had 22 multi-homer games in his career, and this was number 22. They were all two-homer games. It was good news for the Sox when Dewey hit a pair as they went 19–3 in those games.

This was one of 139 games in which Dwight had at least three hits. This was one of 229 games in which Cal Ripken Jr. had at least three hits. I do love my stats.

Greg Olson only allowed 46 homers in his career, 23 at home and 23 on the road, including three walk-offs to Dante Bichette, Vinny Castilla, and Evans. Only four hitters hit as many as two homers off Gregg Olson: Vinny Castilla, Jim Thome, Ivan Rodriguez, and Evans. Olson was lucky he faced Evans only six times, allowing a walk and three hits.

While Evans was the star of this game, it is also noteworthy that in this game, Roger Clemens pitched nine innings and did not allow an earned run. Baltimore scored one unearned run in the 3rd on a ground ball double play after a Wade Boggs error and one unearned in the 8th on a Jody Reed error. Clemens had 53 starts in which he went nine innings without allowing an earned run. He went 49–1–3 in those starts. Walter Johnson threw 131 games in which he pitched nine innings and did not allow an earned run, with a record of 126–4.

Here's a Clemens stat that surprised me: this was one of 51 games in which he walked at least five batters. It's a lot less shocking when I realized that Nolan Ryan threw 233 games with five-plus walks. Clemens and the bullpen held the O's to 0–9 with runners in scoring position in this game.

Enjoy your day in the sun.

ROMINE & RYAN

BOSTON 3 TEXAS 2 | FENWAY PARK, BOSTON, MA
TIME: 2:50 • JULY 2, 1990

BOB RYAN

Nolan Ryan had done his job, leaving with the score tied at 2–2 after eight innings and 144 pitches. The Red Sox were, I'm quite sure, happy to see him leave.

Kevin Romine celebrated the most. He hit a 9th inning leadoff/walk-off homer off Kenny Rogers to win the game.

When Ryan fanned Carlos Quintana in the 4th, he reached one of his countless milestones: It was a record 22nd year he had fanned 100 or more.

Dewey Evans was summoned to discourse on The Master. "When they asked me last year, when I faced Nolan Ryan for the first time in a long time, 'How does he throw?' I said, 'He doesn't throw as hard as he used to, but he still throws harder than everybody else.' That's how I summed it up.

"Back then, he was a total fastball and curveball pitcher," Evans continued. "I mean, that was it. He could tell you the fastball was coming and then throw it by you. I *know* there's nobody I've ever faced that threw as hard as he did then. Now he's got a forkball and some kind of off-speed pitch—I don't know if it's a fork, a changeup, or what, but it reacts differently. He's changing speeds on his fastball. He's more of a pitcher now. Plus, he still throws 96, 97 miles an hour."

Interestingly, Ryan's last Fenway win had been in 1977. Who knew?

BILL CHUCK

Nolan Ryan was a great pitcher… just not at Fenway Park in Boston. Ryan had a career record of 2–8 with a 4.92 ERA and a 1.589 WHIP at the Fens. He was an even worse pitcher at Veterans Stadium in Philadelphia, where he had a career record of 1–9, a 5.52 ERA, and a 1.541 WHIP. Although in Connie Mack Stadium in Philly, he was 1–0 with a 0.90 ERA and 1.400 WHIP.

Maybe Ryan just wasn't an East Coast kind of guy. In Baltimore's Memorial Stadium, his record was 4–10 with a 4.21 ERA and a 1.556 WHIP. At Camden Yards in Baltimore, he was 1–0 but had a 6.75 ERA and 1.333 WHIP. At Yankee Stadium, he was 2–2 with a 5.87 ERA and a 1.598 WHIP.

So, when you're asked who you would have on the mound to win one game, while I would never choose Ryan, I might ask where the game is being played.

The KRs

Here's something impressive about Kevin Romine: In his career (331 games), Romine hit a total of five homers (that's not the impressive part). Of those five homers, he hit one grand slam and two walk-offs (that's the impressive part).

Kenny Rogers allowed three walk-off homers in his 762-game career. On 30 occasions in his career, he faced one batter, recording eight strikeouts and two walk-off homers, one to Romine and one to Pat Tabler of the Royals. In each case, he came in to relieve Nolan Ryan.

CLEMENS AND QUINTANA

BOSTON 2 MILWAUKEE 0 | COUNTY STADIUM, MILWAUKEE, WI
TIME: 2:38 • JULY 25, 1990

BOB RYAN

Roger wasn't talking afterward. He was irked about coverage of what may have been a shoulder injury. Or whatever. Roger was sometimes hard to decipher.

But his pitching was Churchillian, a three-hit shutout. "That's the best I've ever seen him throw," gushed Milwaukee skipper Tom Trebelhorn. "He had incredible velocity. All we could hope for is maybe they'd come up with a costly error or something."

Milwaukee starter Chris Bosio was pretty good himself. You can't say he was done in by a "mistake" pitch when the game-winning two-run homer was a lazy fly ball off the bat of Carlos Quintana that struck the right-field foul pole exactly 316 feet from home plate.

It was a rare moment of glory for the man known as "Q," but it was but one of countless dazzling shows orchestrated by Roger Clemens. "I saw a guy with incredible determination from the beginning to the end," said Joe Morgan. "He was firing *mani*—that's peanuts in Spanish…. If we lose today with Clemens pitching like that, you've hit rock bottom."

BILL CHUCK

Roger Clemens threw 46 complete-game shutouts. So did Tommy John. They are tied for 26th all-time, considerably behind Walter Johnson's 110 shutouts. But it was how dominant Clemens was while tossing a shutout that really stands out.

For example, Nolan Ryan and Tom Seaver each threw 61 shutouts. In those 61 games, Ryan whiffed at least 10 batters 43 times (70 percent), the most of any pitcher. Seaver did it 17 times (28 percent). Randy Johnson "only" tossed 37 shutouts but had double-figure strikeouts in 27 of them (73 percent!). Roger, in his 46 blankings, struck out at least 10 in 22 games (48 percent), the third most of any pitcher.

On this afternoon in Milwaukee, he struck out a paltry nine batters, including future Hall of Famer Robin Yount twice, who picked up the only walk.

The Brewers' bratwurst fans saw their team muster only three hits. Clemens and Bob Feller each had 23 shutouts proffering only three hits or fewer. Ryan had 37 such games. Clemens only faced 30 batters in this game. Chris Bosio, who really pitched well, faced just one fewer in his seven innings.

Only two times in Carlos Quintana's career did he drive home all the runs that resulted in his team's victory. There was this game on Wednesday, July 25, 1990, and then again in the Sox next win on Friday, July 27, 1990, when they defeated Detroit, 1–0, on a Quintana sac fly off Jack Morris.

In this game, Clemens wore a patch that read, 'N "300" R' as a salute to Nolan Ryan, who would win his 300th game on July 31, less than a week later.

REUSS FOUR-DECADE MAN

MONTREAL 4 PITTSBURGH 1
THREE RIVERS STADIUM, PITTSBURGH, PA
TIME: 2:53 • SEPTEMBER 7, 1990

BOB RYAN

He pitched one inning, giving up two hits and a walk. He didn't figure in the decision. But Jerry Reuss made news. He had thus become an official four-decade man in the Bigs.

"In a sense, I'm glad it's over, that it's finally done. I spent a lot of time wondering if I'd even do it," he said. "Probably too much time. It's an asterisk by my name in the record book and the answer to a trivia question, but what it really means to me is that for 22 years, I've been able to perform at the major league level, and not many guys have been able to do that."

Two of the Expo runs had come in kind of a Little Leaguey way in the fifth. Junior Noboa and Mike Fitzgerald were aboard with the Expos trailing 1–0, when starter Oil Can Boyd laid down a bunt. First baseman Sid Bream thought he had a play at third, but his wild throw past third baseman Jeff King allowed both men to score. Pirates skipper Jim Leyland had seen enough baseball to be philosophical.

"It's a game played by human beings, not mechanical men," he said. "I have no problem with that. That didn't beat us."

Reuss joined Bill Buckner, Rick Dempsey, Carlton Fisk, and Nolan Ryan as four-decade men that season.

BILL CHUCK

Jerry Reuss prompts the trivia question: Who are baseball's four-decade players? I'm here to answer that thanks to our friends David Adler and Andrew Simon at MLB.com. Please excuse me if I stick to the 29 players from the 20th and 21st centuries.

Nick Altrock (1898–1933)—five-decade man
Eddie Collins (1906–1930)—on-base machine
Jack Quinn (1909–1933)—one of the last spitballers
Bobo Newsom (1929–1953)—pitched for nine different teams
Mickey Vernon (1939–1960)—won two batting titles
Ted Williams (1939–1960)—you've heard of him
Early Wynn (1939–1963)—he won exactly 300 games
Minnie Minoso (1949–1980)—another five-decade man
Jim Kaat (1959–1983)—a pitcher who won 16 Gold Gloves
Tim McCarver (1959–1980)—HOF broadcaster
Willie McCovey (1959–1980)—"Stretch"
Bill Buckner (1969–1990)—Aaron's 715th went over his head
Rick Dempsey (1969–1992)—the most fun in the rain
Carlton Fisk (1969–1993)—"Pudge"
Jerry Reuss (1969–1990)—the star of this scorecard
Nolan Ryan (1966–1993)—you've heard of him
Rickey Henderson (1979–2003)—thief
Mike Morgan (1978–2002)—you may not have heard of him
Jesse Orosco (1979–2003)—ubiquitous reliever
Tim Raines (1979–2002)—great leadoff batter

Omar Vizquel (1989–2012)—all you need is glove

Jamie Moyer (1986–2012)—old guy

Ken Griffey Jr. (1989–2010)—"Junior"

It will be a while (at least 2030) before there is an addition to this club, since no active players played in 1999.

- Jerry Reuss played for the Dodgers, Pirates, Cardinals, Astros, White Sox, Angels, Reds, and Brewers in his 22-season career. He went 220–191 with a 3.64 ERA.
- In 1969, he appeared in one game for the Cardinals and pitched 7.0 innings of shutout ball in his debut start. He was 1–0 with a 0.00 ERA.
- From 1970 to '79, Reuss appeared in 323 games, starting 287, for the Cards, Astros, Pirates, and Dodgers. He was 114–108 with a 3.79 ERA.
- From 1980 to '89, Reuss appeared in 300 games, starting 258, for the Dodgers, Reds, Angels, White Sox, and Brewers. He was 105–83 with a 3.48 ERA.
- In 1990, he appeared in four games for the Pirates, starting once, and pitched 7.2 innings. He was 0–0 with a 3.52 ERA.

In Reuss' debut on September 27, 1969, at Parc Jarry in Montreal, his catcher was Tim McCarver, another member of the four-decade club. What are the odds of a battery like that?

In his final start, pitching against the Mets, Frank Viola won his 20th game. Viola's batterymate was Todd Hundley. Hundley was born May 27, 1969, four months before Reuss's first game.

LAST (RED) SOX TRIP TO COMISKEY

CHICAGO 4 BOSTON 2 | COMISKEY PARK, CHICAGO, IL
TIME: 2:37 • SEPTEMBER 16, 1990

BOB RYAN

I doubt if Red Sox manager Joe Morgan left town with a scoop of commemorative Comiskey Park dirt. Truth is, he hated the joint.

His club had just lost, 4–2, in the last visit a Red Sox team would ever make to Comiskey Park. "Have you ever seen so many cheap hits in all your life?" he moaned. "I think they manufacture them here."

Before the game, he was recounting his first time in the park. "I was 0-for-1 here in my career," he said, referencing his single season as a Kansas City Athletic. "I popped up on Labor Day in '59 with the bases loaded against Turk Lown. This ends it. Turk Lown, a guy—a high fastball pitcher—a guy I could murder most of the time. But as a pinch-hitter, I was a failure."

The ending was tortuous. The Red Sox loaded the bases with two away in the 9th off Bobby Thigpen. But the game ended when, as was reported in the *Globe*, "Jody Reed lined a 100 mile an hour bullet into the pitcher's glove."

Thus ends a Red Sox–Comiskey history that had begun on August 9, 1910, with a 7–4 setback. Boston didn't make sufficient use of 14 hits off Doc White, and legendary *Boston Globe* baseball writer T.H. "Tim" Murnane explained why. "The White Sox had all the luck in the way of several scratch hits (JOE WAS RIGHT!) while the Boston men lost runs by reckless baserunning, overrating their own speed, and underrating the throwing arms of the home players," Murnane declared.

However, Murnane was charmed by the new facility, which had opened on July 1. "The new park here is by all odds the finest in the country," he maintained.

Joe Morgan would respectfully disagree.

BILL CHUCK

Chicago Ballparks History 101

In 1910, Comiskey Park was designed by the famed Chicago architect Zachary Taylor Davis, who in 1914 designed Weeghman Park for the Chicago Whales of the Federal League, and then in 1916 for the Cubs. By the end of 1918, with owner William A. Weeghman's fortunes failing, he surrendered his interest in the Cubs to the chewing gum magnate, William Wrigley. Starting in 1919, Weeghman Park was renamed Cubs Park, and it stayed that way until the start of the 1927 season, when it was officially renamed Wrigley Field.

Back on the South Side, in 1900, Charles Comiskey moved a ballclub from St. Paul, Minnesota, to Chicago, and that was the birth of the Chicago White Stockings. The team played in South Side Park until July 1, 1910, when the now Chicago White Sox (shortened for headlines) played the St. Louis Browns in the first game at White Sox Park. Not long after, White Sox Park was renamed Comiskey Park.

Joe Morgan, the Player, History 101

There have been two Joe Morgans who played in the majors. One was a Hall of Famer, and the other eventually managed the Red Sox. The Red

Sox Joe Morgan played in a total of 88 games over parts of four seasons in the bigs, playing for the Braves, Athletics, Phillies, Cleveland, and Cardinals from 1959 to 1964. He started just 40 games and was a pinch-hitter in 45 games.

Joe was the pride of Walpole, Massachusetts. In 1959, Morgan was a 28-year-old rookie, and on August 20, 1959, had been purchased by the Kansas City Athletics from the Milwaukee Braves. After all, who wouldn't want a player who was hitting .315 in Louisville, even though he had been hitting .217 for the Braves? The A's were using him as a pinch-hitter since they brought him up from the minors, and from August 21 to September 10, Joe was 2–10 with two walks. On September 12, Morgan, pinch-hitting for Ray Herbert, hit a run-scoring triple. His first triple in the majors, he then scored on a groundout. More importantly, Joe Morgan had his first and only at-bat at Fenway Park, and he retired with a 1.000 batting average in his favorite ballpark.

It's hard to feel bad for Joe's experience at Comiskey in light of the fact that he was a lifetime .193 hitter. Also, Joe was actually 0–2 at Comiskey. On September 7, 1959, in the first game of a doubleheader, Joe pinch-hit for Joe DeMaestri and did indeed pop to second against Turk Lown with a runner on second as the Sox beat the Athletics, 2–1. In the second game of the twin bill, Joe pinch-hit again. This time striking out against Gerry Staley with a runner on third as the Sox completed the sweep, 13–7.

It's odd that Joe felt a bitterness toward Comiskey, where he was a mere 0–2, considering he was 0–7 at Tiger Stadium, 0–8 at Busch Stadium, and 0–9 at both Candlestick Park and Yankee Stadium. It's no wonder that Joe felt most at home at Fenway with his 1.000 batting average.

HEART OF STONE

BOSTON 7 TORONTO 6 | FENWAY PARK, BOSTON, MA
TIME: 3:13 • SEPTEMBER 28, 1990

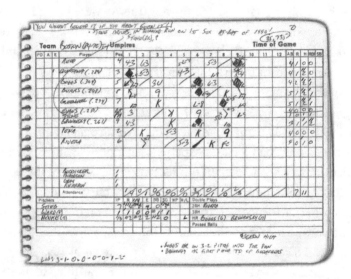

BOB RYAN

Any self-respecting Red Sox fan would happily buy Dave Roberts a drink. It would take a highly discerning one to extend a similar courtesy to Jeff Stone. But it should be considered.

The soon-to-be–30-year-old journeyman made a very big contribution in a pennant race. His single drove home the winning run in Game 157 to give the Sox a one-game lead in a tough race with the Blue Jays. It culminated in a game in which so much had happened that Mike Greenwell said as follows: "It was the most exciting game I've ever been involved with. I wished I'd taped this because I might watch this three or four times this winter." How about *that*?

Let's see…

- Wade Boggs hit a 3–2 pitch into the Sox pen for his sixth homer.
- Tom Brunansky hit the first pitch into the center-field bleachers for his 12th.
- Toronto third baseman Kelly Gruber had made back-to-back E-5s to aid the Sox to a run in the 8th.
- Junior Felix gave the Blues Jays a 6–5 lead with a two-run homer in the top of the 9th.

So now we're in the bottom of the 9th. The game is on the line, and Joe Morgan had to decide if he'll allow Stone, who had entered the game as a pinch-runner in the 8th, to bat when he had such pinch-hit options as Mike Marshall and Danny Heep. I might mention that Stone was a classic September call-up who had yet to bat in the 1990 season. He was known strictly for his speed, not his bat. He had been hanging around for 27 days, waiting to get the call.

Not to worry. Stone banged one to right off Tom Henke. Sox win!

"Everybody in the world wanted a pinch-hitter," said Morgan. "If I'd had Ted Williams, I would have run him up there. I figured Stone, with this speed, was loose. I thought he'd do it. With his speed, he was going to avoid the double play. I turned to (coach) Richie Hebner and he said, 'What if Greenwell gets on?' (He had singled.) 'Well,' I said, 'I'll stay with him.' The way baseball is, Mr. Stone took a big monkey off my back."

This was Stone's fourth big-league team (Philadelphia, Baltimore, Texas). "It was the highlight of my career," he said. "I've never been in that situation before."

Waiter. Give my man Mr. Stone a drink.

BILL CHUCK

The Sox and the Jays entered this game with identical 84–72 records, tied for first place. There were six games remaining to the season. Boston was starting a season-ending homestand with three against Toronto and closing it out with three against the White Sox, who on this date of September 28 were in second place in the AL West, nine games behind Oakland, *but* they had a record of 91–66, significantly better than either the Sox or the Jays. Each game was crucial: you either won your division or you went home, there were no wild card entries.

After the Jeff Stone walk-off hit, the Sox moved into first place and were never displaced. In the final six games, Boston went 4–2 and Toronto went 2–4. The Blue Jays had battled back in this game after trailing 4–0 by scoring four in the 7th and then again after trailing by a run in the 9th, they scored twice to take their first lead of the game. Jeff Stone's one out single broke their heart.

Jeff Blair of the *Montreal Gazette* wrote the next day that Stone claimed he was "On Cloud 10." Stone continued about his first at-bat of the season, "Pressure? Heck, I didn't have none. If I'd struck out, I'd have an excuse. If I'd hit… well, look at me now. The happiest man in the world." Blair added, "We know, we know. Cloud 10."

Stone had had a walk-off hit before: a home run in the bottom of the 11th on August 1, 1986, when he played for the Phillies. Since then, he had 78 hits in 167 games over four seasons. But there he was at the plate when it absolutely could not have mattered more, and he came through.

Boston won the second game of the three-gamer with Toronto behind Roger Clemens' 21st win. Toronto won the third game, 10–5. This time Stone pinch-hit with one down in the 9th and he whiffed.

And that was it. Those were the last two plate appearances of Jeff's career. But as you prepare to buy the man a drink, just remember that when the game was on the line, when the season was on the line, the heart of Stone brought the Red Sox to Cloud 10.

THE CORNERBACK

ATLANTA 6 NEW YORK 1 | SHEA STADIUM, QUEENS, NY

TIME: 3:10 • MAY 30, 1992

BOB RYAN

Let's see… four hits, three runs scored, three runs batted in, three stolen bases, and scoring from second on an infield hit. That's a pretty good day for a Half of Fame cornerback.

Deion Sanders remains the only man to play in both a Super Bowl and a World Series. And he is more than likely the only cornerback-turned-center fielder who spent the morning of a very big afternoon baseball game performance by filming a NIKE commercial in Central Park. But nothing about Deion Sanders was ever ordinary. Regarding his big day, Sanders said, "I'm feeling really comfortable up there. I'm real focused right now, like the team."

What could he have accomplished had he concentrated on baseball? We'll never know. But here was a glimpse.

BILL CHUCK

Before there was Amazon, "Prime Time" was Deion Sanders. Here is a guy who has three seasons on his Baseball Reference page with the designation "Did not play in major or minor leagues (Pro Football)."

This is a guy who played for the Yankees, Braves, Reds, Falcons, 49ers, Cowboys, Washington football team, and Ravens.

This is a guy who hit 39 major league homers off 37 different pitchers, including Mike Hampton, David Cone, Curt Schilling, Bruce Hurst, and two off Orel Hershiser.

This is a guy who hit three inside-the-park-homers and stole 186 bases, including 56 for the Reds in 1997. He was second in the league in steals that season, just like he was in 1994 when he stole 38 in 92 games.

This is a guy who had six four-hit games and 34 three-hit games.

Sanders played 115 games in 1997 and had no other season of over 97 games.

In 1992, he led the NL in triples with 14.

He was never an All-Star but was an eight-time Pro Bowler in the NFL. He played in Super Bowl XXIX with the 49ers and Super Bowl XXX with the Cowboys. He played in the 1992 World Series with the Braves and hit .DXXXIII.

A few others in this game

- Hall of Famer Eddie Murray was playing first for the Mets.
- Dick Schofield played short for the Mets. (Bob also saw his father—also Dick Schofield—play.)
- Todd Hundley was the Mets catcher. (Bob also saw his father, Randy Hundley—also a catcher—play.)
- Bobby Bonilla was the Mets right fielder, and unless this book is beamed into your cerebrum in 2036, he is still being paid each year by the Mets.

LOFTON BREAKS CLEVELAND'S STOLEN BASE RECORD

BOSTON 6 CLEVELAND 4 | FENWAY PARK, BOSTON, MA
TIME: 2:44 • SEPTEMBER 24, 1992

BOB RYAN

Kenny Lofton walked to lead off the game and immediately stole second. It was his club record 62nd stolen base, and the magnanimous home squad gave him the base. How thoughtful.

Cleveland starter Scott Scudder didn't have an enjoyable outing. He threw 12 pitches, and 11 were out of the strike zone. He was replaced on a 3–1 count to Wade Boggs and was later diagnosed as having a strained triceps.

I cannot tell you why Sox starter Danny Darwin left with two out in the 9th so Greg Harris could pick up a one-out save.

BILL CHUCK

I'm not here to make a Hall of Fame case for Kenny Lofton, but if the Hall of Fame equivalence of the "Mendoza Line" is Harold Baines, then Kenny deserves a second look. Lofton, who received just 3.2 percent of the voting in 2013, his one year on the HOF ballot, played 17 big-league seasons and finished with a .299 BA. Lofton was a six-time All Star and four-time Gold Glove winner. For five consecutive seasons, from 1992 to '96, playing for Cleveland, he led the league in stolen bases. He finished his career with 622 steals, 15th on the all-time list, nine of whom are HOFers.

On April 7, 1996, Lofton swiped third, his 255th steal for Cleveland, breaking the franchise record previously held by Terry Turner for more than 77 years. In parts of his 10 seasons with Cleveland, Lofton ended up with 452 steals, 173 more than runner-up Omar Vizquel. Unless baseball finds a way to re-introduce the steal to energize the fans, Lofton's record won't be broken. Besides holding the rookie record for most steals with 66, Lofton holds the record for most career stolen bases in the postseason with 34, including 11 in 1995.

Do stolen bases make a difference? Unlike my sabermetric friends, I think so, not just because it adds excitement to the game, but Lofton and Red Rolfe of the 1939 Yankees hold the record with 18 consecutive games with a run scored. You can't teach speed.

Lofton played for a lot of teams and played well: He played 10 seasons for Cleveland and parts of one season for Pittsburgh, San Francisco, Philadelphia, Atlanta, Texas, the Dodgers, the Cubs, the Yankees, Houston, and the White Sox.

One final piece of the Kenny Lofton puzzle that my esteemed colleague (that's Bob) will appreciate. The 1987–88 Arizona Wildcats finished their *basketball* season with a 35–3 record and reached the Final Four. One of their stars at guard was senior Steve Kerr, and one of his backups was a junior guard, the 5'11" Kenny Lofton.

1992 ALCS GAME 4

TORONTO TAKES A 3–1 LEAD IN THE ALCS
TORONTO 7 OAKLAND 6 (11 INNINGS)
OAKLAND-ALAMEDA COUNTY COLISEUM, OAKLAND, CA
TIME: 4:25 • OCTOBER 11, 1992

BOB RYAN

People automatically assume the famous Kirk Gibson 1988 World Series Game 1 home run caused Dennis Eckersley his most career grief. They would be wrong. The homer, which has had Dennis Eckersley beating himself up all these years, is the 9th inning Robbie Alomar hit off him to tie this game in the 1992 ALCS.

This was the Cy Young/MVP Eck season, and he was thought to be rather invincible. But when he entered the game in the 8th to protect a 6–2 lead, he knew he didn't have his best stuff, and he promptly gave up two base hits before settling down. He ended the inning with a punch-out of Ed Sprague, and he celebrated with a fist pump and yell. The Blue Jays were not amused.

"I felt like coming out of the clubhouse in my street clothes and letting him have it," exclaimed Game 1 starter Jack Morris.

"At that point, I thought I had stopped the bleeding," said Eckersley. "I was very excited, and I reacted instinctively, like I always react."

Devon White opened the 9th with a single. And then it happened. Robbie Alomar hit one out in right. Eck had blown the whole lead. He was mortified. The Jays pushed one across off Kelly Downs in the 11th, and the Jays had a 3–1 series lead en route to winning their first AL pennant in six games.

Eck was morose afterward. "I thought the bleeding would stop, and then I make the worst pitch I could make to Roberto Alomar, who is such a great player," he said. "I've had my good times, and I've had my bad times. And this is one of the worst feelings I've had in a long time."

Ask him about it today. It hasn't gotten much better.

One thing I will never forget is that it was an absolutely perfect postcard/Chamber of Commerce 80 degree, no humidity Northern California day. I doubt Eck remembers.

BILL CHUCK

As I looked back at this game, and what Eck went through, I couldn't help but wonder if R.E.M. based their lyrics on what Dennis had gone through when they wrote,

"That's me in the corner
That's me in the spot-light
Losing my religion."

Dennis Eckersley was so frequently the man in the "spot-light" and most of the time, he thrived, nay, excelled. He was so good that it is his rare anomalies that are the ones we remember.

This Hall of Famer appeared in 710 regular season games as a reliever. On 108 occasions, he pitched at least 1.2 innings but no more than 2.0 innings. Of those 108 appearances, only in two games did he allow as many as the five hits he permitted in this game. Two games!

Once in 1987 and once in 1993. That's it. This game meant it occurred three times in his magnificent career. And of those three times, this time was the only time that a homer was one of the five hits permitted.

Eck made 27 postseason relief appearances (this was his 20th and last for Oakland) going 1–2, with a 2.05 ERA in 30.2 IP, and had 15 saves. He had two postseason blown saves, and you can now call them Kirk Gibson and Robbie Alomar.

This was a particularly egregious appearance for Eck in light of his 1992 season, in which he recorded 51 saves. He was an All-Star, the Cy Young Award winner, and the MVP. Not bad for a guy who pitched just 80 innings. All regular season, he allowed 17 earned runs and just two of 31 inherited runners to score (he allowed two in this game). The A's were 64–5 in the regular season when Eckersley pitched.

I could go on about this, but back to R.E.M.

"Oh no, I've said too much
I haven't said enough."

Back to Bob Ryan for one last note about right-field ump Al Clark. Clark was Bob's Little League teammate... Bob beaned him pitching BP.

RED SOX SMITE NINE DOUBLES

BOSTON 12 CLEVELAND 7 | FENWAY PARK, BOSTON, MA
TIME: 3:13 • APRIL 14, 1993

BOB RYAN

There is a long-standing misconception that Fenway Park is a home run paradise. The truth is that Fenway Park is Two-Bagger Heaven, as this game illustrates. The Red Sox knocked out nine doubles in this one, and that isn't even close to the team record (12, in 1990). But nine is still a hefty number.

Offense ruled the day. The Red Sox batted around in both the third and fourth innings. Mo Vaughn and Scott Cooper each had four hits (Vaughn for the first time). Mo's 4-for-5 day raised his early season average to .429 and included the first Red Sox wall-job double of '93. Cooper exited the game with 13 hits in his last 29 at-bats. His RISP average was .727.

Mo's explanation for success: "You need an idea because the pitchers have a plan for you."

Cleveland starter Mike Bielecki has had better days. He left after going 3.2 innings, having given up seven earned runs while throwing 101 pitches, only 57 for strikes.

BILL CHUCK

- From 1990 to 1999, no team in the majors hit more doubles in a season than the Red Sox of 1997, who hit 373.
- From 1990 to 1999, no team in the majors hit more doubles than the Red Sox, who hit 3,042.
- From 1990 to 1999, no team in the majors hit more doubles in a season at home than the Red Sox of 1997, who hit 197. In second place was the Sox of 1993, who hit 193 at Fenway.
- From 1990 to 1999, no team in the majors hit more doubles at home than the Red Sox, who hit 1,747, over 200 more than the Mariners, who were in second place.

The record for doubles in a season is 376, held by the 2008 Texas Rangers. They are followed by the 1997 and 2004 Red Sox and the 1930 Cardinals, each with 373; the 2003 Red Sox with 371; the 2013 Red Sox with 363; and the 2010 Red Sox with 358.

And if you think that the oddly configured Fenway Park has anything to do with the spate of doubles, you are very insightful. Fenway holds seven of the top 10 slots for most doubles in a season. Entering the 2021 season, Fenway had over 2,000 more doubles than the combined locations of any other franchise.

The record for doubles in a season at home is 218, held by the 2004 Red Sox. The sportsmen at St. Louis' Sportsman's Park in 1931 are tied with the 2003 Fenway denizens (or, if you will permit me to lighten up this list by referring to them as the "Fenizens") with 216. Next would be the 1936 Clevelanders, who played in both League Park (the original home of the Cleveland Spiders) and the enormous Cleveland or Municipal Stadium (it sat over 78,000 fans), who, along with the Red Sox of 2008 and 2012, had 211 home doubles.

EMPTY THOSE BENCHES

BOSTON 6 TEXAS 5 (12 INNINGS) | FENWAY PARK, BOSTON, MA
TIME: 4:14 • MAY 30, 1993

BOB RYAN

Nobody could say Kevin Kennedy and Butch Hobson weren't trying everything they could think of to win. Both the Rangers and Red Sox skippers emptied their benches of position players before the Red Sox finally prevailed in the 12th.

Kennedy managed himself into a pickle that resulted in pitcher Jeff Bronkey having to bat for himself in the 12th. He failed to get a hit, of course.

Shortstop John Valentin's 8th inning error had put what turned out to be the tying run on base, but he was able to redeem himself with the game-winning double in the 12th.

Each team scored in the 10th. That's always fun. The winning pitcher was Jose Melendez, whose Red Sox debut had come the day before. It was his first AL win.

BILL CHUCK

Sometimes, I just look at Bob's scorecard to see what I can find:

- The Texas Rangers used 18 players in this game. The Red Sox used 19 players in this game. That's a lot of players for two teams with 25-man rosters at the end of May.
- The Red Sox used four players at third base: Luis Rivera, Ernie Riles, Scott Cooper, and Scott Fletcher, the most they have ever used in one game.
- David Hulse of the Rangers was a pinch-runner (for Juan Gonzalez), DH, and center fielder in this contest.
- It was Jeff Bronkey's first major league loss (and his only loss as a Texas Ranger) and while he did appear in 45 major league games, it was his only time to the plate. Only four American League pitchers had an at-bat in 1993: Bronkey, Gregg Olson (who also took the loss for the Orioles), Jesse Orosco, and Matt Maysey.
- Geno Petralli pinch-hit for Tom Henke, but before he could come to the plate, Jose Canseco pinch-hit for him and struck out.
- The ageless Julio Franco pinch-hit an RBI single in this game. Franco was 34 at the time and would play in the majors for another 12 seasons (counting this one).
- Billy Ripken, "the brother" pinch-ran and played shortstop for Texas.
- For Boston, Tony Pena pinch-ran (for HOFer Andre Dawson) and then became the DH. That was the only time in his career, he had those credits in one game.
- Pena wasn't the only future manager in the game for Boston as Bob Melvin was their starting catcher.

Going down the rabbit hole alert

Since Bronkey, only one Texas Rangers pitcher has gone to the plate against an American League club; that was John Wetteland on August 16, 1997, who was facing his old team, the Yankees. Wetteland had been signed by Texas following the 1996 season, because the Yanks decided that their closer would be some guy named Mariano. Wetteland had experience at the plate after pitching for the Dodgers and Expos in the NL (at a time when pitchers still hit). In this contest, Mo Rivera pitched a scoreless 9th inning (replacing Jeff Nelson), and the game went into extras, tied 5–5. The combustible Ramiro Mendoza came in and, after allowing a single, sac bunt, and a run-scoring single, allowed a run-scoring double to Wetteland, and another single that scored Wetteland. Texas won 8–5, with Wetteland going 1–1 with an RBI, run scored, and the win to his credit.

Worth the rabbit hole

This made John Wetteland the only AL pitcher to have a hit (an extra-base hit at that), an RBI, and a run scored against another AL club, until Shohei Ohtani on April 4, 2021. The difference is that Wetteland earned the win and Shohei got a ND. Wetteland had a double, while Shohei homered.

NELSON TO LEFT FIELD

SEATTLE 3 BOSTON 2 | FENWAY PARK, BOSTON, MA
TIME: 3:00 • JULY 15, 1993

BOB RYAN

"Who's that big guy out there in left field? Omigod, it's *Jeff Nelson!*"

That, I'm sure, was the reaction of any Seattle Mariners fan after mad-scientist skipper Lou Piniella channeled his inner Paul Richards by taking his 6'8" right-handed reliever from the mound and placing him in left field so southpaw Dennis Powell could face left-handed hitting Mike Greenwell with the tying run on first in the 8th. Greenwell popped to second, ending the inning. Nelson resumed duty on the mound in the 9th.

Nelson had last been in the outfield in high school. What if something had been hit his way? "He shags pretty good before the game," reasoned Piniella.

No, seriously, what if…? "He just told me to keep the ball in front of me and not allow any extra-base hits," Nelson explained. "Any ball that was over my head was going off the wall because I was standing on the warning track."

Powell, meanwhile, was clueless. "(Right fielder) Jay Buhner came over to me and said, 'Hey, thanks for keeping the ball out of left field,'" said Powell. "That's when I found out about Nelson."

The aforementioned Paul Richards had employed this strategy aplenty while managing the White Sox and Orioles in the '50s. Piniella said he saw Whitey Herzog do it in the National League.

Of course, in the AL, it does involve losing the DH. But Lou Piniella never sweated the small stuff.

BILL CHUCK

If you've gotten to this point in the book, you can be pretty confident that Bob and I would be way more excited about a pitcher playing the outfield than an outfielder, infielder, or catcher assuming the role of a pitcher.

I checked on MLB.com as to what the definition of a "hold" is, and the site explains, "A hold occurs when a relief pitcher enters the game in a save situation and maintains his team's lead for the next relief pitcher, while recording at least one out…. A pitcher cannot receive a win or a save in a game in which he records a hold. However, more than one relief pitcher can record a hold in a single game."

Here are the machinations that took place in the 8th and 9th inning at Fenway:

- With two down and a runner on first in the bottom of the 8th, Powell entered the game and replaced left fielder Greg Litton, pitching and batting second.
- Simultaneously, Nelson replaced the DH Marc Newfield and went to left field.
- Greenwell popped to second to end the bottom of the 8th.
- Tony Fossas, LOOGY extraordinaire, replaced Sox starter Frank Viola to start the 9th and face lefty Tino Martinez.

- Bob Melvin replaced Steve Lyons, who had entered the game in the bottom of the 7th as a pinch-runner for first baseman Mo Vaughn and stayed in the game as the first baseman. Melvin, the future manager, came in to catch because Carlos Quintana pinch-hit for Boston catcher Tony Pena and faced Nelson to lead off the 8th. Quintana stayed in the game as the new first baseman.
- Fossas did his job and struck out Martinez.
- In came Greg Harris, an ambidextrous pitcher who spent most of his career as a right-handed pitcher; he was also a switch-hitter. He made one appearance as a lefty in which he faced two batters. This wasn't that game. With two down and runners on first and second, Harris retired Pete O'Brien, who pinch-hit for Dennis Powell to end the top of the 9th.
- Nelson, the momentary left fielder, now returned to the mound as Mike Felder replaced Pete O'Brien and went to left field.
- Nelson quickly retired Andre Dawson and Bob Melvin. But with two down, Ernie Riles pinch-hit for Bob Zupcic. Riles hit a grounder that Tino Martinez booted, and now the tying run was aboard, and the potential winning run was at the plate in the hands of Scott Cooper.
- So, what does that magnificent bastard Lou Piniella do? He brought in Mike Hampton, who, at 20 years old, was the youngest player in the majors. Hampton had appeared in nine major league games and had an ERA of 7.98. He had started against the Sox about two weeks earlier and, in 3.0 IP, had allowed five runs, four earned, after allowing six hits, including two homers. So, of course, Lou brought him in for his first appearance at Fenway.
- Well, Hampton retired Scott Cooper for his first major league save. And in 16 years in the majors, it was his last, and only major league save.

How fabulous was that?!?

Jeff Nelson was credited with his seventh hold of the season, but I think he should have been credited for his seventh *and* eighth hold of the season. Nelson got credit for his hold when he replaced starter Dave

Fleming. Then, Powell got credit for his fifth hold when he replaced Nelson. It is my contention that when Nelson replaced Powell, he should have gotten credit for another hold. The appearance was listed as a hold but not counted as a hold.

If Piniella doesn't sweat the small stuff, I should let this one go.

DAWSON BEATS OUT BUNT

BOSTON 7 TEXAS 3 | FENWAY PARK, BOSTON, MA
TIME: 3:01 • AUGUST 30, 1993

BOB RYAN

I'm gonna guess that when Andre Dawson got out of bed on this day, he was not expecting to help create a run by beating out a bunt.

But a pro's a pro, and when he came to the plate in the 5th inning with the Red Sox ahead, 1–0, he saw two men on base and third baseman Jeff Huson, playing somewhere near the Rhode Island line. So, he thought, "What the hell?" and laid one down. It was a hard bunt, but Dawson easily beat the throw, as the *Globe*'s Nick Cafardo said, "in a scene reminiscent of the climax of *Major League*."

"Oh, that was bee-beautiful," gushed Frank Viola. "Nobody was expecting that."

There was more unexpected craziness three batters later, when Texas pitcher Kevin Brown stumbled while making his first pitch to Scott Cooper, thereby balking home a run.

But Andre Dawson was The Story. Wrote Nick Cafardo, "The bunt he laid down toward third base was like Pee Wee Herman giving an award-winning performance of *Othello*—unexpected, to say the least."

Glad I was there.

BILL CHUCK

On the Hall of Fame website, this is written about The Hawk, "Just one knee surgery can derail a baseball player from his major league career. Andre Dawson had 12 knee surgeries and finished his career in Cooperstown. Dawson, known as 'The Hawk,' was only the second player in baseball history to reach 400 home runs and 300 stolen bases."

Hall of Fame writer Jerome Holtzman wrote of Dawson in the *Chicago Tribune* as he was approaching retirement and compared his painful playing years to Mickey Mantle. "Don Zimmer, the former Cubs manager, was among the first to express the Mantle and Dawson similarities. 'We'll never know how good Mickey Mantle would have been because he played on bad knees,' Zimmer said. 'In my time, Andre Dawson was Mickey Mantle. If Andre hadn't had all those knee operations, he would have 600 home runs and 500 stolen bases.'"

Baseball Reference only has hit data since 1988, so I am limited in my reporting regarding Andre's MLB hitting career, which began in 1976. However, I can tell you that from 1988 to 1996, Andre Dawson bunted in a game on three occasions: once he failed, once he successfully sacrificed, and once he had a hit, and this was it. Dawson laid down 24 successful sac bunts in his career, 15 in his first four seasons, and none after 1988. But there has always been so much more to Andre Dawson than his numbers.

In retirement, Dawson owns a small chain of funeral homes and is far from an absentee owner. He dedicated himself to his work at the Paradise Memorial Funeral Home in Richmond Heights, a small city in southwest Miami-Dade County, which he owns and runs. Andre devoted himself during the pandemic, making sure that residents had a supportive environment to bid farewell to their loved ones. Bob Nightengale, in *USA Today*, spoke with Dawson in April 2020, who related the torment of that side of the pandemic. "You can't have a proper burial like you would under normal circumstances. You can't have the ideal send-off. You can't have people coming in here and making arrangements. You're just trying to expedite the process as quickly as possible. You see the sadness of people not even being able to see them in the hospital when they're sick. I can't even imagine what these people are going through. It's just awful."

As a result, according to *Deadline*, CBS has put in development *Closure*, a one-hour drama loosely based on the life of baseball Hall of Famer-turned-funeral-home-owner Dawson.

In October 2020, the Major League Baseball Players Association chose Dawson as the winner of the inaugural Curt Flood Award, given to a former player who "demonstrated a selfless, longtime devotion to the Players Association and advancement of players' rights."

"No player in baseball history worked harder, suffered more, or did better than Andre Dawson," said Hall of Famer Ryne Sandberg during his Hall of Fame induction speech. "He's the best I've ever seen."

And on August 30, 1993, he bunted for a base hit.

BRETT'S FENWAY FAREWELL

KANSAS CITY 5 BOSTON 2 | FENWAY PARK, BOSTON, MA
TIME: 2:54 • SEPTEMBER 5, 1993

BOB RYAN

It was a day for both Firsts and Lasts. Let's start with the major Last.

This was George Brett's last ever game at Fenway. He went 1-for-5. The hit was an 8th inning double off The Wall—Oh, how he would have flourished at Fenway. The 32,012 privileged to be in attendance did the Right Thing, giving Brett a Standing O. Unfortunately, he did bat once more and ended his Fenway career with a routine 4-3.

The minor First was the major league debut of rookie outfielder Greg Blosser. The major First was a 6th inning grand slam by Gary Gaetti. It was the first granny ever surrendered by Roger Clemens.

Brett was strangely unsentimental about Fenway. "Boston was just another stop along the way," he said. What he did rhapsodize about was attending the 1967 World Series in support of his big brother Ken, a Red Sox rookie pitcher.

There was one more New England first on this day: Drew Bledsoe made his NFL and Patriots debut (though technically he did so in Buffalo).

BILL CHUCK

Do you sometimes wonder, when it comes to a player as great as George Brett, about what has meaning for him as he winds down his career? Brett played in 97 games at Fenway, starting in 95 of them. He hit .298 in Boston with seven homers and 46 ribbies. But for a guy with a lifetime BA of .305, it was just another stop on the road.

In 1980 and then again in 1985, he had four-hit games at the Fens. He never hit more than one homer in a game in Boston, although in 1984, he had a 3–5 game with a homer and a triple and six RBI. But, after all was said and done, in games Brett played in Boston, the Royals went 49–48. No wonder it held no magic for him.

While this was the first granny allowed by Clemens, he ended up giving up six grand slams in his career. Gary Gaetti hit 11 grannies in his career. Oh, and Greg Blosser's major league career consisted of 22 games and 45 plate appearances.

While there are those who might cherish Drew Bledsoe's debut, it was the horrible hit on Bledsoe on September 23, 2001, that produced severe injuries and led to the start of the Tom Brady era.

GREENWELL'S BOMB

BOSTON 9 DETROIT 6 | FENWAY PARK, BOSTON, MA
TIME: 3:25 • APRIL 7, 1994

BOB RYAN

With 130 career home runs and a one-season high of 22 in 1988, Mike Greenwell was not known as a home run hitter. So it caused quite a stir when he led off the Red Sox 3rd inning by launching a Tim Belcher offering into an area of Fenway Park seldom visited by a baseball.

My notation at the top of the scorebook page was as follows: "Greenwell titanic wallop only 20 rows below the Red Seat! 440 feet!"

The "Red Seat" high up in the Fenway bleachers commemorates the colossal Ted Williams home run he deposited there in 1946. People (David Ortiz, for one) still doubt it actually happened, but there is ample documentation that it did. Few homers come as close to it as this inexplicable Greenwell smash. "It was one of the best swings I've had in a long time," he said. "You don't see that many get that far up in the seats. I've hit some to center that might have been farther, but I hit that awfully good."

There was a moment of mirth in the Detroit 2nd when Red Sox right fielder Greg Blosser simply couldn't locate Mickey Tettleton's liner, turning it into a three-base error. After the ball bounced off his glove, he just couldn't find it. "I looked down and was looking around, and there was nothing but grass," Blosser said. "Nobody told me. I wish somebody would have yelled at me."

The game also marked Detroit pitcher Bill Gullickson's first relief appearance since 1980. He marked the occasion by getting himself tossed out of the game by plate ump John Shulock.

BILL CHUCK

Now you have to admit between three-base errors and a pitcher ejection, this game seemed like a lot of fun. But Bob Ryan's 1994 imitation of Statcast is worth the price of admission.

Here are some connections between Greenwell's blast and Ted's iconic homer, which landed 33 rows up in the bleachers and bounced off the head of fan Joseph A. Boucher, puncturing his straw hat, and *then* bounced another 12 rows higher. It is hard to figure out which was the better postgame response from Boucher, who said that he didn't keep the ball that Ted struck, commenting, "After it hit my head, I was no longer interested." Or when he asked the *Boston Globe*, "How far away must one sit to be safe in this park?"

- On April 7, 1994, the game in which Mike Greenwell homered off Tim Belcher of the Tigers in Boston's 9–6 win, was played at Fenway in 3:25 in front of 15,304 fans.
- On June 9, 1946, Ted Williams homered off Fred Hutchinson of the Tigers in Boston's 11–6 win; the game was played at Fenway and took 2:07 in front of 32,800 fans.
- Greenwell's Sox had 16 hits while the Tigers had 10 hits.
- Ted's Sox had 14 hits while the Tigers had 10 hits.
- Greenwell's big blast helped Boston to the completion of a three-game sweep of the Tigers.

- Williams' bigger blast helped Boston to the completion of a three-game sweep of the Tigers.
- It was career home run number 99 for Greenwell.
- It was career home run number 139 for Williams.
- Greenwell tripled for Boston in his game, while Dom DiMaggio and Rudy York tripled in Ted's game.
- Greenwell's Sox had seven extra-base hits.
- Williams' Sox had 10 extra-base hits.
- Andre Dawson was the only HOFer in the Sox lineup the day of Greenwell's blast.
- Hall of Famer Alan Trammell was in the Detroit lineup in 1994.
- Hall of Famer Hank Greenberg was in the Detroit lineup in 1946.
- First baseman Cecil Fielder homered for Detroit in 1994.
- First baseman Greenberg homered for Detroit in 1946.
- HOFer Dawson also homered.
- Hall of Famer Sparky Anderson managed the Tigers in the Greenwell game.
- Hall of Famer Joe Cronin managed the Sox in the Williams game.
- At the time, accounts listed Williams' home run at 450 feet. The Sox later measured the distance and determined it was 502 feet.
- At the time, Bob Ryan listed Greenwell's home run at 440 feet. I'm taking his word for it.

MO VS. ALBERT

BOSTON 6 CLEVELAND 3 | JACOBS FIELD, CLEVELAND, OH
TIME: 2:48 • SEPTEMBER 15, 1995

BOB RYAN

Everybody knew it was Albert Belle vs. Mo Vaughn for the AL MVP. And here they were, duking it out on the day the Cleveland team would establish a new all-time single-season attendance record of 2,634,139. Albert's homer had given his team a 1–0 lead. But it was 1–1 in the 8th when Mo Vaughn stepped in with two on and hit homer number 38 into the right-center-field bleachers. Albert hit his 39th off Rick Aguilera in the 9th, but Mo's was the big blast of the day. Eric Hanson was the happy pitching beneficiary. "I kept us in it, and then Mo gave us an incredible lift," Hanson said. "That could be a very meaningful home run for the rest of the season because it got our offense going."

Vaughn was expressing dismay over his mounting strikeout total, however. He did not wish to lead the league in that category. "I know the strike zone," he explained. "I always *have* known the strike zone."

Homers were the day's big story. Eddie Murray followed Belle's 9th inning homer with his career number 475 shot, tying him with Stan Musial and Willie Stargell.

BILL CHUCK

Let's talk a little bit about the 1995 American League baseball season. Bob, of course, saw the head-to-head matchup between Mo Vaughn and Albert Belle. Here's the tale of the tape for these two very muscular humans. Mo Vaughn was listed as 6'1", weighing 225. Albert Belle was listed as 6'1", weighing 190.

Albert (Don't call me Joey) and Mo were must-see at-bats. Each of these guys was strong and powerful and ended up with very similar numbers for their careers.

- Belle played 1,539 games
- Vaughn played 1,512 games
- Belle had 5,853 at-bats
- Vaughn had 5,532 at-bats
- Belle had 1,726 hits
- Vaughn had 1,620 hits
- Belle had a .295 BA
- Vaughn had a .293 BA
- Belle had a .933 OPS
- Vaughn had a .906 OPS
- Belle had 381 homers
- Vaughn had 328 homers
- Belle had 1,239 RBI
- Vaughn had 1,064 RBI
- Belle walked 683 times
- Vaughn walked 725

Their biggest difference was in strikeouts
- Belle struck out 961 times
- Vaughn struck out 1,429 times

According to Baseball Reference:
- Belle had a 46.2 offensive WAR.
- Vaughn had 31.7 offensive WAR.
- Each had pretty offensive defensive WAR numbers, with Belle at –12.3 and Vaughn at –12.4.

So that was their big picture. Here are their numbers for the strike-shortened 1995 season:
- Belle hit .317 with 50 homers, 52 doubles, 126 RBI, 73 walks, 80 whiffs, a 1.091 OPS, and a 7.0 WAR. He became the only player with 50 doubles and 50 homers in a season. His Cleveland team won the AL Central by 30 games.
- Vaughn hit .300 with 39 homers, 28 doubles, 126 RBI, 68 walks, 150 whiffs, a .963 OPS, and a 4.3 WAR. His Red Sox won the AL East by seven games.

It's pretty obvious who ended up winning the 1995 AL MVP, right? Mo Vaughn.

What?!?

Overall, Vaughn had 308 points to 300 for Belle, with Mo getting 12 first-place votes and Albert getting 11.

So how did this happen? Let's check in with one of the best baseball writers at the time and one of the best baseball minds around today, from the *Baltimore Sun* of November 19, 1995, here's Buster Olney:

"If you believe that part of the reason Boston Red Sox first baseman Mo Vaughn won the voting is that he's a good guy, you are absolutely correct.

"If you believe that a major reason Cleveland left fielder Albert Belle lost is that he's a jerk, you are absolutely correct.

"I know this because I voted in the AL MVP balloting and picked Vaughn first and Belle second, and part of my rationale was based on personality."

Buster added, "Vaughn was a public relations asset for baseball, in a year, after the strike, when the game needed as much public relations as possible. Vaughn is heavily active in community work in and around Boston.

"Conversely, Belle arguably is the game's worst citizen. He was once suspended for hurling a baseball at a fan seated in the stands, and he has long been noted for his obscenity-laced tirades at reporters guilty of nothing more than entering his line of vision."

If you take the personality issue out, which is what Mark Feinsand did in 2020 when he got 13 MLB.com writers to have a re-vote, Belle was the MVP, and Vaughn finished sixth.

These two teams met in the 1995 postseason, and the results were not close. Cleveland swept Boston in the three-game ALDS, as Belle hit .273 with one homer, three RBI, and an OPS of 1.103, while Vaughn was 0–14 with one walk and seven whiffs.

Eddie Murray ended up with 504 homers and is the only one mentioned in this story who is in the Hall of Fame.

SPARKY'S FENWAY FAREWELL

DETROIT 7 BOSTON 5 | FENWAY PARK, BOSTON, MA
TIME: 2:39 • SEPTEMBER 27, 1995

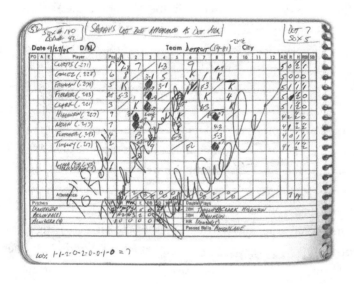

BOB RYAN

I had been in Detroit for Spark's AL debut 16 years earlier, and now I was here for his Fenway farewell. Of course, he wasn't in a sentimental mood since Fenway was far down the list of his favorite ballparks.

"This stadium is the home of Ted Williams," he said. "This is Ted Williams' house, and he was the greatest hitter who ever lived. To think he was here—what people love here is not the ballpark, but they envision the guys who have played here for the last 70 years. When they look at this park, they remember the great ones who were out there. They'll never be able to get that in the new parks—you have to have them, but one part you lose is what you have here and at Wrigley Field and Detroit."

My day was made when he signed my book.

BILL CHUCK

After great success managing the Reds (a.k.a. "The Big Red Machine"), winning back-to-back championships in 1975 and 1976, Sparky joined the Tigers. George "Sparky" Anderson managed the Detroit Tigers from 1979 through 1995. Over those 17 seasons, the Tigers were 1,331–1,248 and a tie. The Tigers' winning percentage of .516 was tied with the Orioles for the fourth best in the AL behind the Yankees, Red Sox, and Royals. Sparky won one pennant and one World Series title, compiling an 8–5 postseason record. He was the AL Manager of the Year in 1984 and 1987.

When he won the championship with Detroit in 1984, Sparky became the first manager to win the World Series in both leagues. One of Sparky's nicknames was "Captain Hook," as he was way ahead of his time in his frequent use of the bullpen (he used eight pitchers in this game at Fenway). The 1984 Tigers team went wire-to-wire in first place, starting the season 9–0 on their way to a 35–5 start. One of those who benefited from Anderson's use of the bullpen was Guillermo "Willie" Hernandez. Willie appeared in 80 games for the Tigers, saving 32 in 33 save opportunities. He was an All-Star, which my buddy Bob doesn't mind. He was also the Cy Young Award winner, and I'm not that confident Bob is in favor of relievers winning the CYA. And he was the AL MVP, which I know really ticks off Bob. Only Sandy Koufax (1963) and Denny McLain (1968) had ever previously won the CYA, the MVP, and the World Series title in the same season.

Sparky kept the Detroit fans happy, compiling a 743–575 record at home. But the Tigers struggled abroad, going 617–699. The Tigers and the Red Sox played 208 games in the Sparky tenure, with the Tigers going 100–108, 57–46 at home, and 43–62 (.409) at Fenway. Sparky's road record was only worse in one ballpark going 40–62 (.392) in the Bronx.

Two Tigers from the Anderson Era are enshrined in Cooperstown, besides Sparky himself. Jack Morris went 198–150 during his Tigers span with a record of 194–144 while Sparky was his manager. Alan Trammell was a .284 hitter in his 20-year career, which was all spent with the Tigers. Trammell played 2,293 games wearing the iconic Detroit "D" and 2,069 of those games were with Sparky in the dugout, sneaking smokes.

I was looking for a Sparky quote to end this homage to Anderson, and I had many choices (Sparky could talk), so I opted for one that showed the respect that he had for the game he loved. On the subject of MLB commissioner Bowie Kuhn, Sparky said, "If I hear Bowie Kuhn say just once more, he's doing something for the betterment of baseball, I'm going to throw up."

I'm so glad he signed Bob's scorecard.

1995 ALDS GAME 2

YANKEES LEAD THE ALDS 2–0
NEW YORK 7 SEATTLE 5 (15) | YANKEE STADIUM, THE BRONX, NY
TIME: 5:12 • OCTOBER 4, 1995

BOB RYAN

There were a whole lot of tired, frustrated, and downright angry people in the ballpark when Jim Leyritz came to the plate to face Tim Belcher with Pat Kelly on first in the early morning hours of October 5. It was the 15th inning. Leyritz was 0-for-5 with a hit-by-pitch way back in the 6th. But he insured a spot in Yankee lore with a two-run shot to provide the Yanks with a 7–5 victory, giving them a 2–0 lead in the new, expanded "Division Series" playoffs.

Any lengthy game produces frustration. Seattle may have thought they had it when Junior Griffey homered off John Wetteland in the Seattle 12th. But the Yankees tied it in their half and thought they may have won it when Ruben Sierra doubled home pinch-runner Jorge Posada. But Bernie Williams was cut down via an Alex Diaz–Luis Sojo great relay throw.

Anger? Yankee fans were all over Seattle's Vince Coleman, whom they thought had once thrown firecrackers near children. Seriously. *Everyone* was angry with plate ump Dale Scott. And the Yanks were furious with first-base ump Jim McKean, whom they believed had badly blown a play on Coleman at first that led to a run in the 7th.

Almost forgot. A Yankee highlight was back-to-back bombs to the distant center-field black seats by Sierra and Don Mattingly in the 6th. The 57,126 in the house were forced to stick around for 5:12, but they got their money's worth.

BILL CHUCK

This is a game filled with **bold-type** names.

Let's start with the winning pitcher in this game. Making his first appearance *ever* in a postseason game, **Mariano Rivera** pitched 3.1 innings of scoreless baseball, striking out five, including all three batters he faced in the 14th inning.

Jorge Posada made his postseason debut… *as a pinch-runner.* He never appeared in another postseason game as a pinch-runner, and in his career, the less-than-fleet afoot Posada appeared in two regular season games as a pinch-runner. Posada was the Yankees' third-string catcher in this series: **Mike Stanley** was the starter, **Jim Leyritz,** who started in this game, was the backup, and there was Posada, who had played in just one big-league game and had never been on base in the majors.

Posada, number 62 on your program, had entered the game in the bottom of the 12th, pinch-running for Hall of Famer **Wade Boggs** (who had a sore hammy) playing in his first Yankees postseason.

Speaking of HOFers, **Edgar Martinez** was playing in his first post-season and in this game went 3–6 as the Mariners DH.

And speaking of Mariners HOFers, **Junior Griffey** was playing in his first postseason, and in this game, he went 2–6, and here in Game 2, he hit his third homer of the ALDS.

The Mariners also had HOFer **Randy Johnson,** who was await-
ing New York in Game 3. Their first baseman was the Yankees' first
sacker of the future, **Tino Martinez. Luis Sojo** was their shortstop, and
he ended up playing seven invaluable seasons for the Yankees. Their
manager was the Yankees' former manager, **Lou Piniella.**

Bernie Williams, who ended up his Yankee career starting more
Yankees postseason games than anyone not named **Derek Jeter,** was
playing in his first postseason series. And this was the last postseason
the Yankees would play without Derek Jeter for a lot of years.

In this series, **Paul O'Neill,** a longtime Yankees favorite (and broadcaster), made his New York postseason debut (he homered in this
game), and **Darryl Strawberry** made his Yankee postseason debut (he
pinch-whiffed). Another favorite Yankee broadcaster, pitcher **David
Cone,** won Game 1.

It was **Andy Pettitte's** postseason debut, and although he allowed
four runs in 7.0 IP, he picked off both Tino and **Jay Buhner.**

Not only were these the first Division Series, but they were also
among the first postseason games since 1993 because the players-strike/
owners-lockout caused the cancellation of the 1994 postseason.

The ALDS were the first postseason appearance for the Mariners
and the first postseason appearance for the Yankees since 1981, a span
which was the New York equivalent of forever.

This game that started on October 4th and ended in the rain on
October 5th was a treat. Check out the nine innings of scoring:

- Mariners lead 1–0 top of the 3rd
- Yankees tie it 1–1 bottom of the 5th
- Mariners lead 2–1 top of the 6th
- Yankees lead 3–2 bottom of the 6th
- Mariners lead 4–3 top of the 7th
- Yankees tie it 4–4 bottom of the 7th
- Mariners lead 5–4 top of the 12th
- Yankees tie it 5–5 bottom of the 12th
- Yankees win it 7–5 with a Jim Leyritz two-run, walk-off homer
  with one out in the bottom of the 15th

In Jim Leyritz's 11-season career, he hit 90 career home runs and just one walk-off. This was the first of eight homers that Leyritz hit in just 72 postseason plate appearances and his only walk-off. When you watch a replay of this blast, you'll see that amongst the Yankees celebrating the homer was the non-roster No. 2 uniformed Derek Jeter.

This was the last win in the major league career of **Dan Mattingly** (he went 3–6 with a homer) and the last in the Yankees career of manager **Buck Showalter**.

1995 ALDS GAME 3

NEW YORK LEADS THE ALDS, 2–1

SEATTLE 7 NEW YORK 4 | KINGDOME, SEATTLE, WA
TIME: 3:04 • OCTOBER 6, 1995

BOB RYAN

Bernie Williams hit a homer batting right-handed off Randy Johnson in the 4th. He hit a homer off Bill Risley batting left-handed in the 8th. But his team lost the game, and few took note, even though no one had ever switch-hit homers from each side of the plate in a postseason game. (Nope, not even The Mick.)

What people did gush about was the gutsy pitching of Johnson, who fanned 10 in seven innings of work while allowing four hits and two runs. "Tonight, pitching on three days' rest, I was obviously physically and mentally drained," he said. "I was mostly pitching on adrenaline and the importance of the game. I didn't have my best stuff tonight. I proved I could win without it."

This didn't surprise Yankee skipper Buck Showalter. "Even when he's not on top of his game, he's better than the majority," Buck said.

One oddity in this game was a Vince Coleman chopper that bounced over the head of Yankee first baseman Tino Martinez to lead off the 6th. By the time Coleman had stopped running, he was on third to ignite a four-run inning. It had been a bona fide turf triple.

BILL CHUCK

The Seattle Mariners were born in 1977, and from the start, played in the Kingdome. Eighteen years later, this was the first postseason game ever in Seattle and the Mariners' first ever postseason win. There were only eight postseason games played in the Kingdome (the Mariners moved to Safeco Field on July 15, 1999), and the Mariners went 4–4 in those contests. At the time of this writing (following the end of the 2021 season), the Mariners have altogether only played 17 postseason home games and won just eight of them (they haven't reached the postseason since 2001), so we don't take anything about this win lightly.

There have only been 15 occasions in which a switch-hitter hit multiple homers in a postseason game. Pablo Sandoval in the 2012 World Series is the only one to have three. Carlos Beltran did it three times; Williams, Mantle, and Chipper Jones each did twice. Both of Mantle's games were in the World Series, while Sandoval, Eddie Murray, and Willie McGee are the others to do it in a Series game.

Bernie matched his own feat of homering from each side of the plate in Game 4 of the 1996 ALDS against the Rangers. Chipper Jones became the first NLer to do it when the Braves HOFer went deep twice against the Cubs in the 2003 NLDS. And Milton Bradley played his own game against the Tigers in Game 2 of the 2006 ALCS (yet his A's still lost, 8–5).

While Bernie Williams had a great game, Don Mattingly did not. The fact that Mattingly went 0–4 against Randy Johnson that night is not meant as a putdown to Donnie Baseball, but simply to show you how dominant the Big Unit was that night. Mattingly, in his regular season career against Johnson, was a .381 hitter, going 16–42 with two walks and two whiffs. That night in the Kingdome, Johnson struck out Mattingly three times, swinging, looking, and swinging (with the bases loaded and two outs in the 6th and the Yankees trailing 2–1). Mattingly never struck out more than three times in a game in his 1,785-game career, and he had only done it five times before this night. The final bit of irony, of course, is that the M's first baseman was Tino Martinez, who went 3–4 with a homer and three ribbies and was the Yankees' first sacker on Opening Day in 1996.

The baseball gods certainly do have a sense of humor. They decided that somebody was going to lose to Johnson that night, and it was going to be Black Jack McDowell. In McDowell's 12-season career, he compiled a record of 127–87, and in the regular season was 10–1 entering this game against the Mariners. By the time McDowell finished his career, he was 11–1 against Seattle in the regular season, and by the time McDowell finished this ALCS, he was 0–2 against Seattle.

1995 ALDS GAME 5

MARINERS WIN THE ALDS 3–2
SEATTLE 6 NEW YORK 5 (11 INNINGS) | KINGDOME, SEATTLE WA
TIME: 4:19 • OCTOBER 8, 1995

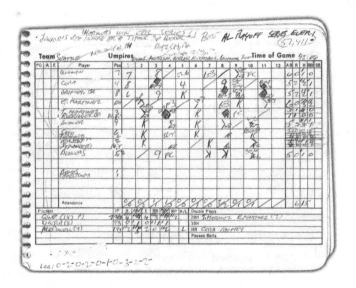

BOB RYAN

The two things I remember most about this epic game, which concluded an epic series:

1. Aiming my binoculars at the Yankee bullpen located down the right-field line from my perch in the left-field auxiliary press box and proclaiming, "Holy Shit! That's Jack McDowell!" It was the Seattle 9th, and there were two on and one out in a 4–4 game. Keep in mind that Randy Johnson had already entered the game and had snuffed out a Yankee uprising in the Yankee 9th.

2. The sight of Junior Griffey rounding the bases, cutting second and third perfectly, with the winning run on the Edgar Martinez double

into the left-field corner in the 11th. This was the same Junior Griffey who had brought the Mariners within a run with a titanic blast to the third deck off David Cone in the 8th.

I am unashamedly quoting myself in the *Boston Globe* on Randy's pitching in the 9th. Again, there were men on first and second, none out. "He was the Marshal come to restore order in this here town, and he acted with dispatch," I wrote. "Eight pitches later them varmints were back in the hoosegow where they belonged." Oh, and the 10th went as follows: K, K, K.

McDowell did get out of that 9th inning jam. He had a chance to get the W when New York reached Randy for a run in the 11th. In the fateful Seattle half, Joey Cora beat out a bunt, and Griffey singled. Martinez knocked one down the left-field line, and... "Junior can really eat up some ground," said Seattle manager Lou Piniella. "I knew when the ball stayed in the corner, he'd have a chance. He cut the bases beautifully."

It was throwback baseball managing. In Ye Olden Days, Walter Johnson had once relieved. Allie Reynolds had once relieved. Orel Hershiser had once relieved. And now Randy and McDowell had relieved *in the same game and were the pitchers of record.*

I get the last word. It had been an absolutely enthralling five games of baseball. As I told my *Globe* readers, "This series had more perambulations than an Italian seaside highway."

BILL CHUCK

Baseball was recovering from the 1994 lockout, and things were particularly bleak in Seattle as their ballpark, the Kingdome, was falling apart. In July 1994, tiles fell from the ceiling, nearly hitting Cal Ripken Jr. in what would have been an ignominious end to his playing streak. In August 1994, there were two fatalities as workers were repairing tiles. Despite the damages, despite the fans hating to go inside to watch baseball on a beautiful Seattle day, there was little enthusiasm by voters to pay for a new ballpark via taxes. The Mariners were going to be the second MLB team to move from Seattle.

And then something happened. Actually, someone happened: Edgar Martinez.

"Refuse to Lose" was the mantra of the 1995 Mariners, who on August 2 had a record of 43–46 and were in third place in the AL West. They trailed the Angels by 13.0 games. From that point on, the M's went 36–20 and the Angels went 22–34. The season ended on October 2 as the Mariners defeated the Angels 9–1 in a one-game playoff.

The M's of October 8 were on a tear. Jack McDowell came on in the bottom of the 9th with one down and runners on first and second in relief of Mariano Rivera(!) and struck out Edgar Martinez. "But you do not get him out forever," wrote Mike Lupica the next day in the *New York Daily News*.

It is still referred to as "The Double." It was the most significant hit in Edgar's Hall of Fame career and the most important hit in Seattle baseball history. It was that win, that hit, that ballplayer, that fan enthusiasm that influenced the Washington state legislature to provide funding for a new ballpark. That, and the fact that at one point, only a third of the voters wanted a new ballpark, but after a "Refuse to Lose" referendum, the vote was too close to ignore.

Don Mattingly, in the top of 10th, struck out looking against Randy Johnson. It was his final major league at-bat. Donnie Baseball hit .417 in the ALDS.

- Hall of Famer Ken Griffey Jr. went 2–5 in this final game and hit .391 for the ALDS.
- Hall of Famer Edgar Martinez went 3–6 in this final game and hit .571 for the ALDS.
- Hall of Famer Randy Johnson appeared in two of five ALDS games and won them both. In 10.0 IP, he had a 2.70 ERA with 16 strikeouts and six walks. He inherited two baserunners, and neither scored.
- Hall of Famer Wade Boggs went 0–5 in this final game and hit .263 for the ALDS.
- Hall of Famer Mariano Rivera appeared in three of five ALDS games and had 5.1 IP with a 0.00 ERA and eight strikeouts. He walked one batter (intentionally). He inherited six baserunners, and none of them scored.

- Hall of Fame Mariners' announcer Dave Niehaus said his favorite call was "The Double."

"They would take a fly ball. They would love a base hit into the gap, and they could win it with Junior's speed. The stretch and the 0–1 pitch on the way to Edgar Martinez. Swung on and lined down the left-field line for a base hit. Here comes Joey, here is Junior to third base. They're gonna wave him in. The throw to the plate will be late! The Mariners are going to play for the American League championship! I don't believe it!"

Yankees postscript

George Steinbrenner did not re-hire Buck Showalter after that loss. The next season, Showalter became the first manager of the Arizona Diamondbacks, and Joe Torre was at the helm in the Bronx as the Yankees won it all. Soon after hiring Torre, the Yankees GM Gene Michael, who brought the Yankees Derek Jeter, Jorge Posada, Andy Pettitte, and Mariano Rivera, was fired as well. The Yankees reached the postseason for 13 consecutive years after The Stick was let go.

SPEEDY GORDON

BOSTON 8 TORONTO 0 | FENWAY PARK, BOSTON, MA
TIME: 2:00 • AUGUST 7, 1996

BOB RYAN

Please, Lord, take me back to see this one. Let me see Tom Gordon at the top of his game one more time.

Gordon didn't mess around. He allowed three hits. He walked nobody. Tony Rodriguez (his career first), Mo Vaughn, and Mike Greenwell hit homers off Pat Hentgen, and Gordon concluded his business in two hours on the nose. Yes, it was the shortest game of the year.

"The key for Tommy is throwing strikes," said manager Kevin Kennedy. "He did that tonight and didn't walk anybody. It's about command. If he has it, he's hard to beat."

Full disclosure: the air on that 83-degree evening was very, very heavy. The Blue Jays hit three shots in the 7th with nothing but aerial outs to show for it. But that's baseball.

BILL CHUCK

On April 22, 1999, the Tigers beat the Red Sox, 1–0. The Tigers had three hits, and the Sox had two. Tigers' pitchers struck out seven and walked one. Sox pitchers struck out three and walked no one. The game lasted 1:49, or 109 minutes.

On September 3, 1997, the Expos beat the Red Sox, 1–0. The Expos had one hit, and the Sox had two. Carlos Perez, the Montreal pitcher, struck out eight and walked none. Sox pitchers struck out four and walked four (Tom Gordon pitched in this one in relief, one inning, and three whiffs). The game lasted 1:54, or 114 minutes.

The two games above are the only games that were faster than the one Bob attended since the start of the 1996 season. Bob's game lasted 120 minutes, and he saw an 8–0 win.

On May 2, 2002, the Angels defeated Cleveland, 8–0. The game lasted 3:34, or 214 minutes.

On April 30, 2016, the Red Sox defeated the Yankees, 8–0. The game lasted 3:30, or 210 minutes.

Since this game that Bob saw on August 7, 1996, there have been 334 regular season, nine-inning games that ended with an 8–0 score. Not one was as speedy as the game that Flash Gordon threw.

I could go on, but you don't have the time to waste. You get the point.

1996 NLCS GAME 5

CARDINALS LEAD THE NLCS 3–2
ATLANTA 14 ST. LOUIS 0 | BUSCH STADIUM, ST. LOUIS, MO
TIME: 2:57 • OCTOBER 14, 1996

BOB RYAN

It was an elimination game, but I guess the Braves weren't ready to go home. They rocked Todd Stottlemyre for nine hits and seven runs in an inning-plus en route to a postseason-record 22 hits and a post-season-record victory margin (tied with the Yankees, who in 1936 defeated the Giants 18–4 in Game 2 of the World Series).

The flip side was John Smoltz, who not only tossed seven innings of seven-hit shutout baseball, but who also went 2-for-4 with an RBI and a run scored. The run cushion was a bit of overkill for a man who had gone 24–8 in a Cy Young season. As the envoy from the *Boston Globe* observed (well, me, actually), "Giving the 1996 John Smoltz 14 runs to

209

work with is like giving an All-You-Can-Eat certificate to an offensive lineman."

Speaking of overkill, the final two Atlanta runs came via a 9th inning two-run homer by Fred McGriff. And it appears no Braves game that season was considered to be official without an appearance by Brad Clontz, who worked a league-high 81 games and who was given the privilege of shaking everyone's hand at the end by getting the last two outs in the 9th.

BILL CHUCK

The Cardinals held a 3–1 lead in this series, and all they had to do was win one game. All they had to do was defeat John Smoltz, Greg Maddux, or Tom Glavine, who combined during the regular season had gone 54–29 with a 2.88 ERA. Piece o' cake.

The Braves had scored a combined 12 runs in the first four games and then 14 on this night. Their five runs in the 1st inning were more runs than they had scored in any single game to this point.

There have been seven postseason games in which a team has had 20-plus hits. This remains the only one in the NLCS. There were 11 different Braves with at least one hit in this game. That's tied for the most in a nine-inning NLCS game with the Cubs, who beat the Padres, 13–0, in the opener in 1984. Mark Lemke and Javy Lopez each went 4–5, the only NLCS game that two players from a team had four hits each. On nine occasions, a pitcher has had two hits, a run scored, and an RBI in an NLCS game. Smoltzie and Don Gullett are the only ones who did it twice.

Four starters have the dubious distinction of pitching an inning or less and allowing a record seven earned runs. In the 2020 NLCS, Kyle Wright lasted two-thirds of an inning for the Braves against the Dodgers. In the 1999 ALDS, Bartolo Colon lasted an inning for Cleveland against the Red Sox. In this game, Todd Stottlemyre lasted an inning (plus three batters in the 2nd), and in the 1992 NLCS, Tom Glavine lasted an inning for the Braves against the Pirates. Stottlemyre is the only pitcher in postseason history to allow nine hits in just one inning of work.

To date:

Bob wrote that the Braves tallied "a postseason-record 22 hits and a postseason-record victory margin." They both remained a record until the Red Sox topped Cleveland 23–7, recording 24 hits in Game 4 of the 1999 ALDS. The run margin record in the NL held up for all of three days until Game 7 of this NLCS.

1996 NLCS GAME 7

ATLANTA WINS NLCS 4–3
ATLANTA 15 ST. LOUIS 0
ATLANTA-FULTON COUNTY STADIUM, ATLANTA, GA
TIME: 2:25 • OCTOBER 17, 1996

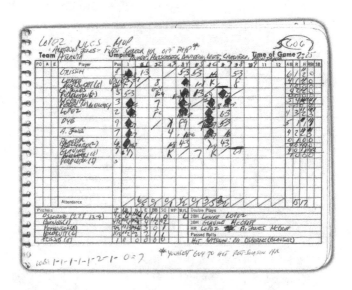

BOB RYAN

Four days earlier, the Cardinals had taken a 3–1 Series lead. Had someone said to them, "Okay, hope you're enjoying yourself now because you're going to be outscored 32–1 in the remainder of the series," how loud would have been the laughter? But it happened.

This one was over after a six-run Atlanta 1st inning. Apparently, Donovan Osborne (six earned runs on five hits, a walk, and a hit batsman) didn't have it. The happy mound recipient for Atlanta was Tom Glavine, who emulated John Smoltz in Game 5 by throwing seven innings of three-hit shutout ball. But he more than likely was equally happy with his 1st inning liner to right. Ron Gant tried in vain for a shoestring catch, and Glavine thus became the first pitcher to hit a triple in LCS history, and it was a bases-clearing triple, to boot.

Andruw Jones, a tender 19, made history by becoming the youngest man to hit a postseason homer. It was off Mark Petkovsek, and so it was also his first career homer off a right-handed pitcher.

Cardinals Hall of Fame reliever Dennis Eckersley spoke for his entire organization. "Okay, they're better than us," he conceded. "Did they have to beat the hell out of us to prove it?"

BILL CHUCK

This marked the first time an NLCS team had come back from a 3–1 deficit.

Prior to this 15–0 massacre, the largest run differential in a sudden-death postseason finale was 11 runs. The Cards beat the Tigers, 11–0, in Game 7 of the 1934 Series, and because the baseball gods are crazy, the Royals beat the Cards, 11–0, in Game 7 of the 1985 World Series. And because karma is a bitch—and so that the Cardinals can be involved in every sudden-death blowout—in Game 5 of the 2019 NLDS, St. Louis topped Atlanta, 13–1.

How quickly does it take for a pitcher to be in deep trouble? In this October 17 game, Marquis Grissom singled on Donovan Osborne's first pitch, and Mark Lemke doubled on his second pitch. After two outs and just 23 pitches, the Braves had batted around and were winning 6–0. Osborne never pitched in the postseason again.

The Braves in the NLCS outscored the Cardinals 44–18 and outhit them .309 to .204.

- Javy Lopez went 2–4 in this game and was the NLCS MVP, hitting .542 (13–24).
- Hall of Famer Chipper Jones hit .440.
- Hall of Famer Ozzie Smith hit .000, going 0–9.
- Hall of Famer Tom Glavine was 1–1 with a 2.08 ERA.
- Hall of Famer Greg Maddux was 1–1 with a 2.51 ERA.
- Hall of Famer John Smoltz was 2–0 with a 1.20 ERA.
- Hall of Famer Dennis Eckersley was 1–0 with one save and a 0.00 ERA in 3.1 IP.

In the top of the 6th of Game 7, Ozzie Smith, as a pinch-hitter, fouled out to right field. It was his final appearance in the majors.

Andruw Jones, at 19 years old, became the youngest player to ever homer in the postseason. I don't ordinarily care about those things, but Mickey Mantle had held the record previously, homering when he was almost 21.

Every now and then, there is an event to savor. Tom Glavine's bases-loaded triple meets that category. The HOFer did hit two regular season triples in his 22-season career, so it wasn't a fluke (please appreciate my sarcasm). The first postseason pitcher-hit triple was hit by Cy Young in 1903. The Babe hit the second one in 1918. Both HOFers, both two-run triples. Dutch Ruether's triple was also a two-run shot. Ruether isn't in the Hall; neither is the pitcher he hit it off of, Eddie Cicotte, one of the eight permanently ineligible Black Sox players from that 1919 Series. Dontrelle Willis' triple in 2003 came with the sacks empty, and Archie Bradley's triple in 2017 drove home two. So, there have been six pitchers with postseason triples, and Tommy Glavine's was the only one worth three runs.

UNASSISTED TRIPLE PLAY SUMMIT

BOSTON 5 PHILADELPHIA 4 (10 INNINGS)
FENWAY PARK, BOSTON, MA
TIME: 3:34 • JUNE 16, 1997

BOB RYAN

John Valentin said something had indeed "crossed his mind" with regard to the impending first-ever Red Sox interleague game with the Phillies. He was aware that he'd be meeting up with an opposing player who, like himself, had an unassisted triple play on his résumé.

The player was Phillies shortstop Mickey Morandini, and what neither man knew was this would be the first time since 1930 two unassisted-triple-play guys would be opponents. Well, I sure knew and made it my business to have them each sign my scorebook.

When Morandini was so informed, he said it was "awesome." Another thing he didn't know was that on the day when he pulled off his triple play (9/20/92), Valentin hit a home run. Yet again, can't make this stuff up.

It was actually a pretty cool game in which Troy O'Leary tied it with a pinch-hit double in the 9th and won it when Ricky Bottalico hit him with a pitch to force home the winning run in the 10th.

BILL CHUCK

I can't help but think of the 671 regular season games that Bill Wambsganss played from 1921 to the end of his career in 1926. I imagine at each one, someone said, "There he is, the man who pulled off an unassisted triple play in the 1920 World Series."

Wamby played for Cleveland, and he hit just .154 in seven games as his team won the title in the best of nine Series against the Brooklyn Robins. But it was in Game 5 that history was made… twice. In the bottom of the 1st inning, the future Hall of Famer and the most famous spitballer, Burleigh Grimes, was on the mound for Brooklyn. Charlie Jamieson led off with a single, Wambsganss followed with another single, and another future Hall of Famer, Tris Speaker, bunted for a single to load the bases. Up stepped Elmer Smith, who led Cleveland with 12 home runs during the regular season, and he did something that had never been done before in the World Series. He hit a grand slam homer. Smith ended his game going 3–4 with a homer, triple, and single, and four RBI. Not only was it the first time a granny had been hit, but the first time one player had a homer and a triple in a Series game, a feat that would not be duplicated until Gil McDougald did it in 1953. Everybody would be talking about Smith after a game like this, right? Wrong.

In the top of the 5th inning, the Robins trailed 7–0 when Pete Kilduff and Otto Miller led off with singles. Up stepped pitcher Clarence Mitchell, who had come in the game in relief of Grimes. Mitchell was more than a pitcher. I mean, he was no Babe Ruth or Shohei Ohtani, but he did start 11 games at first and four in the outfield that season. With the runners moving, Mitchell hit a liner that was headed to center field, but fate and the glove of Bill Wambsganss stepped in. Wamby reached out and stabbed the ball, and his momentum took him right to the second base bag, which he stepped on to double up

Kilduff, and as Wamby turned toward first, there was Otto Miller just waiting to be tagged. Triple play. The only unassisted triple play to date in World Series history and only the second recorded in modern baseball history.

Before I get to Bob's game, I want to mention George Burns, not Gracie Allen's George Burns, but the Clevelanders' backup first baseman, who played in five of the games of the 1920 Series but missed the Smith/Wambsganss classic. Burns was dealt to the Red Sox following the 1921 season and in 1923, became the only first baseman to pull off an unassisted triple play.

One more backgrounder on this oddest of oddities, on May 30, 1927, Jimmy Cooney of the Phillies pulled off the third NL unassisted triple play. *The next day*, Johnny Neun of the Tigers completed the seventh unassisted triple play in the bigs.

At the time of this writing, there have been just 15 TP-U, and Bob immediately took notice that two of the executioners were to be on the field that evening at Fenway. After Cooney in 1927, there wasn't an unassisted TP until September 20, 1992, when Jeff King of the Pirates hit a liner off a Curt Schilling pitch that was snagged by second baseman Mickey Morandini of the Phils, who doubled off

Andy Van Slyke and tripled off Barry Bonds. The Phils lost that game on a 13th inning walk-off.

Baseball's next unassisted triple play occurred on July 8, 1994, at Fenway Park as the Red Sox topped the Mariners, 4–3. John Valentin had one of baseball's most unusual nights.

- In the 5th inning, he committed an error that led to an unearned run.
- In the top of the 6th inning, he picked off a line-drive hit by Marc Newfield that led to an unassisted triple play.
- In the bottom of the 6th, Valentin led off the inning with a homer.

A few other notes from that game: Newfield was the Seattle DH in that game as Edgar Martinez, who reached the Hall of Fame based on his DH skills, was the M's third baseman (he committed his seventh error of the season). Junior Griffey, another HOFer, tripled in this contest. And the Mariners' 18-year-old rookie shortstop, Alex Rodriguez, made his major league debut.

This almost brings us to Bob's game on June 16, 1997. But first, a brief detour to September 28, 1930, and the final game of the season between the Boston Braves and the Brooklyn Robins at Ebbets Field. You remember I mentioned Johnny Neun, who pulled off a TP in 1927 for Detroit? He was now the Braves first baseman (and leadoff batter, something else we don't see that frequently), and playing short for Brooklyn was Glenn Wright, who had executed the second triple play in NL history in 1925 playing for Pittsburgh against the Cardinals (Rogers Hornsby was the third out).

We visited that game because that was the last time two unassisted triple players had faced each other until Bob's game. In Bob's game, Morandini was 0–3 with a run scored, and Valentin was 2–3 with a run scored. And just like the game in which Morandini pulled off his triple play, the Phils lost in a walk-off or plunk-off if you wish.

A SINGLE SHORT

BOSTON 3 OAKLAND 0 | FENWAY PARK, BOSTON, MA
TIME: 2:22 • JULY 23, 1997

BOB RYAN

They had been teammates in Double A Trenton, and now they were doing their thing at the highest level for the parent club. Jeff Suppan and Nomar Garciaparra were front and center in this one.

Suppan had a dominating 7.2 innings on the mound, allowing four hits while fanning six. I gave it a "Suppan Superb!" atop my scorebook page.

By this time, it was a given that this rookie shortstop seldom made a soft out. After grounding to third in the first, Garciaparra doubled down the left-field line in the third, tripled to the triangle adjacent to the Sox bullpen in the 5th, and hit a rocket homer to dead-center in the

219

8th. Yup, three-quarters of a cycle, in order, lacking only the needed single.

But Nomar's praise was reserved for Suppan. "People make great plays behind him because you can feed off him," Nomar said. "He's got a great rhythm out there."

BILL CHUCK

A curmudgeon is defined by Merriam-Webster as "a crusty, ill-tempered, and usually old man." Okay, I will admit that both Bob and I have been described in that fashion. I will also share that we wear the label as a badge of honor. One thing that regularly sets us off down the curmudgeon conduit is when a media member describes a player as "being a triple shy of the cycle."

A triple is not that common and the "missing triple" in a game in which a player hits a single, double, and a homer, is barely newsworthy. Lou Gehrig hit for the cycle twice in his career. He fell a triple shy of the cycle on 42 occasions. That's the most of any player. Gehrig is also tied for the record of most times a player fell a single shy of the cycle along with Babe Ruth, Henry Aaron, Frank Robinson, and six others. They each fell a single shy of the cycle three times. For a guy like Lou, it was almost as hard to fall a single shy as it was to hit for the cycle.

Since this game was in the '90s, here are some numbers from 1990 to 1999:

- There were 24 cycles that were hit, and no player had more than one.
- From 1990 to '99, Juan Gonzalez, by himself, fell a triple shy of the cycle 25 times.
- In the 1997 season, there were 231 occasions in which a player fell a triple shy of the cycle. Can you imagine how frequently the dreaded phrase was uttered or written about?
- But from 1990 to '99, there were only 50 occasions when a player fell a single shy of the cycle.
- In 1997, there were two cycles and seven in which a player fell a single shy like Nomar did in this game.

- Just to satisfy your curiosity, in 1997, there were 22 games in which a player fell a double shy of the cycle and 43 games when the only hit that was missing was a homer.

Like Babe Ruth, Nomar Garciaparra never hit for the cycle. Nomar fell a triple shy 18 times. He fell a homer shy four times. He fell a double shy once. And this was the first of two times in his 1,434-game career that he fell a single shy of the cycle.

THE FIVE-STAR CATCH

BOSTON 4 SEATTLE 0 | FENWAY PARK, BOSTON, MA
TIME: 2:19 • JULY 29, 1997

BOB RYAN

I pride myself on being somewhat judicious with my stars. It's got to be a good defensive gem to get a star. Sometimes I grant two stars, or even three. But in all my scorebooks, there is only one five-star catch, and it belongs to Jay Buhner.

It was the Red Sox 8th. Scott Hatteberg led off against reliever Edwin Hurtado and got hold of one, sending it to deep-right. Back, back, back went right fielder Buhner, who somehow made a spectacular what I call bring-'em-back-alive catch before tumbling into the Red Sox bullpen.

"Greatest catch of bring-back alive I've ever seen in Fenway," I wrote on one side of my scorebook. On the other side, I wrote "Buhner's 5-star catch on Hatteberg!" I guess you get the picture. What's freaky is that he had also made a one-star catch off Mike Stanley in the 4th. A 6-star performance!

My colleague Michael Vega on The Catch: "The catch was worthy of an ESPY nomination at the very least."

What I had pretty much forgotten was that Tim Wakefield had thrown a masterpiece, a five-hit shutout in which, believe it or not, the only official base hit to leave the infield had been a Russ Davis triple in the 5th. Yup, four infield singles and a triple; that's all.

Loser Randy Johnson was certainly impressed. "I pitched just well enough to lose," he said. "It wouldn't have mattered if I gave up just one run. I still would have lost. He pitched better."

Seinfeld fans may recall that George Costanza's dad, Frank, used Jay Buhner as a frequent reference point.

BILL CHUCK

Do me a favor and simply Google "Jay Buhner catch," so I don't have to further elaborate on how incredible this home run heist was. The video comes complete with the stunned reactions of NESN announcers Sean McDonough and Jerry Remy. But if you really want to hear amazement, watch the Seattle feed and listen to the great Dave Niehaus, a treat unto itself. The cherry on the top is that after the Buhner catch, he got a "bear hug" from Junior Griffey. I'd give five stars for that alone. Trust Bob, this was worth a look.

You may not be aware, but in one of my prior professional lives, I was a television critic (okay, "critic" may be a little too strong), and I was known as the "Czar of Entertainment." I mention this because I'm giving five stars to the great scene in which Estelle Harris ("Estelle Costanza") and Jerry Stiller ("Frank Costanza") are talking to George Steinbrenner (seen from the back only and voiced by Larry David), who has just mistakenly told them about the death of their son, George. Steinbrenner, in expressing sympathy to the grieving parents, refers to George as "a human dynamo." Estelle immediately responds, "Are you sure you're talking about George?" At this point, amid this condolence call, Frank snaps at Steinbrenner, "What the hell did you trade Jay Buhner for?" It is a great performance, great writing, and a great question. Five stars.

Jay Buhner played 15 seasons in the majors, 14 with the Mariners. He was a lifetime .254 hitter with 310 homers. He was traded by the Yankees to Seattle in July 1988 for Ken Phelps. Phelps played 11 seasons in the majors, two with the Yankees, and had a .239 career BA with 123 homers. Buhner was beloved in Seattle, wearing No. 19. The number has not been retired since Buhner retired in 2001, but it has also not been issued to any other player.

The Czar would like to also speak of Chris Pratt. He is the actor who brilliantly played Andy Dwyer on the sitcom *Parks and Recreation*. On the big screen, you know him from his leading roles in *Guardians of the Galaxy*, *Jurassic World*, and in the *Avengers* films.

Why does the talented Mr. Pratt get attention in this story? You might recall the movie version of *Moneyball*. A critical part of the film and the book by Michael Lewis was the conversion of catcher Scott Hatteberg (the guy who hit the ball that Buhner made the catch on) to first baseman Scott Hatteberg. Yes, Chris Pratt, after losing 40 pounds, played Hatteberg, the Oakland A's pinch-hitter who hit a walk-off homer to give the team a 20-game winning streak. Five stars.

1997 ALCS GAME 2

SERIES TIED ONE APIECE
CLEVELAND 5 BALTIMORE 4
ORIOLE PARK AT CAMDEN YARDS, BALTIMORE, MD
TIME: 3:53 • OCTOBER 9, 1997

BOB RYAN

When you think "Jimmy Key," you think, "Crafty lefty. Efficient." You don't think of him setting a postseason record by hitting three batters in an inning, in this case, the 1st. That's baseball, however. You can never say you've seen everything… until you do.

Key got Bip Roberts looking to start the game. But before the inning was over, he had hit Omar Vizquel, Dave Justice, and Tony Fernandez. Oh, and after hitting Vizquel, he had given up a homer to Manny Ramirez.

What was going on? The *Baltimore Sun*'s Roch Kubatko said this: "He continually fell behind on the count, then took aim as if he was trying to win a kewpie doll at a carnival."

The big controversy came in the O's 8th. Everyone in the entire state of Maryland thought Armando Benitez had gotten rid of a check-swing pinch-hitter Jim Thome at 3-and-2 with two away and one on, the O's leading by a 4–2 score. But third-base ump Larry McCoy answered plate ump Jim Joyce's look by saying, "Nope, he held up." Benitez wasn't pleased. You know what's coming. Marquis Grissom hit a three-run go-ahead and ultimately game-winning homer.

Asked if he thought the notoriously volatile Benitez was "rattled," Oriole skipper Davey Johnson said, "I think everyone did, but that's no excuse for not making good pitches on the next guy. The next guy is the one who can beat you."

BILL CHUCK

This is a series that went six games, but after it was over, you realized it was the 8th inning here in Game 2 that dictated the direction the ALCS would take.

The fact that Cleveland came back against Armando Benitez was a power boost to their psyche. The Orioles had tied the game 2–2 in the 2nd, and after Manny's 1st inning homer, Cleveland stopped hitting. Scott Kamieniecki pitched three innings and faced 10 batters allowing just a walk and no hits (and no hit batsmen).

During the regular season, in 69 save opportunities, the Orioles were successful 59 times, an 86 percent success rate, the best in the league. When O's were leading entering the 8th inning that regular season, they had a record of 79-4. Add three more wins from the ALDS and one more from Game 1 of the ALCS, and this team had a record of 83-4 when leading after seven innings.

That brought the game to 8th and Armando. Benitez had held batters to a .191 BA during the regular season and just .162 in save situations, and this was indeed a save situation. There were two outs, and batters had hit .120 against Benitez with two outs. He faced 307 batters during the regular season and allowed just seven homers and none with two runners on base.

And that brings us to Marquis. Grissom had hit just 12 homers in 1997, none with two runners on base. In 1997, he hit .195 against the Orioles and .095 (2–21) at Camden Yards. One more item of note, Grissom had been suffering from the flu, and before Game 1, he was so dehydrated that he was in the clubhouse getting fluid intravenously. The home run was more than a game changer; it's what makes baseball great.

One more thing...

Philadelphia is the City of Brotherly Love, but this was the ALCS of Brotherly Love. The Orioles had future HOFer Roberto Alomar at second base, and the future Guardians had his older brother Sandy Alomar Jr. behind the plate.

1997 ALCS GAME 3

CLEVELAND LEADS THE ALCS 2–1
CLEVELAND 2 BALTIMORE 1 (12 INNINGS)
JACOBS FIELD, CLEVELAND, OH
TIME: 4:51 • OCTOBER 11, 1997

BOB RYAN

Start with this: Mike Mussina fanned an LCS record 15 and had naught but an elegant no-decision to show for it. And the winning run came on a controversial botched suicide squeeze. No kidding.

Marquis Grissom was on third, and Tony Fernandez was on first with one out in the top of the 12th. Mike Hargrove called for the squeeze against Randy Myers. Omar Vizquel squared to bunt, but he missed the pitch, and the ball eluded catcher Lenny Webster as Grissom scored the winning run. Webster disagreed. "He tipped it," Webster protested.

228

"I saw contact. I *heard* contact." That wasn't the opinion of plate ump John Hirschbeck, nor of Vizquel.

"I didn't foul the ball," said Vizquel. "I bunted right through the pitch."

The Orioles had scored a funky run themselves in the 9th. It involved a misjudgment by Tony Fernandez, a career shortstop who was in the game as a second base replacement for Bip Roberts. Baserunner Jeff Reboulet fell to his feet as Fernandez fielded a grounder. Rather than tag him, Fernandez threw to first. Jim Thome's return throw hit Reboulet. Brady Anderson followed with a relatively easy fly to center that was misjudged by Grissom for a run-scoring double. Got all that?

The game had started at 4:07 local time; i.e. dreaded twilight time. Mussina took full advantage with his nefarious knuckle-curve, fanning those 15 while allowing three hits and one run before leaving after throwing 120 pitches through seven.

That botched suicide squeeze was a source of fascination. "I never saw a run scored on a missed squeeze," marveled Cleveland's starter Orel Hershiser IV. Nor has anyone else, before or since.

BILL CHUCK

Let's talk strikeouts for a moment. With two down in the top of the 1st, Oral Hershiser recorded his first strikeout. In the bottom of the 1st, Mike Mussina recorded his first three whiffs. In the top of the 2nd, it was Orel's turn to strike out the side. Mussina responded with one K in the bottom of the 2nd, and Hershiser did the same in the top of the 3rd. In the bottom of the 3rd, Mussina struck out the side (again). Through the first three innings, 12 of 18 outs were whiffs. As Bob pointed out, the afternoon shadows wreaked batter hell.

Mussina pitched seven innings of one-run ball and struck out at least one batter in each inning and struck out the side in three separate innings. Mussina's 15 Ks were a career-high he matched two times in the future in regular season games.

Let's talk about double plays for a moment. Cleveland pulled off four after the O's leadoff batter got on in the top of the 3rd, top of the 4th, top of the 5th, and top of the 6th. If you think this was a fluke, think again. Orel Hershiser pitched 18 seasons in the majors, and in 1997, at the age of 38, the Bulldog produced 31 GIDP, the most of his career. And yes, from 1983 to 2000, Hershiser led all pitchers producing 314 double plays.

As for the controversial "botched suicide squeeze" ending to this game that Bob so ably described, perhaps you are wondering about the scoring on such a play? At the time, it was scored as a Lenny Webster passed ball. But an hour before the fourth game, a further explanation of the rules forced a scoring change. Baseball-Almanac.com list 35 games that have ended with a steal of home. Marquis Grissom, who felt sick about his misjudgment of the fly ball, lost in the lights in the 9th, which enabled the Orioles to tie the score, was credited with the only steal of home that has ever ended a postseason game. No game of any sort has ended with a steal of home since that strange afternoon, evening, and night at the Jake.

1997 ALCS GAME 6

CLEVELAND WINS ALCS, 4–2
CLEVELAND 1 BALTIMORE 0
ORIOLE PARK AT CAMDEN YARDS, BALTIMORE, MD
TIME: 3:52 • OCTOBER 15, 1997

BOB RYAN

When he arose that morning, Tony Fernandez was not in the lineup. But there he was in the Cleveland 11th, taking an Armando Benitez slider over the right-field fence to give Cleveland a 1–0 victory and the American League pennant. Wait, there's more.

He was in the lineup because a ball off his own bat during batting practice had struck starting second baseman Bip Roberts on the right thumb, causing a contusion that knocked him out of the lineup. No, folks, you truly can't make this stuff up.

Now, talk about squandering… the Orioles left a man on base in every inning but the 6ᵗʰ, 14 in all. They were 0-for-12 with RISP.

Worse yet, the O's squandered yet another dazzling performance by starter Mike Mussina, who threw eight innings of one-hit, 10 K ball for a second frustrating no-decision in the series. This, on top of his 15 K start in Game 1.

In the Oriole 7ᵗʰ, Cleveland snuffed out a bid with an artfully executed (and starred by me) "Wheel Play," with third baseman Matt Williams and shortstop Omar Vizquel turning a Robbie Alomar bunt down the third-base line with men on first and second and none out into a rare 5-6 force-out at third. Geronimo Berroa then hit into a 5-4-3 DP, and that was that.

It turns out Fernandez has some celestial aid on his game-winning homer. "I just asked God to guide the ball," he explained. "I needed help."

The *Baltimore Sun*'s John Eisenberg summed up an amazing six games of baseball, saying, "The series was the closest thing to an Alfred Hitchcock movie you will ever see at Camden Yards."

BILL CHUCK

Tony Fernandez was always a player you could like and appreciate for what he added to a game. His presence made teams better. In his postseason career, Tony played 43 games. In 42 of them, he did not homer. On October 15, he chose an opportune moment to go deep.

In baseball history, there have only been 14 occasions in which a 1–0 postseason game has been decided by a solo homer. Only seven times has the winning team played the game on the road. Only once has this occurred in extra innings, and only once has it occurred in a potential clinching game, and this was it. Way to go, Tony.

Fernandez was a one-year rental for Cleveland, signing with them in December 1996; they granted him free agency October 1997. He spent most of his career in three stints with the Blue Jays and was outstanding, going to the All-Star Game with them four times (he went five times in total) and winning four Gold Gloves. In 2001, Fernandez was named a member of the Toronto Blue Jays Level of Excellence. The Jays traded him to the Padres in 1990 in one of baseball's great deals going with Fred McGriff to San Diego for Roberto Alomar and Joe Carter. Then in June 1993, Fernandez was traded back to the Jays (he was now with the Mets), which meant he was with the team when Carter won the 1993 Series with his walk-off homer. Interestingly, as Bob pointed out, Roberto Alomar was with the Orioles in this game (Robbie and Tony each played for the Padres, Blue Jays, Cleveland, and Mets but played together only for the 1993 Jays). This game ended when Jose Mesa struck out Alomar with a runner on base.

- Cleveland won Game 2, 5–4
- Cleveland won Game 3, 2–1 in 12 innings
- Cleveland won Game 4, 8–7
- Cleveland won Game 6, 1–0 in 11 innings

Note that all four victories were by one run.

Tony Fernandez had indeed found an opportune time to go deep.

DIAMONDBACKS FIRST GAME

COLORADO 9 ARIZONA 2 | BANK ONE BALLPARK, PHOENIX, AZ
TIME: 2:50 • MARCH 31, 1998

BOB RYAN

It was the first-ever major league baseball game in Arizona and team owner Jerry Colangelo received the biggest ovation of the evening. "Tonight's game was the most significant day in the history of Arizona," he said. "It's the beginning of a new era of baseball in Arizona."

It was also the beginning—and very likely the end—of swimming pools in ballparks. Indeed, Bank One Ballpark (aka "The Bob") opened with an honest-to-God swimming pool you could rent out beyond the right-center-field fence.

Colorado's Vinny Castilla hit the first homer in the new park. Actually, he had two. Arizona rookie Travis Lee had Arizona's first. Let the record show that the fans started heading home in droves after the Rockies concluded a five-run 7th.

BILL CHUCK

Here is a timeline of the first games, and first home games, of baseball's expansion franchises:

- The Washington Senators (now the Texas Rangers) played their first game on April 10, 1961 (at home). They lost to the White Sox, 4–3.
- The Los Angeles Angels played their first game on April 11, 1961. They beat the Orioles, 7–2.
- The Los Angeles Angels played their first home game on April 27, 1961. They lost to the Twins, 4–2.
- The Houston Colt .45s (now the Astros) played their first game on April 10, 1962 (at home). They beat the Cubs, 11–2.
- The New York Mets played their first game on April 11, 1962. They lost to the Cardinals, 11–4.
- The New York Mets played their first home game on Friday, April 13, 1962. They lost to the Pirates, 4–3.
- The Seattle Pilots (now the Milwaukee Brewers) played their first game on April 8, 1969. They beat the Angels, 4–3.
- The Montreal Expos played their first game on April 8, 1969. They beat the Mets, 11–10.
- The San Diego Padres played their first game on April 8, 1969 (at home). They beat the Astros, 2–1.
- The Kansas City Royals played their first game on April 8, 1969 (at home). They beat the Twins, 4–3 in a 12-inning walk-off. They won their second game against the Twins as 4–3 in another walk-off, this one in 17 innings.
- The Seattle Pilots (now the Milwaukee Brewers) played their first home game on April 11, 1969. They beat the White Sox, 7–0.
- The Montreal Expos played their first home game on April 14, 1969. They beat the Cards, 8–7.
- The Seattle Mariners played their first game on April 6, 1977 (at home). They lost to the Angels, 7–0.
- The Toronto Blue Jays played their first game on April 7, 1977 (at home). They beat the White Sox, 9–5.

- The Florida Marlins played their first game on April 5, 1993 (at home). They beat the Dodgers, 6–3.
- The Colorado Rockies played their first game on April 5, 1993. They lost to the Mets, 3–0.
- The Colorado Rockies played their first home game on April 9, 1993. They beat the Expos, 11–4.
- The Tampa Bay Devil Rays (now the Tampa Bay Rays) played their first game on March 31, 1998 (at home). They lost to the Tigers, 11–6.
- The Arizona Diamondbacks played their first game on March 31, 1998 (at home). They lost to the Rockies, 9–2.

And this about the game…

- Daryl Kile earned the win, and Andy Benes took the loss.
- Travis Lee made his MLB debut and got both the first hit and the first homer for Arizona.
- Renowned GM Jerry Dipoto pitched the final inning for Colorado.
- Bob was there because of a personal invite from Jerry Colangelo, of Phoenix Suns fame.

F.P. SWITCH-HIT PLUNKS

BOSTON 7 MONTREAL 4 | FENWAY PARK, BOSTON, MA
TIME: 2:50 • JUNE 30, 1998

BOB RYAN

Check out F.P. Santangelo's line in the Expos' box score. There were two 1-3s (one a bunt) and two HBPs. Love it.

But the real fun part for me was that the hit batsman in the 5th came when he was batting right-handed against Steve Avery and the hit batsman in the 7th came while he was batting left-handed against Rich Garces. Switch-hit hit plunks in successive at-bats. How cool is that?

This game marked the American League debut of rangy (6'7") veteran Billy Ashley, who introduced himself to the Fenway crowd with a golden sombrero, i.e., four Ks. Even Rob Deer couldn't do that.

Four Montreal errors made life easier for the Red Sox.

BILL CHUCK

Dan McGann is a name I was unfamiliar with before this Bob Ryan story brought me to Baseball-Reference.com. McGann leads all switch-hitters with two hit-by-pitches in eight games. McGann played between 1901 and 1908 for the Cardinals, New York Giants, and Boston Braves, and records are sketchy during that time period, so it's hard to determine if there were games in which McGann was plunked on each side of the plate. I can say that relief pitchers were not in common use, so the occasions in which McGann would switch during a game were limited.

Next on the list with four games each are Danny Espinosa and F.P. Santangelo. In the four games that F.P. was plunked twice, the Expos lost all four. So much for the value of taking one for the team. All the events took place in 1998, starting on April 29 against the Cardinals, when lefty Kent Mercker got him and righty Mike Busby got him. On May 8, a pair of Rockies righties rocked him. Then there was Bob's game on June 30. Finally, on July 31, against the Padres, Kevin Brown got him twice.

Santangelo played seven years in the bigs and was hit by 83 pitches. In 1997, he was hit 25 times, the most in any season by a switch-hitter.

And there's this…
- This was the first appearance by the Montreal Expos at Fenway Park
- Derrick May, son of Dave May, and Damon Buford, son of Don Buford, played in this game.

1998 NLCS GAME 5

PADRES LEAD BRAVES IN NLCS 3–2
ATLANTA 7 SAN DIEGO 6 | QUALCOMM STADIUM, SAN DIEGO, CA
TIME: 3:17 • OCTOBER 12, 1998

BOB RYAN

Definition of managerial genius: the player comes through for you. Definition of managerial idiocy: he doesn't. That is to say, Bobby Cox's decision to relieve with Greg Maddux worked out. Bruce Bochy's decision to relieve with Kevin Brown didn't.

Bochy brought in Brown to protect a 4–2 lead in the 7th. Forty-one pitches and a Michael Tucker three-run homer later, he was gone, and he would be the loser. Oops. "We had our best out there," shrugged Bochy. "We went for it, and it just didn't work out."

Cox brought in Maddux for his first relief appearance in 11 years after a Greg Myers pinch-hit two-run homer made it a 7–6 game in

239

the 9th. Sixteen pitches later, the game was over. Save, Maddux. Bobby, you're a genius.

The game also included a botched suicide squeeze by the Braves in the 4th and many weak swings. Said (ahem) the *Boston Globe*'s Bob Ryan, "There might have been a world's record for dribblers and infield hits (five of these)."

Also noteworthy was John Rocker's first big-league plate appearance, which resulted in a base on balls and a run scored via a Tony Graffanino double. Something to tell the grandchildren.

BILL CHUCK

A pair of aces from the 'pen. It would be fair to say that this game saw each team's ace come in. Greg Maddux had gone 18–9 during the regular season and led the league with a 2.22 ERA. Kevin Brown went 18–7 with a 2.38 ERA. You just don't see two relievers like that every game. Brown had pitched a three-hit shutout to win Game 2 of this NLCS, while Maddux had gone five innings, allowing two runs, and was the loser of Game 3.

While Brownie didn't do the job in this game, he was on his way to his second straight World Series, having pitched for the 1997 world champion Marlins.

The one and only Greg Maddux earned the one and only save of his major league, regular season, or postseason career in this game. The final out was a grounder to first hit by HOFer Tony Gwynn (who hit .429 against Maddux in their regular season careers).

On that botched suicide squeeze Bob told you about, John Smoltz was the batter, and Andruw Jones was charged with a caught stealing at home.

More on John Rocker

John Rocker's plate appearance delighted Bob and me. The rookie reliever came up in the top of the 8th immediately following Michael Tucker's three-run blast, which turned the game from a 4–2 Braves deficit to a 5–4 lead. Donne Wall relieved Kevin Brown and walked Rocker on five pitches. Rocker scored the Braves' seventh run (the deciding run) and picked up the win. Rocker had his second and final PA the following postseason against Houston in NLDS Game 3, and once again, Rocker walked. Rocker appeared in 280 regular season games and never had a plate appearance.

The genius of managing

A moment on Warren Spahn, one of the greatest pitchers the world has ever seen. Spahnie debuted in 1942 for the Boston Braves as a 21-year-old. In 1965, as a 44-year-old, Spahn pitched for the New York Mets for half a season. In each case, his manager was Casey Stengel. Soon after Spahn was released in July 1965, the wry lefty said, "I'm probably the only guy who worked for (Casey) Stengel before and after he was a genius." Now re-read Bob's opening paragraph again.

PULP FICTION MEETS *BULL DURHAM*

BOSTON 8 DETROIT 7 | FENWAY PARK, BOSTON, MA
TIME: 2:57 • MAY 31, 1999

BOB RYAN

"*Pulp Fiction* meets *Bull Durham*." That was the *Globe*'s Dan Shaughnessy's description of this wild-and-wooly game. Oh, and this: "One of the nuttiest and entertaining games of the season."

Start with the one thing that made sense. Troy O'Leary won it with a two-run homer in the 7th. This was the climax of a game which, as Shaughnessy annotated, included "10 pitchers, six homers, four hit batsmen (flag that one), three ejections, one subluxation, and one cleaned-out locker."

Sox starter Mark Portugal was the one with the shoulder "subluxation" sustained when hit by a Deivi Cruz comebacker in the 2nd. He was also the one cleaning out his locker in a postgame rant.

The ejections were Detroit's when plate ump Chuck Meriwether tossed Matt Anderson, as well as catcher Brad Ausmus and manager Larry Parrish after hitting Mike Stanley, the man up after O'Leary's homer.

Detroit's Damion Easley tied a record by being hit by a pitch three times. The best part is he was hit by three different pitchers. If it sounds as if he was target practice, consider that, according to Mr. Shaughnessy, "Actually, he was grazed all three times."

Hey, it wasn't just Dan Shaughnessy. "There was a lot of weird stuff out there today," observed Jason Varitek.

BILL CHUCK

There have been a mere 35 games when a player has been plunked three times. The honor has been given to 29 different players, with Reed Johnson of the Blue Jays having three such games: first on 4/16/2005 against Texas, then against Tampa Bay on 4/7/2006, and then again later that same month on 4/29 against the Yankees.

Jurickson Profar was hit three times twice in two weeks while playing for Texas in 2018: first on June 9 against the Astros and then on June 23 against the Twins.

The Cubs' Frank Chance (of Tinkers to Evers to Chance fame) was the first to get hit three times, in 1902 by the Reds while playing for the Cubs and then again in 1904 by the Reds while playing for the Cubs. And what are the odds of another player getting hit twice while playing for the same team and hit by the same team? Pretty long, I would imagine, but it happened to Damion Easley as well when he was hit thrice by the Red Sox in 1999 (this game) and then again in 2002.

The Red Sox lead all teams in hitting players three times in a game, doing it five times: Sherm Lollar in 1956, Bill Freehan in 1968, Brandon Guyer in 2016 (Toronto also got him three times), and whacking Easley twice.

Mel Ott is the only HOFer with a three HBP game to his résumé; the Pirates got the Giants' outfielder in 1938.

Here's an interesting line: On August 15, 2005, the Devil Rays' Jonny Gomes went 1–1 with three HBP and a homer against the Yankees. He is the only player to homer in the same game he was hit three times.

In case you are curious, Sandy Alomar played 1,481 games, the most for any player who was hit three times in his career. And now that I've piqued your curiosity, Mark Lemke played the most games of any non-pitcher, 1,069, without ever getting hit by a pitch.

A little more on Damion Easley (and Cal Ripken Jr.)

Easley was hit by 132 pitches in his career, which lasted 1,706 games. The pain of getting hit so frequently, I surmise, was less than the pain Easley suffered from never playing in a postseason game. Perhaps Easley should be better known not for his getting hit by pitches but for a pop-up that ended the 5th inning on September 6, 1995, off Mike Mussina. It was that pop-up that made the game official, thereby certifying that Cal Ripken Jr. had broken Lou Gehrig's record for most consecutive games played, this being his 2,131[st].

MATCHING LEADOFF HOMERS

BOSTON 6 PHILADELPHIA 4 | FENWAY PARK, BOSTON, MA
TIME: 2:50 • JULY 15, 1999

BOB RYAN

Leadoff homers are always cool. *Two* guys starting off their team's 1st inning by going deep is waaaay cooler. And pretty rare.

We have one here. Doug Glanville did it for the Phillies in the top of the 1st, and Jose Offerman did it for the Sox in the bottom of the 1st

Making this game even more distinct was that Jason Varitek (2nd) and Brian Daubach (7th) also homered for the Red Sox, and each was also a man leading off an inning.

Brian Rose was the winner. Tim Wakefield picked up his 11th save in 12 attempts.

BILL CHUCK

Okay, maybe you don't think hitting a leadoff homer is that big a deal. I think that would be a good example of recency bias. Since we're talking about the Red Sox, let me point out that of the 12 seasons in which they banged 200-plus homers, eight have occurred after 1999. In 1999, when Bob saw this game, the Sox hit 176 homers. Through the 2020 season, that ranked 23rd on their all-time list. Through the 1999 season, it was 10th.

Home runs in 1999 were much more of an event. And leadoff homers in a game were a particularly big deal. Even in the home run decade of 2011–2020, there were only 26 leadoff homers hit at Fenway Park; 12 by the Sox and 14 by the visitors.

You know how many leading off the game homers the Sox hit in 1999?

One… this one. It was indeed the game Bob attended, and Jose Offerman hit it on the third pitch from Paul Byrd (Glanville's homer came on the second pitch from Brian Rose).

The Phillies hit three game leadoffs, and Doug Glanville hit two of them. The only other time that season that Doug hit a leadoff homer, the other leadoff batter, Eric Young, Sr. hit a weak pop-up to third off Curt Schilling, and had Bob attended that game, you wouldn't be reading this right now.

So, here's to Rickey Henderson, who holds the career record with 81 leadoff home runs. And another tip of the cap to Alfonso Soriano, who hit 54. And let's toast Craig Biggio, who holds the National League career record with 53 leadoff homers.

Say what you want, but a leadoff homer is waaaay more fun than a weak pop-up to third.

Five more things...

1. This was the first game back to action following the All-Star Game that was played that season at Fenway Park. The Red Sox' Pedro Martinez was the AL starting and winning pitcher in the 1999 Midsummer Classic. In 2.0 innings pitched, he struck out five NLers.

2. Jose Offerman pinch-hit for the AL in the ASG and did not homer.

3. Leadoff home runs in the All-Star Game have been hit by Frankie Frisch (1934), Lou Boudreau (1942), Willie Mays (1965), Joe Morgan (1977), Bo Jackson (1989), and Mike Trout (2015).

4. Paul Byrd was on the NL squad but did not get in the game. The Phillies' Curt Schilling started the 1999 All-Star Game for the NL and was the losing pitcher. By 2004, he was a member of the Red Sox.

5. And speaking of 2004, the Phillies manager in this 1999 game was Terry Francona, who would lead the Sox to the promised land in 2004.

TIGER FAREWELL WEEKEND

BOSTON 11 DETROIT 4 | TIGER STADIUM, DETROIT, MI
TIME: 2:37 • JULY 24, 1999

BOB RYAN

Tiger Stadium was my all-time favorite ballpark. Period. So, my wife and I had to say goodbye, choosing a weekend series in July with the Red Sox just happening to be the foe. I requested low-row upper deck seats, and we were thus staring down at first base all weekend. In quiet moments you could hear the voices of the first baseman, first-base coach, and any baserunners. That's how close we were.

Trot Nixon entered the game with three home runs. He left the game with six after receiving a pregame lesson from batting coach Jim Rice. He had been hitting too many ground balls.

"When I roll my top wrist over, you get those grounders," Nixon explained. That was before hitting one into the left-center-field seats in the 2ⁿᵈ, one into the deeper left-center seats over the 410-foot sign in the 4ᵗʰ, and into the right-field upper deck in the 8ᵗʰ. The one to center got everyone's attention because, as the *Globe*'s Larry Whiteside pointed out, "there was a near gale blowing in from left field."

Nixon agreed. "That was the best of the home runs because it was right into the teeth of the wind, and I hit it hard. And it put us ahead."

He did this while batting ninth, and that made him just the fourth man ever to make that claim. Wind or no wind, the ball was flying all over the place. The Red Sox hit seven homers, and the Tigers hit three.

Oops, almost forgot. Nomar Garciaparra hit two homers himself, but he did it without any known pregame batting help from Jim Rice.

BILL CHUCK

Tiger Stadium, previously known as Navin Field and Briggs Stadium, was the home of the Detroit Tigers from 1912 to 1999.

On only 20 occasions, a ballplayer had a three-homer game at this park despite it being located in the Corktown region of Detroit. No one ever hit four homers in a game in this beautiful structure. Not only were there only 20 three-homer games, *no one ever did it twice.*

It's not that it was that difficult a ballpark to homer in. On July 18, 1921, Babe Ruth hit what many people consider the longest verified homer, clearing the center-field fence and going 575 feet. Of course, we don't know precisely since this was the pre-Statcast era, and we don't know the spin rate of the pitch he hit either. The Babe also hit No. 700 there. It was where Ted Williams hit a walk-off homer in the 1941 All-Star Game, during an era when all-stars stayed in the game. Reggie Jackson broke the lights with a shot in the 1971 All-Star Game. In the 1984 World Series, Kirk Gibson hit an 8ᵗʰ inning blast in Game 5 that secured the title. And you thought Gibson only hit one famous World Series homer.

No one hit more homers in Tiger Stadium than Al Kaline, who slammed 212 of his 399 homers at his home. Yes, Al is one of the 20 with a three-homer game there, as are other HOFers such as George Brett, Carl Yastrzemski, and Johnny Mize. No visitor hit more homers at Tiger Stadium than Babe Ruth, who appropriately hit 60 (in 180 games). Ted Williams is next with 55.

The final game at Tiger Stadium was on September 27, 1999 (not counting the reimagined games played there when Billy Crystal filmed *61** at the vacant ballpark). Robert Fick had the final major league hit, a rooftop grand slam, which was Tiger Stadium's 11,111th home run. And Trot Nixon had the final three-homer game at Tiger Stadium.

DAUBACH'S EPIC AT-BAT

BOSTON 6 OAKLAND 5 | FENWAY PARK, BOSTON, MA
TIME: 3:13 • AUGUST 16, 1999

BOB RYAN

Sox relievers Mark Guthrie and Rich Garces were joined by clubhouse man Pookie Jackson, all three standing on a couch in the middle of the Red Sox clubhouse. They were watching on TV as Brain Daubach battled Tim Worrell through nine pitches and five two-strike foul balls, the last of which Daubach hit far down the right-field line, screaming past the Pesky Pole, juuuuuuust foul.

And then he hit the 10th pitch off the left-field wall, clearing the bases to give his team a rousing 6–5 win in what had been billed as a wild card showdown series. "One of the most incredible at-bats I've ever seen." praised Guthrie.

First-base coach Dave Jauss was a seasoned baseball lifer. "You see things like that," he said, referring to the foul home run on pitch nine. "*That's* your hit, then they get you out on the next pitch. That's what they do in baseball."

Say this: Daubach was the right man to have up there. That hit gave him 15 RBI in his last four games.

Major Oakland offense had been supplied by catcher A.J. Hinch, a name to remember. He had a three-run homer off Brian Rose in the 3rd.

BILL CHUCK

Bob's story of this one at-bat sums up Brian Daubach perfectly. Here's a guy who will just keep working it and working it until he can make it work for him.

He was a 17th round draft choice of the Mets in 1990, and through the 1997 season, he continued to ply his trade in the minor leagues before having an uneventful cup of coffee playing 10 games with the 1998 Florida Marlins. He played for nine different minor league teams, from the Rookie League to Triple A. Back down in Charlotte in 1998, Daubach hit .316 with 35 homers and 124 RBI and was named the Marlins organizational player of the year. In November, he was released.

For the second time in minor league career he was a free agent, and in December signed with the Red Sox, who immediately assigned him to Pawtucket in the International League. The Sox were looking for a replacement for Mo Vaughn, who had left to play for the Angels in free agency, and Daubach became another possible lefty replacement.

With a strong spring training, Daubach, the Belleville Basher, made the team as Midre Cummings was cut and DH Reggie Jefferson was recovering from minor injuries. Then, when Jefferson recovered, Daubach was briefly sent back to the minors (he had options) before he was brought back to the big club.

But there was just something about Daubach, the kid from Belleville, Illinois, that struck the fancy of the Fenway faithful. By June, when Daubach was hitting .368 for the month, Gordon Edes had a SportsPlus front page article about the nine-year minor league veteran. The call-out quote came from Daubach, who said, "The weirdest thing is, the

Mets always thought I was a better player defensively. The Marlins thought I could hit, but they didn't think I could play anywhere."

By the time the 1999 season was completed, Daubach had hit 21 home runs with a slash line of .294/.360/.562 in 420 PA. In the ALDS against Cleveland, Daubach had a big home run in Game 3. He even finished fourth in the American League in Rookie of the Year voting.

When Daubach's career ended in 2005, he had spent eight seasons in the majors and hit 20 or more home runs in four straight seasons (1999–2002). In 2003, he played for the White Sox, and then in 2004, he played 30 games for Boston and collected a World Series ring. He ended his career in 2005 with 15 games with the Mets, the team that had originally drafted him.

In that first Boston spring training, Dan Shaughnessy showed his Hall of Fame instincts by singling out Daubach in a column about the patience exhibited by Daubach and his family and friends. He also showed how prescient Daubach would prove to be. Daubach told Shaughnessy, "Obviously, everyone wants to play in the majors," he says. "But I enjoy playing and competing. I've enjoyed every day of this. I've got zero regrets. There's a lot of people like myself who played eight or nine years in the minors. Whenever I'm done playing, I'd like to be a coach." And Dan adds, "He could teach young men how to hit. And how to be patient."

Since 2008, Daubach has been a minor league manager and coach, doing exactly what he and Shaughnessy said he would do.

1999 ALCS GAME 3

THE YANKEES LEAD THE ALCS, 2–1
BOSTON 13 NEW YORK 1 | FENWAY PARK, BOSTON, MA
TIME: 3:14 • OCTOBER 16, 1999

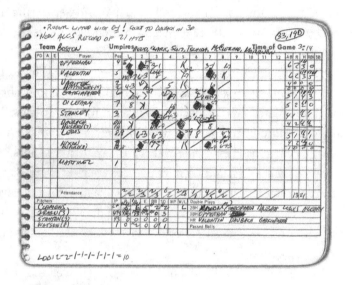

BOB RYAN

Pedro vs. Roger was supposed to be epic. Well, it *was* interesting.

The Red Sox banged out an ALCS record 21 hits, 10 for extra bases. Pedro was quite vintage Pedroey, allowing two hits while fanning 12 in 7.0 IP.

Roger? Let's just say that when you are lifted with an 0–1 count after allowing five earned runs in two-plus innings you put it in the "can't-win-'em-all" category and move on. You kinda knew it might not be Roger's day when Jose Offerman led off the Red Sox 1st with a triple and John Valentin hit a two-run homer.

Here's the really interesting part. Pedro swore he was hurting and actually had very little in the way of, you know, stuff. "I doubt if I threw my fastball better than 88 (mph)," he insisted. "I'm hurting every pitch." He went on to say he "mixed his pitches."

Joe Torre was in awe. "He *is* an artist out there," Torre said. "It's just that he uses a baseball instead of a paintbrush. There is no question he carves up the plate pretty good."

BILL CHUCK

It was one of those matchups that baseball fans dream about. Pedro Martinez was 23–4 with a 2.07 and on his way to the Cy Young Award. Roger Clemens was 37 and pitched like a 37-year-old (Cy Old?) going 14–10 with a 4.60 ERA but had been the CYA winner the prior two seasons with the Blue Jays. We didn't know what would happen in the years ahead, but we assumed both of these masters of the mound were on their way to Cooperstown. Well, we were half right. We were also half right in assuming that these pair of aces would rise to the occasion of meeting each other in the ALCS.

As we look back at his career, Clemens did not excel in the postseason, going 12–8 with a 3.75 ERA and a WHIP of 1.221. Quite honestly, the postseason really wasn't Pedro's milieu either. His career numbers were 6–4 with a 3.46 ERA and a 1.080 WHIP.

But in the 1999 postseason, Pedro was brilliant. In three games (two starts), Pedro threw 17.0 IP and allowed five hits, six walks, struck out 23, and permitted no—as in zero—runs against Cleveland and New York.

In the 1999 postseason, Roger started against Texas in the ALDS and pitched seven innings of shutout ball. In the World Series against Atlanta, he threw 7.2 IP and allowed one run. So, we are left to wonder what happened to Roger in front of his former Fenway faithful on that Saturday afternoon when he went 2.0 innings and allowed six hits and five runs?

Look at Bob's scorecard and you can see how dominant the Sox batters were that day:

- Nomar Garciaparra had four hits.

- Jose Offerman, John Valentin, and Trot Nixon each had three hits.
- Troy O'Leary, Mike Stanley, Brian Daubach, and Darren Lewis each had two hits.

In baseball history, there has never been another postseason game in which one team had eight players with multi-hit games. The 38 total bases set an LCS record, and it has since been topped just once, in 2004 Game 3, when the Yanks picked up 45 bases against the Red Sox.

At the time of this game, the 21 hits the Yanks allowed this Saturday afternoon were the most they had permitted in their long postseason history. This has since been topped (only once) by the 22 hits permitted in Game 6 of the 2001 World Series against Arizona. The six doubles allowed remains tied with four other games for the most the Yanks have allowed in a postseason game. BTW: At the time of this game, Roger had only allowed a leadoff triple to the first batter of the game just once before and that was way back in 1992, by Hall of Famer Tim Raines.

In Boston's robust postseason history, the 21 hits they picked up was only the second time (and the last time) they had 20-plus hits in a game. The first time had been less than a week before when they had 24 on October 10.

This Sox win ended a Yankees postseason winning streak at 12 games.

In the 1999 postseason:

- In the ALDS, the Yankees defeated the Rangers, 3–0.
- In the ALCS, the Yankees defeated the Red Sox, 4–1.
- In the World Series, the Yankees defeated the Braves, 4–0.

One postseason loss for New York, in one matchup for the ages: Pedro over Roger, one masterpiece, one mess.

BILL CHUCK ON THE 1990s

- The Atlanta Braves led the 1990s with a .595 winning percentage, going 925–629.
- The Yankees led the AL in the 1990s with a .548 winning percentage, going 851–702, second best in the majors.

The World Series of the 1990s

1999	4–0	New York Yankees (98–64, AL) vs. Atlanta Braves (103–59, NL)
1998	4–0	New York Yankees (114–48, AL) vs. San Diego Padres (98–64, NL)
1997	4–3	Florida Marlins* (92–70, NL) vs. Cleveland (86–75, AL)
1996	4–2	New York Yankees (92–70, AL) vs. Atlanta Braves (96–66, NL)
1995	4–2	Atlanta Braves (90–54, NL) vs. Cleveland (100–44, AL)
1994		No Postseason
1993	4–2	Toronto Blue Jays (95–67, AL) vs. Philadelphia Phillies (97–65, NL)
1992	4–2	Toronto Blue Jays (96–66, AL) vs. Atlanta Braves (98–64, NL)
1991	4–3	Minnesota Twins (95–67, AL) vs. Atlanta Braves (94–68, NL)
1990	4–0	Cincinnati Reds (91–71, NL) vs. Oakland Athletics (103–59, AL)

chapter 4

THE
2000s

BOB RYAN

I never bought into the idea of "The Curse of the Bambino." Let's start with that. But I was acutely aware of the tortured Red Sox history, and thus it was a genuine thrill to be a witness to the long-awaited World Series triumph in 2004 and the follow-up title in 2007.

Who could have imagined that an obscure Twins farmhand named David Ortiz would become a genuine Red Sox icon?

It was a wildly exciting decade featuring monumental "Ups" and crushing "Downs."

EVERETT'S MEMORABLE DEBUT

BOSTON 13 MINNESOTA 4 | FENWAY PARK, BOSTON, MA
TIME: 3:00 • APRIL 11, 2000

BOB RYAN

The hardest thing for Carl Everett in his Fenway debut was finding the ballpark. If you've never been there, be advised that Fenway Park is smack dab in the middle of what is, unquestionably, the hardest city for a newcomer to negotiate by car in all of America.

He was only there remotely on time for his first home game thanks to the efforts of traveling secretary Jack McCormack, who talked him in. Gordon Edes of the *Globe* wrote that Everett arrived "with traveling secretary Jack McCormack bringing him in by cellular phone, like an air traffic controller guiding an airplane in distress to a safe landing."

What then? Well, Everett, a self-proclaimed "semi switch-hitter," did indeed switch-hit two homers, but only because new teammate John

Valentin wouldn't let him bat lefty against left-hander Mark Redman in the 6th. Everett homered lefty in his first at-bat against rightly Joe Mays. But he sometimes chose to bat lefty versus a lefty because of "feel."

"Uh-uh," said Valentin, when Everett indicated he was going to bat lefty against Redman in the 6th. "'You're not hitting lefty against no lefty with that Green Monster out there,' he told me," Everett explained. So, of course, he hit one out off Redman. Right-handed.

The chief subplot was the pitching of starter Ramon Martinez, after sitting through a lengthy eight-run Red Sox second, allayed any fears about getting stale with an 11-pitch Twins 3rd. "Eleven pitches," said pitching coach Joe Kerrigan. "1-2-3, boom. We had the momentum the rest of the way."

Is it necessary to add that Everett was the first person to switch-hit homers in his Fenway debut?

BILL CHUCK

It is easier to climb Mount Everest than it is to understand Carl Everett.

On July 15, 2000, in a game against the Mets (Carl's 82nd game with the Sox), Everett headbutted umpire Ron Kulpa, hurled a bat from the dugout onto the field, knocked over a water cooler and exchanged (un)pleasantries with teammates, all in front of a national television audience.

"This is embarrassing, uncalled for," Fox broadcaster Joe Buck told the nation as Sox coaches Tommy Harper and Wendell Kim, along with teammate Jose Offerman, fought to contain Everett. "He is right now out of control. One hundred percent out of control."

The next day, Dan Shaughnessy in the *Boston Globe* wrote, "The Sox are afraid of Jurassic Carl. He is a wonderful talent, so just leave him alone and hope the next explosion isn't directed at a teammate, umpire, or law officer."

The nickname did not come out of the blue. In the June 19, 2000, edition of *Sports Illustrated*, Tom Verducci quoted Everett, "'God created the sun, the stars, the heavens, and the earth, and then made Adam and Eve. The Bible never says anything about dinosaurs. You can't say there were dinosaurs when you never saw them. Someone actually saw Adam and Eve. No one ever saw a Tyrannosaurus rex.'"

What about dinosaur bones? "'Made by man,' he says."

But as they say in infomercials, "But wait… there's more."

Verducci adds, "Everett has trouble too, with the idea of man actually walking on the moon. After first rejecting the notion, he concedes, "'Yeah, that could have happened. It's possible. That is something you could prove. You can't prove dinosaurs ever existed. I feel it's far-fetched.'"

The guy could hit, that's for sure. In 2000, he hit 34 homers and drove home 108 runs, the same amount he had driven home for the Astros the season before. And though he hit an even .300, he was an odd one who just talked and talked. Verducci threw this in, "'Carl Everett is the best player in the major leagues,' says Marlins right-hander Ryan Dempster. 'Just ask Carl Everett.'"

After all was said and done, Boston would have been better off had he never found his way to Fenway Park.

TRACHSEL OUTDUELS PEDRO (17K)

TAMPA BAY 1 BOSTON 0 | FENWAY PARK, BOSTON, MA
TIME: 2:36 • MAY 6, 2000

BOB RYAN

If the guy next to you at the bar says his name is Steve Trachsel, and he once beat Pedro Martinez on a day when Pedro fanned 17, believe him. It's true.

Pedro was coming off a five-game suspension and was really fired up. He had 15 Ks entering the scoreless 8th. With two out, Dave Martinez singled and stole second. Up stepped Greg Vaughn, who had whiffed three times. Pedro thought he had him for a fourth time, but plate umpire Mike Fichter wouldn't give him a close 2–2 pitch, and Vaughn singled on 3–2.

"I was just battling and trying to find a way bat to put the bat on the ball," Vaughn said. "That's all I was trying to do. He probably made a mistake, and I was just fortunate enough to get a hit."

"I totally tip my hat to Vaughn," said Pedro. "There's no whining. No crying in baseball." Yes, I heard that somewhere.

As for Trachsel, who threw a masterful three-hitter, Tiger manager Larry Parrish said, "You can't pitch better than that unless you're Pedro."

BILL CHUCK

At this point, I'm sure we agree that there have been a ton of games Bob attended that you wish you could have been there to see. I really wish I was at this game, not so much to see the 17 strikeouts, which of course, would have been cool, but I wish I were there to enjoy Bob's reaction as he recorded K after K on his magnificent scorecard.

- Ten times in the history of a baseball, a pitcher has struck out 17 *and lost.*
- Five times the games were extra innings affairs, and only five times the game has been nine innings or less, like this one.
- Every batter who came to the plate for the Rays struck out at least once.
- Pedro threw 130 pitches, 91 for strikes.
- In Pedro's Hall of Fame career, he struck out at least 15 on 10 regular season occasions, hitting a high 17 twice, once in this game and once against the Yankees.
- In the 10 games that Pedro struck out at least 15, this was his only loss.
- Pedro lost three 1–0 games in his career, one with the Dodgers, one with the Expos, and one with the Red Sox.
- This was Steve Trachsel's only complete-game, 1–0 win.
- This was Pedro's only complete-game, 1–0 loss.
- 12 Devil Rays struck out swinging, and five Rays struck out looking.
- Vinny Castilla earned a golden sombrero, striking out four times.
- In 1,854 games in the majors, this was Castilla's only sombrero.

For the record

- 1st inning—Pedro struck out three
- 2nd inning—Pedro struck out three
- 3rd inning—Pedro struck out one
- 4th inning—Pedro struck out two
- 5th inning—Pedro struck out three
- 6th inning—Pedro struck out one
- 7th inning—Pedro struck out two
- 8th inning—Pedro allowed a run, and struck out one
- 9th inning—Pedro struck out one

THOMAS' SAC 4

BOSTON 3 CHICAGO 2 | FENWAY PARK, BOSTON, MA
TIME: 2:31 • MAY 8, 2000

BOB RYAN

Frank Thomas had 1,704 regular season runs batted in, but perhaps none stranger than this one. Ray Durham was on third base with one out in the 6th when Thomas hit a pop-fly to shallow center. Second baseman Jeff Frye made the catch, whirled around, and threw home, but the throw was to the right side of the plate, and then fleet Durham beat Jason Varitek's sweeping tag.

That, folks, goes into the book as a "Sac 4."

This being baseball, Thomas already had a more traditional sacrifice fly to right in the fourth, "Sac 9" in the book.

BILL CHUCK

Frank Thomas hit 121 sac flies in his career, eight at Fenway Park. This was the only time of those eight that he hit two in one game. Okay, if you must know, it's the only time he ever hit two sac flies in one game. And Ray Durham scored both of the runs.

The Big Hurt twice hit a sac fly to a second baseman. On June 20, 2005, Thomas hit a sac fly that was fielded by Royals' second baseman Ruben Gotay in foul territory behind first base, and Pablo Ozuna (Marcell's cousin) scored from third base.

Thomas was proficient at hitting sac flies. He led the league with 12 in 1995. His career ranged from 1990 to 2008, and during that time he hit the most of any player. Rafael Palmeiro was next with 109.

All-time, Eddie Murray hit the most sac flies with 128, Cal Ripken was next with 127, in third place is Robin Yount with 123. Are you beginning to get the feeling that this is a great Hall of Fame club? And tied for fourth, with 121, is Frank Thomas, who is tied with the greater than great Hank Aaron.

One more thing…

At the time of this writing, there are 27 members of the 500-plus home run club. Only Eddie Murray had more sac flies, and Hank and Frank are next. Need I mention that between the three of them, they had six first names?

Eddie Murray hit 504 homers. Hank hit 755. Frank hit 521 homers. Harmon Killebrew hit 573. What is Harmon suddenly doing here? Killebrew and Thomas are the only two 500-homer hitters without a sac bunt in their résumé.

ORTIZ 0–0–0–3

BOSTON 11 MINNESOTA 8
HUBERT H. HUMPHREY METRODOME, MINNEAPOLIS, MN
TIME: 3:44 • JULY 3, 2000

BOB RYAN

The Red Sox had on their hitting shoes during a trip to the Twin Cities. How about four homers in a nine-run 4th inning? One of them was the first major league homer by a comet flashing across the sky named Morgan Burkhart, a 28-year-old rookie who had already worked his way to third in the batting order.

But the primary object of my attention was a young Twins player named David Ortiz. I love funky box scores, and he produced one of the neatest in this one: 0–0–0–3. It just so happened I wrote the game story and looked at it this way: "…and David Ortiz brought home (Ron) Coomer with a sacrifice fly, his second of the game, which, combined with a bases-loaded walk, gave him the intriguing box score line of 0–0–0–3."

File that name in the back of your mind. David Ortiz.

BILL CHUCK

I know you love Bob, and you like me, but you wouldn't be reading this book if you didn't thrill at the flukes of filled-out scorecards.

And here you have a one-of-a-kind in the history of traceable major league scorecards. No other player has had a line of zero at-bats, zero runs scored, zero hits, and at least three RBI. Long before Big Papi was "Big Papi," he made baseball history.

Ortiz was a great hitter with a runner on third and less than two outs. In 650 plate appearances, he hit .334, drove home 409 runs, of which 92 came in as a result of a sac fly. However, Ortiz played in 2,408 games in his big-league career, and he only had two games in which he had two sac flies, this one and one when he was playing for Boston in 2015, and they beat the Mariners, 22–10. In 242 plate appearances with the bases filled, Ortiz had 214 RBI, 44 came as the result of grand slams, while 17 came as the result of bases-loaded walks.

Additional things of interest from this game:

- Ramon Martinez, Pedro's brother, started this game for Boston. More about Pedro in a moment.
- Brian Daubach went 1–4 for Boston. More about Brian in a moment.
- In the bottom of the 6th, Butch Huskey pinch-hit for Ortiz.
- In the bottom of the 8th, Midre Cummings pinch-hit for Huskey.
- In the top of the 9th, the Twins sent in their 21-year-old rookie, Johan Santana, for mop-up duty. He allowed a Jose Offerman single but struck out the side.

What were they thinking?

On December 16, 2002, the Minnesota Twins released David Ortiz, which means it's time to talk about Jose Morban. The Twins released Ortiz because they were unable to find a team willing to make a deal with them to acquire the 27-year-old first baseman/DH. The Twins were looking to move Ortiz because on that fateful date, they had drafted Morban from the Texas Rangers in the 2002 Rule 5 draft and needed room on the 40-man roster.

In 2002, Ortiz had hit .272 with 20 homers, but only .203 against lefties and just .240 when runners were in scoring position. He had been on the disabled list twice and was expected to jump from $950,000 in salary to $2 million as he entered arbitration for the first time.

On December 17, 2002, the great La Velle E. Neal III, in the *Star Tribune*, quoted Twins' manager Ron Gardenhire speaking about Ortiz, "He's one of our favorites in the clubhouse, but we are trying to move forward here. We've been talking about facing lefty pitching, and this works out for our organization a little better." Morban never played for Minnesota, and in his 61 games with Baltimore in 2003, he hit .141.

On January 22, 2003, the Red Sox signed Ortiz. Gordon Edes in the *Boston Globe*, wrote about general manager Theo Epstein's assessment of his new slugger, "We think, all the scouts think, he has a very high ceiling. You're looking at a player with the potential to be a middle-of-the-lineup bat in the big leagues." That turned out to be the biggest understatement since Noah said it looks like rain.

Ortiz said in Edes article that he was urged to sign with Boston by Dominican countryman Pedro Martinez, "Pedro is like my father to me, Ortiz said. "He gives us a good example to work hard and how to get to the top. That's the message we get from Pedro."

Ortiz was signed to replace Brian Daubach, who was granted free agency by Boston four days after Ortiz had been let go by the Twins. Daubach and Ortiz had eerily similar numbers, but Theo saw into the future. At the time of the signing, both Daubach and Ortiz had .266 career batting averages. In 2002, they had each hit 20 homers. Daubach had 78 RBI, Ortiz had 75 RBI.

You have to wonder if Theo had watched this game along with Bob and said to himself, "If I ever get a chance, I'm going to sign him."

2000 ALCS GAME 4

YANKEES LED ALCS, 3–1

NEW YORK 3 SEATTLE 0 | SAFECO FIELD, SEATTLE, WA

TIME: 2:59 • OCTOBER 14, 2000

BOB RYAN

You trust me, right?

You know I'm not making it up?

Okay, to this day, I can still see first baseman Tino Martinez leaping and juuuuuust missing the Al Martin shot that broke up a chance Roger Clemens had for his only career no-hitter. How close did Tino come to snatching that ball?

"I thought I heard it tick off his glove," sighed Clemens, who had nothing else to feel bad about on this memorable occasion.

No one saw it coming. Roger hadn't thrown like this in a very long time and was coming off a pair of lackluster starts in the ALDS against

Oakland. However… "I knew I was gonna be strong," Roger declared. "I had all three pitches working. My fastball was live, and my splitter was the best it's been all year."

Did he say "strong?"

Seven of his final nine outs were among his 15 Ks. Consider that Seattle 7th. Martin's hit had become a double. It was still a 3–0 game. Roger went K (Alex Rodriguez), caught looking (Edgar Martinez), walk (John Olerud), and caught looking (Mike Cameron).

"That wasn't the 7-8-9 men," noted Joe Torre. "That was the heart of the order. I can't tell you how impressed I was with Roger Clemens tonight."

Torre let Roger throw 138 pitches. Put that one in the "Never-Gonna-See-That-Again" file.

BILL CHUCK

One of the joys of doing this book with Bob has been finding the buried gems amongst the games he has seen. As I have said before, Bob is not Zelig, he was not there for every great moment and every great game, but some of the games he has seen and memorialized through his scorecards have been historical in nature. Like this one. Bob knew when he had seen history in the making, and my job has been to polish the gem.

The Roger Clemens Regular Season Fact Book

- 24 seasons
- Record: 354–184
- 709 games/707 starts
- 118 complete games
- 46 shutouts
- 110 10-plus strikeout games
- 22 10-plus strikeout shutouts
- 10 15-plus strikeout games
- Three 15-plus strikeout shutouts
- One complete-game one-hitter
- 85 games of 130-plus pitches

The Roger Clemens Postseason Fact Book

- 12 seasons
- Record: 12–8
- 35 games/34 starts
- One complete game
- One shutout
- Two 10-plus strikeout games
- One 10-plus strikeout shutout
- One 15-plus strikeout games
- One 15-plus strikeout shutout
- One complete-game one-hitter
- Four games of 130-plus pitches

ONE STRIKE AWAY

MINNESOTA 6 BOSTON 4 (10 INNINGS)
FENWAY PARK, BOSTON, MA
TIME: 3:25 • APRIL 25, 2001

BOB RYAN

You need 27 outs, not 26 and 2/3.

The Red Sox were one strike away from a 3–2 victory when Jacque Jones and A.J. Pierzynski hit back-to-back wall job doubles off Rod Beck to tie the game.

They won it when Torii Hunter doubled inside the third-base bag with the bases loaded in the 10th.

Way back in the 2nd, there had been a play for the ages. Jason Varitek was on third with one out. Craig Grebeck popped one toward Twins first baseman Doug Mientkiewicz, a noted glove man. He made a sliding catch, quickly got to his feet, and threw to shortstop Denny Hocking, whose throw got Varitek at the plate for a spectacular double play. "I never dreamed he'd make that play," marveled Red Sox third-base coach Gene Lamont. "That first baseman is fantastic. He really popped up quick."

Doug Mientkiewicz. File that name away.

BILL CHUCK

Pedro Martinez started this game for Boston and struck out 10 Twins in 7.0 innings, but he threw 110 pitches, and the bullpen corps was entrusted to win the game. I mention this solely to point out how the game has evolved. For so many years, the goal was to build up the pitch count on the starter and get him out of the game and try to take advantage of weaker middle relievers. Now, one reliever after another comes in the game throwing bullets in excess of 97 miles per hour, and teams wish the starter had remained on the hill.

This also might be a good time to talk about the "Tax Stat," at least that's what I call it because it deals with the IRS. In this case, "IRS" does not stand for Internal Revenue Service but Inherited Runs Scored, both are taxing, and both are painful.

The fact that Rod Beck gave up two out back-to-back doubles off the Monster in 9th, that's going to happen. The Sox had three walk-off wins in 2001, and one of them on June 5 came when Shea Hillenbrand homered over the Wall in the 18th inning to beat Detroit. Stuff happens, particularly at Fenway.

But Jimy Williams decided that Beck should come out to pitch the 10th as well. (Williams was fired on August 17 in large part to a disgruntled clubhouse.) Beck allowed a leadoff single, a sac bunt, and an intentional walk. Beck was pulled at this point in favor of Pete Schourek, who got David Ortiz on a pop-up and walked Doug Mientkiewicz to load the bases. Schourek was pulled, and in came Rolando Arrojo.

Arrojo gave up a bases-clearing double to Torii Hunter before getting Jacque Jones to fly out to deep center field, and the side was retired.

And this is when the Tax Stat enters the game.

- Beck entered the game with a 0.00 ERA and left with a 2.03 ERA and three runs charged to him.
- Schourek entered the game with a 2.08 ERA and left with 3.00 ERA and one run charged to him.
- Arrojo entered the game with a 0.00 ERA and left with a 0.00 ERA and no runs charged to him.

It seems to me that each time a reliever enters a game mid-inning that the Tax Stat should be prominently displayed because, as we saw, Arrojo really didn't do the job. And it wasn't the first time that young season it had happened. Including this game, Arrojo had pitched 9.2 innings and had not allowed a run, when in reality, he had not allowed a run *that was charged to him*. He had inherited six runners in six appearances, and four had scored. And by the time the season had ended, Arrojo finished with a misleading 3.48 ERA because he had inherited 24 baserunners, and he allowed 15 to score.

Now I apologize if I appeared excessively cranky writing about this, but besides this being something that really bugs me, I'm not a good typist, and when Bob has a game with Pierzynski, Mientkiewicz, and "Jimy" Williams, I make many inherited typos.

SIX LEFTY HOMERS

BOSTON 10 TEXAS 4 (GAME 1) | FENWAY PARK, BOSTON, MA
TIME: 3:22 • AUGUST 4, 2001

BOB RYAN

Left-handed hitters who can go the other way do well at Fenway. Left-handed pull hitters often face a daunting task trying to hit a homer in a park where the alley in right is 380 feet. So, it was quite surprising when left-handed hitters bashed six homers in this game, only one—by Carl Everett—to the opposite field. Troy O'Leary and Trot Nixon each hit two. Brian Daubach hit the sixth.

And smashes they were. The *Globe's* Kevin Paul Dupont wrote they had hit "a half mile's worth of homers (six covering 2,700 feet)."

Four of them came off Texas starter Rich Helling, which came as no surprise. He was leading the AL with 27 homers allowed with still two months to play.

BILL CHUCK

"As I grew up, I knew that as a building (Fenway Park) was on the level of Mount Olympus, the Pyramid at Giza, the nation's capital, the czar's Winter Palace, and the Louvre—except, of course, that is better than all those inconsequential places."

—*Baseball Commissioner, Bart Giamatti*

To understand Fenway, the oldest and most unusually configured ballpark in the majors, you must know its very odd dimensions.

- Fenway Park measures 310 feet down the left-field line.
- It then juts out to 379 feet in left-center field and deepens even further to 390 feet in center field.
- Then there is the triangle in deep center field, which is a mere 420 feet away.
- Moving along, it is 380 feet in deep right field, but just 302 feet down the right-field line, where the Pesky Pole is located.
- But the outfield has other dimensions that intimidate both pitchers and batters.
- The left-field wall—also known as "The Green Monster"—is 37 feet high.
- The center-field wall is 17 feet high.
- But the bullpen fences measure just five feet high, and that short right-field fence is only 3 to 5 feet high.

"Fenway Park, in Boston, is a lyric little bandbox of a ballpark. Everything is painted green and seems in curiously sharp focus, like the inside of an old-fashioned peeping-type Easter egg."

—*John Updike*

It is shocking that any batter or pitcher, after spending some time playing at Fenway, doesn't need therapy for their swing and their heads. When the former Red Sox pitcher, Bill Lee, saw the Green Monster for the first time, he asked, "Do they leave it up there during games?"

Somehow, it's the lefties who thrive at Fenway.

Here's a list of players with over two hundred homers at Fenway Park

- Ted Williams—248
- Carl Yastrzemski—237
- David Ortiz—222

They are all lefties. All of them. Jim Rice had 208 homers at Fenway, the most for any right-handed batter.

Here's a list of players with over two hundred doubles at Fenway Park. (The top four are all lefties, and the bottom four are all righties.)

- Carl Yastrzemski—382
- David Ortiz—325
- Ted Williams—319
- Wade Boggs—292
- Dwight Evans—277
- Bobby Doerr—247
- Dustin Pedroia—238
- Jim Rice—207

"That moment, when you first lay eyes on that field—The Monster, the triangle, the scoreboard, the light tower Big Mac bashed, the left-field grass where Ted (Williams) once roamed—it all defines to me why baseball is such a magical game."

—*Jayson Stark*

HATTEBERG TO THE EXTREME

BOSTON 10 TEXAS 7 | FENWAY PARK, BOSTON, MA
TIME: 3:16 • AUGUST 6, 2001

BOB RYAN

Dante Bichette was all over it. Scott Hatteberg had just hit a 6th inning grand slam off Juan Moreno. "I said to (Brian) Daubach and (Doug) Mirabelli," he explained. "'Trivia question: Who's the only guy ever to hit into a triple play and then hit a grand slam in his next at-bat? I think it's a sure thing. I can't imagine it ever happening before.'"

That's exactly what had happened. Hatteberg had hit into the triple play in the fourth when two runners were going, and he hit a smash to shortstop Alex Rodriguez, who had no trouble turning it into a triple play.

After hitting the grand slam in the 6th, he was ushered out for a curtain call. "I'm not used to that," he said.

As for the historic juxtaposition of at-bats, Hatteberg said, "That's from the outhouse to the penthouse right there." But the truth is he probably hit the ball as hard leading to that triple play as to the grand slam. That's baseball in the proverbial nutshell.

Yes, baseball. Brian Daubach was on base for both the triple play and the grand slam. You can't make this stuff up.

BILL CHUCK

Who doesn't love the energy generated by a bases-loaded home run? I can tell you that from 2001 to 2020, there were 2,363 grand slams. Now *that* is a lot of excitement, but not an extraordinary moment. But when you've seen a triple play, you remain astonished because there are so many variables, and they are so rare. How rare? From 2001 to 2020, there were only 73 triple plays.

And since you're asking questions:

Is Scott Hatteberg's triple play/grand slam combo unique?
You bet. Bob saw the only time one player spanned the batting spectrum.

What's the deal with the Red Sox and triple plays?
On July 17, 1990, the Sox were the first team to hit into two triple plays in the same game. The Twins turned a pair yet lost, 1–0.
In Bob's game, the Rangers pulled the triple play, and the Red Sox hit the grand slam.

Have there been occasions when the same team hit a slam and into a triple play in the same game?
Yes, but only four times since divisional play began in 1969. The White Sox in 2019, the Tigers in 2017, the Mets in 2002, and the Blue Jays in 1979. Before 1969, the last time that happened was when Cleveland's Elmer Smith hit a 1st inning grand slam and Brooklyn's Clarence Mitchell hit a line drive to Cleveland's shortstop Bill Wambsganss, who turned an unassisted triple play in Game 5 of the 1920 World Series.

Do some players have a hitting into a triple play proclivity?

Who are the three players who hit into three triple plays?
- George Sisler—Hall of Famer who played from 1915 to 1930
- Joe Start—Who played from 1871 to 1886
- Deacon McGuire—Who played from 1884 to 1912

All three at one time played for a team from Washington, and all three were also managers.

What's the deal with Brooks Robinson and triple plays?
Hall of Famer Brooks Robinson was known as "The Human Vacuum Cleaner." Defensively, he was involved in three triple plays, but Brooksie is the player who has hit into the most triple plays in a career with four (that's 12 outs).

Naps taken in a triple play?
On May 16, 1913, the Philadelphia A's hosted the Cleveland Naps. In the 7th inning, Doc Johnston led off with a single. Ray Chapman doubled, putting runners on second and third. Ivy Olson then bounced a hard-hit ball off shortstop Jack Barry's chest, at which point Johnston originally held and then started running. As Barry got caught in a rundown, Chapman headed to third. As Johnston was finally caught, Chapman, for reasons unknown, started to head back to second, which was then occupied by Olson. The A's second baseman, Eddie Collins, tagged both baserunners, and Olson was declared out. Then as newspaper accounts of the game wrote, "Chapman then had another brainstorm and dashed for third, only to be touched out by (left fielder Rube) Oldring." The ball changed hands 10 times, and six different fielders were involved. That means this triple play went (SS) Jack Barry to (C) Ira Thomas to (3B) Home Run Baker to (P) Byron Houck to (SS) Jack Barry to (2B) Eddie Collins to (3B) Home Run Baker to (SS) Jack Barry to (LF) Rube Oldring. And for you scoring at home, 6-2-5-1-5-4-5-6-5-7, the longest scorebook entry for a triple play.

Why don't we talk about Joe Pignatano with the same awe in which we talk about Ted Williams?

Yeah, yeah, yeah, Ted Williams homered in his final big-league at-bat. So did over 50 other players who were nowhere near as good at hitting as Teddy Ballgame. Joe Pignatano, on the other hand, is the only player to ever hit into a triple play in his final big-league at-bat. He did it on September 30, 1962, against the Cubs. Piggy was playing for the Mets (who else?).

One more thing…

Every person in a ballpark wants to see a triple play, including sportswriters like Bob Ryan. Vincent Canby wrote, "Seeing a triple play, to a sportswriter, is what a partial eclipse is to an astronomer." This brings us to the fictional sportswriter Oscar Madison, who, with Felix Unger, was one of the leading characters of the play, movie, and oft-repeated and re-done television show, *The Odd Couple*, written by Neil Simon.

The film included a game-ending fictional triple play that the Mets pulled off against the Pirates. Still, Madison misses it when he was called away to the telephone to speak to Unger, who told him not to eat any hot dogs at the ballpark since that's what they were having for dinner.

In this film version, real ballplayers were used. Bill Mazeroski was pinch-hitting for Roberto Clemente (you know it's fiction when you read that) and hits a ground ball to third for a perfect 5-4-3, "round-the-horn," triple play.

Some backstory is provided by Vincent Canby, the renowned *New York Times* film critic. Maury Wills, the Bucs third baseman, had been advised by his agent to pass up on the role of "baserunner." Clemente bowed out when he learned that for this big-budget Hollywood film he was to be paid a measly $100, the Screen Actors Guild minimum for acting ballplayers. Another version of this story states that the speedy Clemente six times beat the throw to first before he basically walked down the line and subsequently was "pinched-filmed" by Maz.

MUSSINA'S NEAR PERFECTO

NEW YORK 1 BOSTON 0 | FENWAY PARK, BOSTON, MA
TIME: 3:00 • SEPTEMBER 2, 2001

BOB RYAN

I had been waiting my whole life to see a professional baseball no-hit, no-run game, and now I was one strike away from seeing—yes!—a perfect game. So what if it was being thrown in Fenway Park by a Yankee? This was my big night.

The count on batter number 27 went to 1 and 2. One strike away. And then Carl Everett, by this time a pretty much despised member of the Red Sox, hit a soft liner that fell between left fielder Chuck Knoblauch and center fielder Bernie Williams. Bye-bye, everything.

What a night. Ex-Yankee David Cone, the last man to have thrown a perfect game, had himself thrown a great game, shutting out the

Yanks for eight innings before being reached for a run in the 9th. He hadn't gone more than seven innings all year.

Most no-nos need that one defensive gem to preserve it, and Mussina thought he had received it when first baseman Clay Bellinger(Cody's dad), who had entered the game as a pinch-runner and subsequently scored the only run on an Enrique Wilson double, made a sensational, star-worthy stop on a Troy O'Leary smash leading off the 9th.

"I've come in to the ninth inning before (with a no-hitter)," Mussina said. "Maybe it's just not meant to be."

Cone had great empathy with his pitching foe. "It was surreal and eerie to watch him pitching in the 9th, one strike away," he said. "Part of me didn't want him to do it because I was the last one. But part of me wanted him to do it because he's such a great pitcher. I had mixed emotions."

There was turmoil in the Red Sox clubhouse afterward. Pitching coach John Cumberland had been demoted, and many players were upset, the most vocal being Nomar Garciaparra. "That's why no one wants to (expletive) play here," he fumed.

Meanwhile, I'm still waiting for my no-no.

BILL CHUCK

Like Bob, I love baseball.

Like Bob, I've seen hundreds of games (okay, he's seen way more).

Like Bob, I've never attended at a no-hitter.

Am I jealous of those who have? Damn right. I don't care what team I'm watching, what pitcher I'm watching. I always root for whoever is going for the no-no. I'll switch whatever I'm watching to watch the 8th and 9th inning of any game that has a pitcher going for a no-hitter and root like crazy for the completion.

A no-hitter is one of the magic moments that make our sport so great and not just because of the uniqueness of the feat, the athletic ability of the pitcher and his teammates, the luck involved of a hard liner going into a glove, or the luck involved of a batter so fooled that he hits a roller off the end of his bat that finds grass. A no-hitter makes the ordinary extraordinary for fans.

For example, take the evening that Dave Stewart threw a no-hitter against the Blue Jays, beating them 5–0. I'm sure that the more than 49,000 fans at the Skydome would have preferred their team to win, but on this June night, with close to 90 games left in the season, they got to see the excitement of a no-hitter. The same is true for the over 38,000 happy fans at Dodger Stadium who got to see Fernando Valenzuela turn an unexciting 6–0 win into an incredible night of baseball. And this can happen at any time in the season. In these two cases, both occurred on Friday night, June 29, 1990.

There is a long list of pitchers who lost their no-hitters with two outs in the 9th. The pressure must be unbearable at that point. The adrenaline in your body must be flying wilder than an entire class of junior high school boys hormones. Yet you still have to throw that pitch and get that last out. You want to be relaxed, you want to be under control, you want it to be over.

Think about what Dave Stieb went through on September 24, 1988. Stieb's Blue Jays had never had a no-hitter in team history, and here he was with two outs in the 9th and Cleveland's Julio Franco at the plate with a count of 1–2. Then, foul ball, foul ball, foul ball, ball two, and on the eighth pitch of the bat, Franco hits a chopper to second base… that takes a bad hop and flies over the head of the second baseman into the outfield for a base hit.

Now, think about what Dave Stieb went through on September 30, 1988, his next start following the Franco shocker. Stieb's Blue Jays were at home in Exhibition Stadium with two outs in the 9th and Baltimore's Jim Traber was at the plate with a count of 2–2. Traber had had one hit in his previous 26 at-bats. Traber fouled off the 2–2 pitch. Then, on the sixth pitch of the bat, Traber hits a broken-bat pop-fly over the head of first baseman Fred McGriff that finds the grass in the outfield for a base hit. The next day in the *Baltimore Sun*, correspondent Tim Kurkjian described it as "a broken-bat single that couldn't have been hit more softly." It was Stieb's second consecutive near-miss, his third one-hitter of the season, and the eighth time in the 1988 season that a pitcher took a no-no into the 9th only to lose it.

Then there was this Sunday night game in September of 2001. On a 1–2 count (again!) to Everett, here's how Buster Olney described it the next day in the *New York Times*, "Mussina threw a high fastball, Everett swung, the ball fell in left-center. Posada walked to the mound, unsure of what to say. 'What could I say to him?' Posada asked later."

I'll never forget Mussina's reaction immediately after the Everett hit. He had the look of fate biting him in the butt. I'll never forget Everett's reaction immediately after the hit. He was clapping his hands and celebrating a little too damn much. I'll never forget Fenway's reaction immediately after the Everett hit. They stood in salute to the tremendous near-perfect pitching of Mike Mussina and the excitement of knowing that perhaps the Sox could rally and win this game.

Then Trot Nixon grounded to second to end the game.

The Sox had lost.

And because of that one lousy flare to left, Bob had lost as well.

I felt like I lost as well. If on that Sunday afternoon, you had told me that we would've seen a 1–0 game between the Red Sox and the Yankees, no matter who won, I would have been thrilled. But all I felt was disappointment.

In Buster's words, "One more out. One more strike."

HARGROVE CHANGES PITCHERS

BALTIMORE 8 BOSTON 3 | FENWAY PARK, BOSTON, MA
TIME: 3:12 • SEPTEMBER 13, 2002

BOB RYAN

For years I told people it was Bobby Valentine because it was such a Bobby Valentine thing to do. But, no, the manager who made the most annoying, game-prolonging, intellectually indefensible, showoffy pitching change in the history of mankind was Mike Hargrove, a guy I liked and respected.

His team was leading, 8–3. There were two away and nobody on in the Red Sox 9th. The 27th and final out was Shea Hillenbrand, not Ty Cobb, Rogers Hornsby, or even Derek Jeter. But Grover—his insiders' nickname—replaced Jorge Julio with Buddy Groom. And this wasn't a platoon advantage thing, either. He was bringing in a lefty to face a righty. Why, Mike, Why? Why? Why? Why? Let's just get out of here and get the hell home.

Or maybe he knew what he was doing. Hillenbrand struck out.

I don't care.

Atop the page, I wrote, "Hargrove bush move: change P with 2 outs in 9th."

BILL CHUCK

Nomar Garciaparra was famously known for his numerous OCD-like adjustments before each pitch. Nomar was a picture of calm in comparison with Mike Hargrove, the player known as "The Human Rain Delay."

Hargrove drove pitchers crazy. Hargrove drove fans crazy. And, while I have no proof of this, I venture to guess that Hargrove drove teammates crazy.

Chris C. Anderson was kind of enough to describe Hargrove's "twitchy, obsessive, and excessively long batters box routines" for his readers, "Before every pitch, Hargrove would step out of the batter's box following each pitch and: adjust his helmet, adjust his batting gloves making sure they fit exactly right especially around the thumbs, pull each sleeve up about an inch, wipe each hand on his uniform pants, reach back to adjust his rear pockets, knock the dirt from his cleats—both feet—with the bat, flex his shoulders, adjust the gloves again; rub his nose, adjust the rubber ring to protect his thumb, and then *repeat the entire sequence*."

Is it any wonder that Hargrove, the manager, would add "drove Bob Ryan crazy" to his list of accomplishments?

2002 WORLD SERIES GAME 1

FIRST WORLD SERIES GAME IN ANAHEIM
SAN FRANCISCO 4 ANAHEIM 3 | EDISON FIELD, ANAHEIM, CA
TIME: 3:44 • OCTOBER 19, 2002

BOB RYAN

When Barry Bonds came to bat to lead off the 2nd inning of a scoreless game, this is what he saw: second baseman Adam Kennedy was 25-feet deep into right field. Shortstop David Eckstein was playing a standard second base. Third baseman Troy Glaus was playing a standard shortstop. The third base slot was wide open. What went through Bonds' mind we'll never know. But what we do know is that he hit a Jarrod Washburn pitch over everyone's head, becoming the 27th person to hit a homer in his first Series at-bat, the ball landing in—again, we'll never know—A) Neptune B) Saturn C) Jupiter.

In the bottom of the 2nd, Glaus became the 28th to hit a first AB HR. His homer remained on Planet Earth. That we know.

It was a fascinating game. The first three hits in the game were home runs, the other being hit by the Giants' Reggie Sanders. Glaus, the Angels' third sacker, hit another homer in the 6th. Former Angel J.T. Snow struck the actual game-winning homer for San Francisco in the sixth.

As a special bonus for the 44,603 in attendance (and especially me), the first ball was thrown out by the then 89-year-old basketball coaching legend (and one-time high school baseball coach) John Wooden. He was greeted with a hearty handshake at home plate by Giants' outfielder Kenny Lofton, a guard on the 1988 Arizona Final Four team.

BILL CHUCK

The starting pitching decided this game. Jarrod Washburn pitched 5.2 innings, gave up six hits and four runs, and took the loss. Jason Schmidt pitched 5.2 innings, gave up nine hits and three runs, and took the win. None of the six relievers allowed a hit or a run.

Troy Glaus became the sixth player to hit a pair of homers in his first Series game. He ended up as the Series MVP.

Bonds had played 2,439 games before appearing in his first Series; yeah, that was a record. He never appeared in another one, but he hit .474 with four homers in this one. He also set a record by walking 13 times. His 1.294 slugging pct. is the highest for a seven-game Series.

Before this, the Giants hadn't won a World Series game since October 15, 1962.

Angels manager Mike Scioscia was making his only World Series appearance. This was Giants manager Dusty Baker's sole World Series appearance to date. As players, Scioscia was in two Series, both with the Dodgers, winning in 1981 and 1988; Baker was in three Series, all with the Dodgers, in 1977, 1978, and winning in 1981. Yes, the two opposing managers were champs together in 1981. And in 2022, 20 years later, Dusty still is looking for his first world championship as a manager.

2002 WORLD SERIES GAME 2

SERIES TIED 1–1
ANAHEIM 11 SAN FRANCISCO 10 | EDISON FIELD, ANAHEIM
TIME: 3:57 • OCTOBER 20, 2002

BOB RYAN

It was truly a wild, wild west of a World Series game. All those runs. Six homers. Action galore.

But do you think any of the 44,504 on hand knew when they clambered to their cars (it was California, so you know they weren't walking anywhere) they had seen the last World Series game anyone will ever attend in which a pitching staff recorded no—as in Z-E-R-O—strikeouts? But they had.

The Angels sent 42 men to the plate against six Giants pitchers. Not one struck out. Take down the names of the Giants' hurlers: Russ Ortiz, Chad Zerbe, Jay Witasick, Aaron Fultz, Felix Rodriguez, and

Tim Worrell. Not one could coax a swinging strike or a "Steeeeerike Threee" out of plate umpire Angel Hernandez. Nowadays, the over/under on team strikeouts in any given game is about 10.

Encased in this game was a wondrous pitching performance by the 20-year-old Angels' phenom Francisco Rodriguez. After appearing in just five regular-season games, he was en route to a 5–1 postseason, the absolute highlight coming in this game when he entered the game with his team trailing, 9–8, and started off by throwing 12 straight strikes as he retired all nine men he faced. As I told the *Boston Globe* readers, "If someone can conjure up a more phenomenal World Series debut, let him speak now or forever hold his peace." He quickly acquired the nickname "K-Rod," and he went on to carve out a 16-year career, finishing with 437 saves, including a 62-save haul in 2008. But he may never have been more amazing than he was in his World Series debut at age 20 with less than a month of big-league experience.

Back to the game: Tim Salmon won it for the Angels with his second homer of the evening, a two-run shot off Felix Rodriguez (no relation) in the 8th. I don't know about anyone else, but I went back to my hotel talking about a kid named Francisco Rodriguez. I'm not sure I realized the Giants hadn't struck anyone out.

BILL CHUCK

It's hard to believe in a game when 21 runs were scored that the story would be about pitching, but Francisco Rodriguez threw 26 pitches, and 22 were for strikes. He struck out four of the nine batters he faced and "permitted" the Giants three grounders and two fly balls, no line drives, no hits, no walks.

This pitching stat makes sense: There have only been 17 occasions in Series history in which a starting pitcher has gone no more than two innings and allowed at least five earned runs. This game is the only time when both pitchers reached that millstone. Kevin Appier, with 2.0 IP, allowed five earned runs for the Angels. Russ Ortiz went 1.2 innings allowing seven runs. Ortiz tied the dubious record of the most earned runs in the shortest time with Mordecai Brown, who also went 1.2 innings and allowing seven earnies. Three-Finger Brown made it to the Hall of Fame. Ortiz did not.

As Bob pointed out, Giants' pitchers failed to strike out a batter. The last time this had happened in the Series was October 13, 1960, in Game 7, when neither the Pirates nor the Yankees pitchers struck out a batter.

Tim Salmon played 14 seasons with the Angels, and this was his only World Series appearance. He made the most of it with two two-run homers in this game and hitting .346 over the seven games. In this game, Salmon became one of five players all-time to garner four hits and a walk in a nine-inning World Series game. No one has done it since.

Take a look at Bob's scorecard, and you will see that in the 1st inning, the Angels pulled off a double steal. Scott Spiezio stealing second is no biggie; Brad Fullmer stealing home is worth mentioning. It was the 14th steal of home in Series history. BTW: Fullmer and Ortiz were teammates at Van Nuys Montclair Prep, a private school in the San Fernando Valley.

And yes, the winning pitcher in this game was F. Rodriguez, and the losing pitcher was F. Rodriguez. You can look it up.

DUBOSE 1U

BALTIMORE 4 BOSTON 2 (GAME 2) | FENWAY PARK, BOSTON, MA
TIME: 2:57 • AUGUST 8, 2003

BOB RYAN

It was just an inning-ending force-out in the third frame of the evening portion of an Oriole day-night doubleheader sweep of the Red Sox. But all force-outs are not created equal.

Johnny Damon was on third and Bill Mueller was on second. Manny Ramirez was on first. David Ortiz hit a high chopper between the plate and the mound. The Orioles hurler Eric DuBose came charging in. He caught the ball and kept on running. He touched home plate for a force-out to end the inning. Yes, a "1U"; that would be "Pitcher Unassisted" force-out in my scorebook. A first!

I got out of my seat in the Fenway press box. I turned around, and there was Gene Michael of the Yankees. Before I could say a word, he says to me, "I've never seen that either."

It was the second start of DuBose's career. He gave up one run in six innings pitched, and Jason Varitek was impressed. "He was able to basically throw three or four pitches any time he wanted to," Varitek said. "He pitched great. You can't take away anything from what he did. We just didn't get it done."

For me, the night was all about the "1U" in my scorebook.

BILL CHUCK

It has been said that each time you go to a ballgame, you have the chance to see something you've never seen before. One of my joys in working with Bob has been his appreciation, nay, sheer joy, for these moments that too often go unnoticed.

Then there are often things we see at a game that just don't take place that frequently; take Casey Fossum's game in which he allowed four unearned runs. That stuff happens, but not often. In fact, it had happened to Fossum precisely 51 weeks before this outing.

But Bob knew the rare moment *exactly* when it happened, and if he needed verification, there was that instant reassurance from Gene "Stick" Michaels, who played in over 2,000 professional games, managed in over 400 more, coached in too many to be counted, scouted in even more than that, and just watched thousands more.

Bob will tell you that he never attended a no-hitter, but how many of you are there who have seen a no-hitter can tell me that you have seen a pitcher record an unassisted put out at home plate?

One more thing...

Eric DuBose won nine games in his MLB career. This was his first. No doubt it was also his first unassisted putout at home plate.

COLON'S TWO-HIT LOSS

BOSTON 2 CHICAGO 1 | U.S. CELLULAR FIELD, CHICAGO, IL
TIME: 2:41 • SEPTEMBER 2, 2003

BOB RYAN

A complete-game two-hitter is pretty good, right? Throwing 98 mph in the 9th is pretty good, right? Bartolo Colon did both these things and wound up with the L because those two hits were solo homers by Trot Nixon and Gabe Kapler, while four Red Sox pitchers were working on a four-hit, one-run game themselves.

Nixon's 2nd inning blast traveled 420 feet to right-center. Kapler's 6th inning clout was the juicy story because the only reason he was in the lineup was that manager Grady Little had benched Manny Ramirez, who had refused a pinch-hitting request the day before during a big comeback win in Philadelphia.

And that was the only reason I was there. I was minding my own business the day before, Labor Day, covering a golf tournament in Norton, Massachusetts, when The Boss called and said to get my butt to Chicago immediately because all hell might break loose in this Manny saga. Well, Grady held his ground and did not play Manny.

Said one insider, "It's very simple. Grady figures that if he didn't do that, he would lose every guy in that clubhouse."

Kapler was just starting to make his mark in Boston. "Boston fans don't know Kap well," said Nixon, "but he's a flat-out gamer who just plays it hard. He's exactly the kind of player Boston fans love." Kinda like Trot himself.

BILL CHUCK

Before you skip over this because you don't think this story about "Big Sexy" is not sexy enough, this was a rare game in the annals of baseball history.

There have only been six pitching performances where a starter pitched a complete game and allowed a total of two runs, on two hits, both homers, and still lost:

1. Jim Slaton in 1973
2. Mark Langston in 1987
3. Jose Rosado in 1998
4. Bartolo in 2003
5. Mark Buehrle in 2007
6. Justin Verlander in 2019

And, if you don't think the pitching feat is rare, try this on for size: This is the only game in Red Sox history in which they scored a total of two runs, on two hits, both homers, and still won. They don't even have a loss with that combination.

This was indeed a one-of-a-kind game. And you got to read about it because Manny Ramirez, the day before, had a sore throat that he said made him feel too weak to pinch-hit despite being asked by coaches and the manager. That meant that Bob was lucky enough to leave some golf tourney and fly to Chicago and write this the next day:

"Oooh, this is getting interesting. Let's go over this one more time, so there is no confusion on anyone's part. The $160 million man, who leads the Red Sox in home runs (31) and second in runs batted in (90), a guy that people who don't have to live with him think is one of the most valuable players in the league, declares his physical readiness for a game in the heat of a pennant race, and the manager says, "No thank you?" Is that what's going on here?

"Ab-so-lutely."

So, thank you, Manny, and thank you, Bob. And thank you, Trot and Gabe. And thank you too, Bartolo. Ab-so-lutely, thank you.

2003 ALDS GAME 3

A'S LEAD RED SOX IN ALDS, 2–1
BOSTON 3 OAKLAND 1 (11 INNINGS) | FENWAY PARK, BOSTON, MA
TIME: 3:42 • OCTOBER 4, 2003

BOB RYAN

Can one playoff game contain three Keystone Kops baserunning episodes? Yes. They're almost too impossible to describe. What's far easier to prove is that Trot Nixon's 11th inning, two-run pinch-homer off Rich Harden saved the Red Sox from elimination.

You ready?

1. Jason Varitek scored the first Sox run when interfered with, sort of, by third baseman Eric Chavez during a rundown.
2. Oakland's Eric Byrnes was tagged out in the 6th when he and Varitek collided, and Byrnes neglected to touch home plate.

3. Also in the 6th, Miguel Tejada collided with Sox third baseman Bill Mueller, then slowed down and was tagged out by Varitek.

You want to talk self-destruct? The A's made three errors in the 2nd, enabling Boston to score an unearned run and reach the 11th inning. The A's matched that, scoring an unearned run of their own in the 6th.

Kinda hidden for the Sox was the combined four innings of hitless relief by Mike Timlin and Scott Williamson.

But it was undoubtedly a night 35,460 Fenway fans weren't likely to forget. The Sox had lived to fight another day.

BILL CHUCK

A little silent film history for those of you who are unaware of Mack Sennett's Keystone Kops. This was a ragtag group of police officers who ran amuck with extraordinary incompetence. They were a well-meaning group who were an integral part of slapstick comedies of the early 1900s. With that background, you can genuinely appreciate the bungling of the A's on this night at Fenway.

The A's were held to six hits (Eric Byrnes had half of them but was one of the Kops when he cost Oakland a run) in 11 innings, and the first five batters in their lineup combined to go 0–23. The Sox only had seven hits with the heart of the order, Bill Mueller, Manny Ramirez, and David Ortiz going 0–13.

Also, kinda hidden for the Sox was the seven innings that Derek Lowe had provided as a starter, only allowing one unearned run. Lowe had taken the loss in relief in Game 1 and then earned the save in Game 5.

In Trot Nixon's regular season career, he was not much of a pinch-hitter going 11–72 (.153) with one homer. He wasn't much of a hitter in extra innings, either going 12–60 (.200) with two homers. But the beauty of baseball is that in any given game, any player can be a star. And so it was for Trot Nixon, who hit a one out two-run pinch homer, the only walk-off homer of his major league career. It was the Red Sox first postseason walk-off homer since Carlton Fisk in 1975.

2003 ALCS GAME 7

YANKEES WIN ALCS, 4–3
NEW YORK 6 BOSTON 5 (11 INNINGS)
YANKEE STADIUM, THE BRONX, NY
TIME: 3:56 • OCTOBER 16, 2003

BOB RYAN

We must start at the end. At 16 minutes past midnight Tim Wakefield threw one knuckleball. Aaron Boone took a swing and hit a home run into the lower left-field stands. Once again, the Yankees had one-upped the Red Sox. Once again, the Red Sox fans had further reason to bemoan their fate.

It will forever be remembered in Boston as the game in which Grady Little left Pedro in too long, that he should have yanked him with a 5–2 lead after seven innings of work. You can go so far as to say it cost him his job. One person who thought that was an unfair indictment was Pedro Martinez. "If anyone wants to point a finger," he said, "point it at me. I gave up the lead. If you want to judge me, judge me for that. I'll take that."

It was downright cruel of the baseball gods to have Wakefield be the loser. He had been Boston's best pitcher, winning Games 1 and 4. I myself invoked Tevye, wondering in print if it would spoil some "vast eternal plan" if the Red Sox were to actually win one of those gut-wrenching confrontations.

BILL CHUCK

There comes a moment in any comeback when the rising party gets the upper hand. They may still be battling, still losing, but they become aware they are up to the challenge. This game was that moment for the Red Sox and their Nation. There are those who might say that Game 4 the following season (the Dave Roberts game) was that moment, but I contend that this Game 7 was when the Red Sox knew the Yankees dynasty was over. They knew that they could beat this curse. They discovered that the Yankees could lose. And even if it didn't happen on this night, the tipping point had arrived.

First of all, it was Martinez versus Clemens, which had been forced when the Sox beat the Yanks in Game 6, in the Bronx. When Clemens was pulled by Joe Torre in the top of the 4th inning in this game, with baserunners on first and third and nobody out, it was already 4–0, Boston. Mike Mussina came in for the first relief appearance of his career and shut down the Sox that inning and in 3.0 IP of scoreless relief, he permitted just two singles.

In the bottom of the 5th and in the bottom of the 7th, Jason Giambi homered for New York. There have only been two occasions in which a player has homered two times in Game 7 of an LCS; this was the first, the next time was Game 7 of the 2004 ALCS, when Johnny Damon went deep twice for the Sox against the Yankees.

Following the second Giambi homer, the score was 4–2 Boston, two outs in the bottom of the 7th. Pedro then allowed back-to-back singles before striking out Alfonso Soriano on six pitches. You didn't need to be a Mark Bittman cooking specialist to know that Pedro was done. Perhaps it was the David Ortiz homer off David Wells in the top of the inning to make the score 5–2, but Grady brought Pedro back to the mound for the bottom of the 8th. Little did he know what would ensue.

It took seven Martinez pitches to get Nick Johnson on a pop-up, but Pedro stayed in. Derek Jeter doubled to right, but Pedro stayed in. Bernie Williams singled him home, but Pedro stayed in. Hideki Matsui's ground-rule double put runners on second and third, but Pedro stayed in. It was only after Jorge Posada's game-tying double that Pedro came out.

Alan Embree came in and got Giambi on a fly ball and in came Mike Timlin to issue an intentional walk to pinch-hitter Ruben Sierra and that brought in Aaron Boone to pinch-run for Sierra (that should wake you up). Back in the day (like 2003), intentional walks were thrown, not signaled. Those days, I always felt that a relief pitcher shouldn't offer an IBB to the first batter he faces, but that chore should be left to the departing pitcher. I say that because the reliever needs to gain a comfort level in the game and he might then unintentionally walk the next batter, which Timlin did on four pitches. The bases were filled with two outs and on Bob's scorecard it reads, "Groundout: 2B-SS, force-out at second." But it can't describe how the grounder that Alfonso Soriano hit bounded high off the pitcher's mound (!) and Todd Walker had to grab the ball over his head and make the play that retired the side.

The score stayed tied through 10 innings. Mariano Rivera was masterful in relief. There's a shocker. The Sox had a runner on second with two outs in both the 9th and 10th innings. Mo was Mo. Tim Wakefield retired the Yankees in order in the bottom of the 10th before allowing the first-pitch game winner to Aaron Boone.

A few more things…

Tim Wakefield had won his two starts in this ALCS and finished with a 2.57 ERA in 14.0 IP. Had the Sox won (or maybe even if Tim hadn't taken the loss in Game 7), he would have been ALCS MVP.

David Ortiz hit .269 in this ALCS. He and Jorge Posada led their teams, each with six RBI.

And as for Aaron Boone, while working out over the off-season, he tore his ACL while playing basketball (in violation of the terms of his contract). He was unable to play in 2004, and he never played for the Yankees again as they released him. Looking for a replacement at third base, the Yanks traded for Alex Rodriguez and the rest, as they say, is history.

McCARTY WALK-OFF

BOSTON 9 SEATTLE 7 (12 INNINGS) | FENWAY PARK, BOSTON, MA
TIME: 3:54 • MAY 30, 2004

BOB RYAN

David McCarty logged 203 plate appearances in parts of three seasons with the Red Sox. His time with the club would come as news to all but the most devoted Red Sox fan unless he or she were among the 35,046 in attendance on this Sunday afternoon when David McCarty hit a two-run walk-off homer off J.J. Putz in the 12th inning to defeat the Seattle Mariners.

McCarty had entered the game in the 8th during some defensive maneuvering and had doubled and scored. Eddie Guardado and Putz had combined to fan six men in innings 9 through 11, but with one out in the 12th, Putz hit Jason Varitek, and McCarty delivered the big blow.

'It feels good," he said. "I don't know if I've ever had a walk-off homer."

And speaking of *really* forgotten Red Sox players, rookie Andy Dominique has his first major league hit, an RBI pinch-hit single in the 8th, and his second major league hit, an infield single in the 10th.

BILL CHUCK

Take a look at date of this game.

- Forget the May 30th part, the year was 2004. The year the Sox broke the curse.
- Dave McCarty did not play in that famous postseason, but for his 89-game contribution, he got a championship ring.
- Andy Dominique did not play in that famous postseason, but for his seven-game contribution, he got a championship ring. BTW: Those were Dominique's only MLB hits.
- Earl Snyder did not play in that famous postseason, but for his one-game contribution, he got a championship ring. BTW: That one game was his last as a major leaguer.
- Abe Alvarez did not pitch in that famous postseason, but for his one-game contribution, he got a championship ring.
- Phil Seibel did not pitch in that famous postseason, but for his two-game contribution, he got a championship ring. BTW: Those two games were his only as a major leaguer.
- Frank Castillo did not pitch in that famous postseason, but for his two-game contribution, he got a championship ring. BTW: Those two games were his only as a Red Sox, and he only pitched one more game in the majors.
- Joe Nelson did not pitch in that famous postseason, but for his three-game contribution, he got a championship ring.
- Sandy Martinez did not catch in that famous postseason, but for his three-game contribution, he got a championship ring. BTW: Those three games were his last as a major leaguer.
- Bobby Jones did not pitch in that famous postseason, but for his three-game contribution, he got a championship ring. BTW: Those three games were his last as a major leaguer.

- Jamie Brown did not pitch in that famous postseason, but for his four-game contribution, he got a championship ring. BTW: Those four games were his only as a major leaguer.
- Pedro Astacio did not pitch in that famous postseason, but for his five-game contribution, he got a championship ring.
- Jimmy Anderson did not pitch in that famous postseason, but for his five-game contribution, he got a championship ring. BTW: Those five games were his last as a major leaguer.
- Byung-Hyun Kim did not pitch in that famous postseason, but for his seven-game contribution, he got a championship ring.
- Anastacio Martinez did not pitch in that famous postseason, but for his 11-game contribution, he got a championship ring. BTW: Those 11 games were his only as a major leaguer.
- Ellis Burks did not play in that famous postseason, but for his 11-game contribution, and his inspirational force, he got a championship ring. BTW: Those 11 games were his last as a major leaguer.

Bob will remind you, pay attention to every player who comes into a game. You may be seeing their first game, their last game, or the game that earns them a World Series ring.

One more thing…
Dave McCarty hit 36 homers in his career, and this was his only walk-off.

2004 ALCS GAME 4

THE YANKEES LEAD THE RED SOX, 3–1 IN THE ALCS
BOSTON 6 NEW YORK 4 (12 INNINGS) | FENWAY PARK, BOSTON, MA
TIME: 5:02 • OCTOBER 17, 2004

BOB RYAN

You almost forget sometimes how it ended, with Big Papi smashing a Paul Quantrill pitch for a two-run homer in the 12th. The lasting memories center around the dramatic Red Sox 9th, where the Red Sox, down a run to the greatest closer of all time, and three outs away from a bitter season-ending sweep at the hands of the hated Yankees, scratched out a run with a walk, stolen base and single to keep the game going.

Kevin Millar drew the walk. Dave Roberts pinch ran. "When I was with the Dodgers," Roberts explained, "Maury Wills once told me that there will come a point in my career when everyone in the ballpark will know that I have to steal a base, and I will steal that base. When I got out there, I knew what Maury Wills was talking about." He drew three throws from Mariano Rivera and then took off. Jorge Posada's throw made it close, and Derek Jeter was the master of the deceptive sweep tag. But Joe West correctly signaled "safe." Mission Accomplished.

Bill Mueller was up with a lighter-than-usual bat he only used for Rivera. He smacked one up the middle. "I was surprised it didn't hit me," recalled Rivera.

Roberts agreed. "He looked like a hockey goalie trying to do a kick save."

It was hit hard and not an automatic RBI, but no matter. "I wasn't stopping at third," asserted Roberts, "even if there *was* a stop sign."

In one trip to the bases Dave Roberts had become an all-time Boston sports icon. "It has truly impacted my life," Roberts said. "People are often remembered for one thing in their career, whether it's good or bad. Fortunately for me, that stolen base is embedded in people's minds."

BILL CHUCK

Let's start with this question: Has there ever been a more famous steal in baseball history? (Feel free to talk amongst yourselves.)

The "Dave Roberts steal" would have to be in most people's Top 10 postseason moments along with Bill Mazeroski's home run, Kirk Gibson's home run, and Joe Carter's home run. I'm sure I don't have to remind you that Bobby Thomson's "Shot Heard 'Round the World" was not in the postseason.

It is amazing how Roberts created a singular moment that was such a flashbang that even the most ardent of Red Sox fans remember very little else about what must be considered the most consequential moment for Boston baseball in 86 years.

Here's a quiz about this game that should be challenging (or easy) for all baseball fans. The answers are below.

The situation was this: the Yankees were leading the best-of-seven ALCS, 3–0. It was a Sunday night, and the game began at 8:20 pm.

Nine to Know?

1. Who were the starting pitchers?
2. The Yankees led 2–0 thanks to a 3rd inning two-run homer hit by whom?
3. The Sox took the lead in the 5th after a single by Orlando Cabrera made it 2–1 and a bases-loaded single by which batter made the score 3–2 Boston?
4. In the top of the 6th, the Yankees scored a pair of runs to take the lead. Who was the Boston pitcher who allowed an inherited runner to score and allowed one run of his own to score?
5. Who is the Yankee who drove home the Yankees fourth and final run? He was a former Red Sox and became a big deal in retirement.
6. After Rivera left the game, another former Red Sox pitched two innings of scoreless relief. He was no flash in the pan, lasting 21 seasons in the majors. Who is he?
7. With one out in the top of the 7th, the Sox brought in their closer and he shut out the Yankees for 2.2 IP, allowing just two walks. The previous season he led the AL in saves. Who was this righty?
8. The winning pitcher in this game pitched 1.1 scoreless innings. It was his last major league appearance. Who was he?
9. Who was the batter and what did he do before the Ortiz walk-off homer in the bottom of the 12th?

BONUS QUESTION: Dave Roberts played in three games for the Sox in the 2004 postseason, how did he do at the plate?

Nine to Know Answers

1. Orlando Hernandez started for New York and was charged with three runs in 5.1 IP and Derek Lowe started for Boston and was charged with three runs in 5.0 IP.
2. The Yankees led 2–0 thanks to an Alex Rodriguez homer.
3. A bases-loaded single by David Ortiz gave Boston the lead. Big Papi ended up with four RBI that night.
4. Mike Timlin was credited with a blown save.
5. Tony Clark drove home the Yankees final run. He later became executive director of the Players Association.

6. Tom "Flash" Gordon.
7. Keith Foulke, who recorded 43 saves for Oakland in 2003 and 32 saves for Boston in 2004.
8. Curt Leskanic made his third appearance of the ALCS in this game. He never pitched again.
9. Manny being Manny Ramirez singled on a 2–1 pitch before Big Papi homered on a 2–1 pitch.

BONUS QUESTION: Dave Roberts pinch-ran once in the ALDS for Boston and was quickly forced at second. He made his first appearance of the ALCS in this game. Pokey Reese took his place at second base in the top of the 10th. In Game 5, Roberts once again pinch-ran for Kevin Millar, this time in the bottom of the 8th. He went to third on a Trot Nixon single and scored on a Jason Varitek sac fly (off Mariano Rivera) to tie the game, 4–4. Doug Mientkiewicz replaced Roberts playing first in the top of the 9th. Roberts never played the field nor came to the plate in the postseason but scored two incredibly important tying runs.

2004 ALCS GAME 7

RED SOX WIN THE ALCS, 4–3
BOSTON 10 NEW YORK 3 | YANKEE STADIUM, THE BRONX, NY
TIME: 3:31 • OCTOBER 20, 2004

BOB RYAN

For Sox fans it was no muss no fuss, no sweat, no stress. Papi hit one out in the first and after Johnny Damon greeted Javier Vazquez with a 2nd inning grand slam it was 6–0 and o-v-e-r. The Yankees weren't going to touch Derek Lowe, who, as I noted in my scorebook, had brought his A-plus-plus-plus game. The Yankee pitching was beyond brutal. Esteban Loiaza's 1–0 pitch to Varitek in the 4th was the 100th Yankee pitch of the evening. Say no more. The Red Sox were going to be AL champions.

Thinking back to the doom and gloom following Game 3, I put it this way in The *Boston Globe*. "There was only one place on earth where there was any hope, and that was inside the Red Sox clubhouse."

More specifically, the source of optimism had been one Kevin Millar, and he gets the valedictory. "How many times can you honestly say you have a chance to shock the world?" he asked. "It might happen once in your life or it may never happen. But we had that chance, and we did it. It's an amazing storybook."

BILL CHUCK

Baseball fans across the country knew this one was over before it began. We know that every Game 7 has a sense of finality, but objectively no one could honestly think the Yankees had a chance in this one. Earl Weaver famously said, "Momentum is only as good as tomorrow's starting pitcher." The Yankees could have started Sandy Koufax, Bob Gibson, or Babe Ruth, but would still have been toast. They were done as soon as the Sox scored four times in the 4th inning of Game 6.

The Yankees problem was that they had none of those pitchers; they had Kevin Brown. Brown had started the Yankees final win in Game 3, but it wasn't because of his prowess. Brown had lasted two innings allowing five hits and four runs (three earned). Because of that short start and the fact that the Yanks really had no one else, Brown was starting on short rest.

It did not go well.

In the top of the 1st, Johnny Damon grounded Kevin Brown's sixth pitch into left for a leadoff single. On an 0–2 pitch to the next batter Mark Bellhorn, Damon had the audacity to steal second (after a huge jump). After Bellhorn whiffed (he did that a lot), Manny Being Manny Ramirez grounded a single to short left. Damon was thrown out at the plate on a bang-bang-bang play, Matsui to Jeter to Posada, but it was Damon's aggressiveness that was setting the tone for this game.

Frequently, a defensive play can be inspiring to a ballclub. The Yankees who avoided a run being scored now could change the tenor as David Ortiz stepped to the plate.

It did not go well.

Before the crowd had settled back in their seats after the play at the plate, Ortiz hit Brown's first pitch into the right-field bleachers. It traveled faster than the Acela from New York to Boston. On that one pitch, the Win Expectancy for Boston, according to Baseball Reference, jumped from 47 percent to 65 percent.

Derek Lowe retired the Yankees 1-2-3 in the bottom of the 1st on 13 pitches. When Kevin Brown was pulled with one down in the top of the 2nd with the bases loaded, he had faced nine batters and thrown 44 pitches. Just like they did in Game 3, when Brown failed, the Yankees brought in Javier Vazquez in relief. Vazquez picked up the win in that game. Now, Torre brought him in to face Damon.

It did not go well.

On Vazquez's first pitch, Johnny Damon went deep with a grand slam into the right-field stands. That Win Expectancy dealie now jumped from 76 percent to 91 percent.

Through 2020, there have been 10 slams hit in the ALCS, hit by 10 different players, five of whom wore the Red Sox uni at the time of the blast.

Through 2020, the 2004 Red Sox remain the only team ever to recover fully from an 0–3 deficit in the postseason.

The Sox were the AL Champions and heading back to Boston to face St. Louis. The Cardinals had come back themselves from being down three games to two in the NLCS against the Houston Astros to win in seven games. The Cards felt that they were the team that could stop the momentum of the Red Sox.

It did not go well.

2004 WORLD SERIES GAME 1

RED SOX LEAD SERIES 1–0
BOSTON 11 ST. LOUIS 9 | FENWAY PARK, BOSTON
TIME: 4:00 • OCTOBER 23, 2004

BOB RYAN

It might be a stretch to say, as people might have in those days, that had there been a vote of Red Sox fans, Mark Bellhorn couldn't have been elected dogcatcher in New England. When the World Series began, he wasn't exactly a fan favorite. He had been the starting second baseman for 128 regular season and 10 postseason games. Still, people couldn't warm up to him, largely because a league-leading 177 strikeouts seemed quite unbecoming for a second baseman. Eighty-two runs batted in and a healthy .817 OPS didn't seem to matter. That was all quickly forgotten when he smacked a Julian Tavarez pitch off the Pesky Pole (that's the one in right field, to you non-Bostonians) for an 8th inning two-run homer that gave the Red Sox an 11–9 triumph in as wild a Series opener as anyone had ever seen.

The Red Sox somehow prevailed despite committing four errors. It was the only World Series game in which each starting pitcher gave up five earned runs while failing to get out of the fourth. The Red Sox scored four in the first off Cardinals starter Woody Williams and never lost the lead. The two pitching staffs combined for 14 walks. The Cardinals' Larry Walker set a record for the most total bases (nine) in a Game 1 losing effort. It was a four-hour, nine-inning game. And for Bellhorn, it was the second game in a row hitting the right-field foul pole, having done the same at Yankee Stadium in Game 7 of the ALCS.

"I wanted the ball down," said Tavarez. "A back door slider." The ball drifted over the plate, however, and Bellhorn didn't miss it. "Not the location I wanted," Tavarez said. "When you don't make a pitch, you get hit. That's what happened to me today."

What happened to Mark Bellhorn was that he had become a part of Red Sox history.

My official *Boston Globe* observation the following day: "The 100th World Series is off to a perversely entertaining start."

BILL CHUCK

This game was four hours of some crazy (and not particularly impressive) baseball, the longest nine-inning Game 1 in Series history. It remains the only Game 1 in Series history in which each team scored nine-plus runs (and it's the most runs the Cardinals have scored in a losing Series game). The Red Sox scored four in the 1st and never trailed in this game and, in fact, never trailed in the Series. They led here 7–2 after four but somehow, neither starter was involved in the decision since it was the first and only time in World Series history that both Game 1 starting pitchers went no more than 3.2 IP and gave up five-plus runs. It's only the third time, and the most recent time, this has happened at *any* Series game, and Bob was there for all three (the other two being the 1993 Game 4 between the Phillies and Jays and then again in Game 2 of 2002 between the Angels and Giants). Tim Wakefield walked five in just 3.2 IP, tying him for second-most walks by a Sox starter in a WS game with Sad Sam Jones, who walked five in

Game 5 of the 1918 WS. The most walks in a World Series game by a Sox starter is six in Game 4 of the 1918 Series by Babe Ruth (who won his game, 3–2). I'm relieved to tell you that Bob wasn't there for either of those games. Woody Williams was one of three Series starting pitchers to allow 7 ER in less than 3.0 IP and get a no-decision. Bob was there in 1993 when Tommy Greene did, but not for Russ Ortiz in 2002.

David Ortiz homered in his first World Series at-bat (off Woody Williams). At the time, he was the second Red Sox player to do that. The first was pitcher Jose Santiago off Bob Gibson, no less. Larry Walker became the 11th player to amass four hits (most ever) in a losing, nine-inning, World Series game.

In the top of the 4th, the Cardinals scored three runs without the benefit of a hit. That inning, the Sox made one of their four errors (first baseman Kevin Millar). Pitcher Bronson Arroyo also made an error and Manny Being Manny Ramirez made two.

Bill Mueller had the only two-out RBI for Boston, who went 6–16 w/RISP and left 12 on base. Edgar Renteria and Larry Walker each had a two-out RBI for St. Louis, went 3–14 w/RISP and left nine on base.

Boston's victory came 18 years to the day since the last time the Red Sox won in the World Series, beating the Mets in Game 5 in 1986.

BTW:

The Cards starting shortstop in this game, Edgar Renteria, was the Sox starting shortstop on Opening Day in 2005. Julian Tavarez, who allowed Bellhorn's homer, pitched for Boston in 2006–08 (and not particularly well). Cards' catcher Mike Matheny came back to manage St. Louis and led them to the 2013 World Series, only to lose to Boston once again.

2004 WORLD SERIES GAME 4

SOX SWEEP THE WORLD SERIES
BOSTON 3 ST. LOUIS 0 | BUSCH STADIUM, ST. LOUIS
TIME: 3:14 • OCTOBER 27, 2004

BOB RYAN

There was never an actual Curse, but there was an 86-year frustration and sense of deprivation accentuated by Game 7 losses in the 1946, 1967, 1975, and 1986 World Series. The depths of despair being reached, when with two outs, two strikes, and a two-run lead in the 10th inning of the 1986 Game 6, the Mets rallied, or the Red Sox imploded. Take your pick.

Imagine, therefore, the emotional release felt by Red Sox fans everywhere at 11:40 EDT, when, with two away in the Cardinals' 9th and a 3–0 lead, Edgar Renteria tapped one back to the mound and Keith Foulke underhanded the ball to Doug Mientkiewicz at first base to make official a four-game sweep and make the Boston Red Sox world champions of baseball for the first time since 1918. "This is for anyone who ever played for the Red Sox, anyone who ever rooted for the Red Sox, anyone who has ever been to Fenway Park," said general manager Theo Epstein, who had grown up a sacrifice fly from Fenway Park. "This is bigger than the 25 players in this clubhouse. This is for all of Red Sox Nation, past and present. I hope they're enjoying it as much as we are."

Johnny Damon led off the game with a home run, and Derek Lowe took it from there, hurling 7.1 innings of three-hit ball. Bronson Arroyo, Alan Embree, and Foulke completed the first four-pitcher shutout in World Series history (there have been two more since). The "W" gave Lowe the distinction of being the only pitcher in postseason history to be the winning pitcher in each finale of the three rounds, having been on the mound for clinchers against both Anaheim and New York. It was also Lowe's last appearance in a Red Sox uniform.

Further offense was provided by Trot Nixon, who had three doubles and the other two runs batted in. It had been a true multi-generational triumph of an organization. The starting nine this night in St. Louis consisted of four players signed by Epstein's predecessor Dan Duquette, four by Epstein, and one by general manager once-removed Lou Gorman.

On October 16, the Yankees had pummeled the Red Sox, 19–8, taking a 3–0 ALCS series lead. Now, 11 nights and eight straight victories later (a postseason record), the Red Sox were sipping and spraying champagne. It was the greatest comeback in baseball history... or perhaps all of American sport.

BILL CHUCK

This Series would have been memorable simply by virtue of it being the 100th World Series of all time, but the fact is, this one broke "the Curse" (yeah, Bob, in baseball, there are curses and whammies and gifts from the baseball gods).

Symmetrically speaking, in the four games, St. Louis had 24 hits, Boston had 24 runs (and 24 walks).

Keith Foulke, who closed out this game, joined the Yankees' Jeff Nelson (1999) as the only pitchers to appear in all four games of a four-game Series.

The Sox became only the fourth team to never trail in a game throughout the Series.

Manny being Manny Ramirez tied Hank Bauer and Derek Jeter for the longest hitting streak in postseason history (17 games/14 of them in 2004).

PEDRO'S METS HOME DEBUT

NEW YORK 4 FLORIDA 3 | SHEA STADIUM, QUEENS, NY
TIME: 2:46 • APRIL 16, 2005

BOB RYAN

They came to see Pedro make his home debut in a Mets uniform, but they stayed to see a tremendous 9th when the Mets won it with a two-out run after the Marlins had tied it with a two-out run of their own in their half.

Pedro went seven innings, allowing two runs on three hits. He was charged with three wild pitches, but two were tough scoring decisions and could have been Mike Piazza passed balls.

"Michael did a great job," Pedro said. "I'm not the easiest guy to catch. This is the second time he caught me in a long time (they had been Dodger teammates). Today was 'a struggle day' for my breaking pitch."

"You could tell he was juiced," Piazza explained. "He was pumped. The ball was just exploding out of his hand... There's not many catchers, even in their prime, who are going to control some of those pitches."

BILL CHUCK

When fans picture the great Pedro Martinez, they see him in a Red Sox uniform. Bob wanted to make sure he could see what happened after the page was turned.

Pedro pitched in 476 regular season games in his Hall of Fame career, and less than half of them were with Boston. You might remember he started his career with the Dodgers and pitched in 67 games. Boy, did they miss the boat. He only started three games, but I guess his Dodgers' ERA of 2.97 wasn't worth more than Delino DeShields, the player they got when they traded him to Montreal.

In Montreal, he was a two-time All-Star and a one-time Cy Young Award winner in his 118 games (117 starts), but he was dealt to Boston, not because the Expos preferred Carl Pavano and player-to-be-named-later Tony Armas Jr, but because Pedro was entering his contract year and the Expos could not afford to pay the reigning Cy Young Award winner to the contract that may have saved their franchise.

In the *Globe* the next day: "There has to be a catch," Bob wrote. "He has a rare disease. He can't pitch in any city with seafood restaurants."

But then Bob expressed the thoughts and feelings of Red Sox Nation: "It is a sad day for baseball, frankly, when a player of Martinez's magnitude is dealt away for purely financial reasons. Absent the increasingly insane economics of modern-day baseball, a player such as he would be spending the next 10 years or so where he is."

Further down in the column, Bob wrote words that sports fans should always remember drawing a comment that Pedro had allegedly made about not signing a long-term contract with Boston. "Ladies and gentlemen, this is organized American sport, an enterprise in which the two most irrelevant words are 'always' and, more importantly, 'never.' There are no absolutes. There are only negotiable issues."

And that's how Pedro Martinez ended up pitching for the Mets. In December 2004, The Sox offered Pedro three years and $40.5 million, with a team option for the fourth year. The Mets offered a four-year contract for $53–56 million.

This time, when he changed teams, he wasn't coming off a Cy Young–winning season, but a year in which he went 16–9 with a 3.90 ERA.

Pedro made 79 starts for the Mets before calling it a career with nine starts with the Phils. In those final 88 games, Martinez had a 3.86 ERA, and the difference between his 2.52 ERA with Boston was far greater than a run and a third a game. Bob saw Pedro pitch some of baseball's great games, and he made sure he also saw him pitch for the Mets.

Pedro went 32–23 for the Mets and 5–1 for the Phils. If you ever have trouble picturing him still with Boston, go look at the cap he's wearing on his plaque in Cooperstown.

One more thing...

Remember Carl Pavano, who the Expos got in exchange for Pedro? Pavano signed with the Yankees a week after Pedro signed with the Mets. In three years, he managed just 26 starts and had a 9–8 record with a 5.00 ERA.

2005 ALCS GAME 5

THE WHITE SOX WIN THE ALCS 4–1
CHICAGO 6 LOS ANGELES ANGELS OF ANAHEIM 3
ANGEL STADIUM OF ANAHEIM, ANAHEIM, CA
TIME: 3:11 • OCTOBER 16, 2005

BOB RYAN

Jose Contreras went nine for the win, as did Freddie Garcia in Game 4. As did Jon Garland in Game 3. As did Mark Buehrle in Game 2. Four straight complete-game victories? Yes, this was 2005, not 1905, and, no, White Sox skipper Ozzie Guillen hadn't lost his mind. But he *had* violated a late 20th century managerial code, and it is a complete and utter mortal lock we will never see anything like this again.

This will also always be remembered as "the A.J. Pierzynski Series." The flinty White Sox catcher had been the central figure in Game 2 when he alertly swung at a Kelvim Escobar pitch that may or may not have skimmed the ground before landing in the mitt of catcher Josh Paul. Controversy ensued. But A.J. got on base, and Joe Crede drove in the winning run in a 2–1 game as a result.

This time it was a 3–3 game, and Aaron Rowand was on first in the 8th when A.J. was apparently tagged out on the first baseline by pitcher Escobar. The Angels ran to the dugout. But wait! A.J. was saying that Escobar had tagged him with the glove on his left hand while the ball was in his right. After consultation, crew chief Jerry Crawford upheld the claim, and A.J. was on first. With the runners going, Crede hit a shot on which second baseman Adam Kennedy made a great play, but Rowand was able to score the go-ahead run.

Notice the parallels? Pierzynski? Escobar? Crede?

Have I mentioned you can't make this stuff up?

BILL CHUCK

There was a method to the madness of Sox manager Ozzie Guillen. The team led the AL with 99 wins, and their pitching staff tied for the AL lead with Cleveland, who won 93 games, with a 3.61 ERA. The Sox starters tied with these Angels with 3.75 ERA, for the best in the AL, and the bullpen was second in the AL with a 3.23 ERA. The starters tied with three other clubs for the most complete games with nine, but they alone led the league in innings pitched.

So, it really should come as no surprise that Guillen's staff won the last four games with four complete games. Even in the Game 1 loss, Jose Contreras pitched 8.1, with Neil Cotts making the only relief appearance of any Sox pitcher, tossing two-thirds of an inning.

Needless to say, no other League Championship Series has seen four complete games by one team. The 1973 Mets and the 1992 Pirates each had three complete games. To fully understand the magnitude of this, try this on for size. From 2006 to 2020, there have been two complete games in the LCS. The last time there had been four consecutive complete games was in 1956, when the Yankees had five straight in the World Series.

In 2005, from April 19 to October 2, A.J. Pierzynski went 117 games without committing an error, handling 777 chances. But as Bob pointed out, he was "flinty." There are loads of stories, but it can be summed up in one quote from Ozzie Guillen, "If you play against him, you hate him. If you play with him, you hate him a little less."

Pierzynski is not in the Hall of Fame. Only one HOFer (to date) played in this ALCS, Vladimir Guerrero. So, here's the good news about Vlad's performance: in 20 at-bats, Guerrero struck out only once. The bad news? He only picked up one hit (and that was of the infield variety) and one RBI. He had no walks to help his .050 BA. In addition, he only saw 47 pitches and hit only two out of the infield, grounding out 14 times.

In conclusion, Aristotle said, "There is no great genius without a mixture of madness." My friend Bob Ryan has a touch of madness when it comes to identifying the Angels. When the Angels joined the American League in 1961, they were known as the Los Angeles Angels. Starting in 1965, they became known as the California Angels. That lasted until 1997, when they became the Anaheim Angels. Starting in 2005, as you can see, they became the Los Angeles Angels of Anaheim. That lasted until 2016, when they returned to being the Los Angeles Angels. It is for this reason that Bob now refers to the team as "the Orange County American League Baseball Club."

2005 WORLD SERIES GAME 3

WHITE SOX LEAD SERIES 3–0
CHICAGO 7 HOUSTON 5 (14 INNINGS)
MINUTE MAID PARK, HOUSTON, TX
TIME: 5:41 • OCTOBER 25, 2005

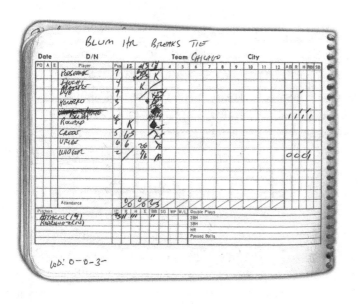

BOB RYAN

Improbable heroics are practically a staple of the World Series. The 1906 White Sox had one in unheralded third baseman George Rohe. And now they had another one in Geoff Blum, who came to the plate in the 14th for the first time in three weeks after a season when he had one homer and three RBI in 99 plate appearances and homered to left, giving the ChiSox the go-ahead run in a 7–5 triumph. It was then the lengthiest (5:41) World Series game ever. Adding to the fictional quality of the Blum blast, he had spent two years in Houston, where he was something of a local folk hero.

This game was not exactly a thing of beauty. White Sox relievers themselves walked 10 men. But, of course, they did fan 10. Clutch hitting, you say? Each team left 15 men on base. Entering the 14th, the White Sox had only scored in one inning, a five-run 5th.

All kinds of records had been set. Blum's homer had been hit on the 440th pitch of a record 482 thrown. The 17 pitchers employed by both teams was also a new record.

The winning pitcher was Damaso Marte, who pitched the 13th. Mark Buehrle finished up. It was the only save in a 16-year career. You can't make this stuff up.

BILL CHUCK

At the time, this was the longest World Series game in time lasting 341 minutes. It was overtaken in Game 3 of the 2018 Series between the Dodgers and Red Sox, which went 18 innings, totaling 440 minutes, meaning the extra four innings of play took an additional 99 minutes. Jim Reeves of the *Fort-Worth Star-Telegram* wrote the next day, "It took 44 years to finally bring a World Series to Texas. It only seemed that long to play the first game…."

The Astros only had eight hits in this game. Of greater interest to me was that Houston jumped out to a 4–0 lead on seven hits in the first four innings, which means over the final 10 innings of the game, they got just one hit, a run-scoring double in the bottom of the 8th. That's not to say they did not have baserunners. Over the final 10 innings, they reached on 11 walks, one hit batsman, and one error. They left 15 on base. In fact, each team left 15 runners on base, tying the record for most by a single team and setting the record for two teams in a World Series game.

White Sox leadoff batter Scott Podsednik played the equivalent of two games as his eight at-bats are the most ever in a World Series game. Podsednik had two hits, which is a lot better than Willy Taveras and Brad Ausmus. The Sox held each of them to 0–6 nights. The only other time in which a team has had two players who went at least 0–6 was in 2018 Game 3, when the Dodgers held Mookie Betts to 0–7 and Xander Bogaerts to 0–8

The Sox pitchers walked 12 and struck out 14, and as Bob pointed out, the Sox bullpen by themselves walked 10 and struck out 10. There have only been two games in Series history in which a team's pitchers had 10-plus walks and 10-plus strikeouts, and this is one of them. The other was in Game 2 of the 1956 World Series, when the Yankees seven pitchers had 11 walks and 10 whiffs. The Yankee starter that game was Don Larsen, who walked four and whiffed none in 1.2 IP. His next time on the mound, he was perfect.

As Bob pointed out, Mark Buehrle, who appeared in 518 games, starting 493 of them, earned the only save of his career as he became the first pitcher to start a game in the Series and save the next one since Bob Turley of the Yankees in the 1958 World Series.

The White Sox used nine pitchers, tied for the most pitchers ever used by a team in a Series game. The 17 pitchers used were the record until the 2018 Game 3 marathon. The 482 combined pitches thrown was the record until the 561 pitches in the 2018 18-inning epic.

Bob wasn't the only headliner attending the game, as former First Lady Barbara Bush was there as well. I do not know whether she kept score throughout.

The two teams played like they were a bit spent that next night, as Chicago completed the sweep with a 1–0 win. (Perhaps too much scoring and too many innings the game before?) The Astros were hoping to start Roger Clemens in Game 5, sore hamstring and all.

FYI: In 1906, George Rohe hit a three-run triple to give the White Sox a 3–0 win over the Cubs in Game 3 of the Series that the Sox took in six. To my knowledge, Bob was not in attendance.

2005 WORLD SERIES GAME 4

WHITE SOX SWEEP

CHICAGO 1 HOUSTON 0 | MINUTE MAID PARK, HOUSTON
TIME: 3:20 • OCTOBER 26, 2005

BOB RYAN

Every once in a while, there might actually be a Team of Destiny. The 2005 Chicago White Sox won their final five games of the regular season before going 11–1 in the postseason, capping a 16 of 17 run with a 1–0 victory over the Astros. Nobody was getting in their way.

It was Freddy Garcia on the mound for the ChiSox and Brandon Backe starting for the Astros. The teams were scoreless until the top of the 8th, and by this time, Brad Lidge was on the mound for Houston. A Willie Harris pinch-hit single, a sacrifice by Scott Podsednik, and an infield grounder to the right side by Carl Everett put a man on third with two away. Veteran Jermaine Dye poked a single up the middle, and that was that for the offense. Cliff Politte, Neil Cotts, and Bobby Jenks nailed it down in the 8th and 9th.

But it wasn't quite that simple (is it ever?). In the bottom of the 9th, the Astros had a man on second with one out when pinch-hitter Chris Burke hit a foul pop-fly down the left-field line. Anxious Chicago fans no doubt thought of a man named Bartman at that moment. Not to worry. Shortstop Jose Uribe reached into the stands to make a beautiful catch that rated a star in my scorebook, especially considering the timeliness of the play. Orlando Palmeiro nudged one toward short, forcing Uribe into a tricky do-or-die play. Yes, he did! White Sox win!

Everyone in Chicago had perennially fixated on the Cubs and the championship drought that had begun in 1908. Fewer wept for the White Sox, whose last World Series win had come in 1917, and whose pain from the 1919 Black Sox scandal was everlastingly acute. Now the glory belonged to the *other* team in town.

BILL CHUCK

It was back-to-back Sox World Series wins in 2004–2005. The White Sox World Series win in 2005 followed the Boston Red Sox win in 2004. The last White Sox World Series win was in 1917, which was followed by the last Red Sox win in 1918. To re-emphasize the Sox connection, it was the last White Sox game for Willie Harris, who scored the sole run in this contest. During the off-season, Harris signed with the Red Sox. As Bob is fond of saying, "You can't make this stuff up."

Bob made a passing reference to "Bartman." This was not a salute to Bart Simpson but a remembrance of Steve Bartman, the Cubs fan who deflected an 8th inning foul ball in the 2003 NLCS, disrupting Cubs' outfielder Moises Alou's ability to catch the ball. Instead of the Cubs being four outs away from the Series, the Marlins rallied for eight runs for the victory. The next night Florida won again and won the NL pennant.

In the bottom of the 7th, Jeff Bagwell pinch-hit for Brandon Backe and grounded out to second. It was his final MLB appearance.

This was Brad Lidge's second loss of the Series, and he finished the postseason (0–3). Only Justin Verlander lost more games in a single postseason (four in 2019). Lidge is tied with the most losses for a relief pitcher.

This was the first, last, and only National League World Series appearance for the Astros.

YANKS SCORE IN EVERY INNING

NEW YORK 17 TORONTO 6 | YANKEE STADIUM, THE BRONX, NY
TIME: 3:48 • APRIL 29, 2006

BOB RYAN

They had actually done it once before, in 1939, against the St. Louis Browns. Score in every inning that is. But it's not something you see every day, week, month, year, or decade, is it?

Well, here it is. The Yanks scored 17 runs on 15 hits and nine walks, and they scored at least once in all eight at-bats. This enabled Randy Johnson to pick up a cheesy W in which he allowed six earned runs in 5 IP.

Before he left, Randy hit Reed Johnson twice. Yup, Johnson hit Johnson twice. Not to be outdone, Tanyon Sturtze also hit Reed, allowing him to tie a single-game HBP record.

Johnny Damon had his ninth career two-homer game. His second homer, a right-field upper decker, prompted his first Yankee Stadium curtain call.

BILL CHUCK

The Yanks scored their runs on 15 hits, and Derek Jeter went 0–4. Alex Rodriguez also went 0–4, but it was particularly odd. A-Rod went 0–4 with three runs scored and one RBI. There have been only 12 occasions in MLB in which players had that line score, and since that date in 2006, the singular occurrence was Stephen Vogt on June 26, 2021. Prior to A-Rod's 2006 line, the most recent had been by Jeff Burroughs 30 years before. Of the 12 times this occurred, a Yankee did it three times. Sandy Alomar (the senior) did it in 1975 for the Yanks, and in 1938, Joe DiMaggio did it when the Yankees beat the Senators, 16–1.

Johnny Damon also had an unusual line with five AB, five runs scored, three hits, three RBI. No other player has ever had a game like that.

In his career, Johnson never had another win in which he threw only 5.0 and allowed six runs. However, Randy Johnson hit Reed Johnson four times in his career, tied with the four Jim Leyritz plunkings for the most assaults.

Scoring in every inning

This is a rare event accomplished only eight times in the modern era in the AL and three in the NL. The AL record is eight innings, and the NL record is nine innings (all away teams).

2006 NLCS GAME 7

CARDINALS DEFEAT METS 4–3 TO WIN THE NLCS

ST. LOUIS 3 NEW YORK 1 | SHEA STADIUM, QUEENS, NY

TIME: 3:23 • OCTOBER 19, 2006

BOB RYAN

New York sports fans take things seriously. They have very long memories. It's not a good thing to make the last out of a Game 7 for the NLCS by leaving the bat on your shoulder.

Carlos Beltran did just that. With the bases loaded and two away in the 9th, trailing by two, he was facing Cardinals' rookie Adam Wainwright. He took a called first strike. He fouled one off. And then… the kid broke off a gorgeous slow curve. Beltran watched *and* watched. And watched. The ball plopped into Yadier Molina's glove on the outside corner. Plate ump Tim Welke raised his right hand. Streeeeerike three! And thus had a great player placed himself into the

337

everlasting consciousness of every Mets fan, forever and ever. No, I'm not kidding.

Poor Endy Chavez. Had the Mets won, he'd have been forever hailed as the Mets answer to Sandy Amoros, whose double-play catch and throw off a Yogi Berra smash punctuated that 1955 Game 7 Dodger victory. It was a 1–1 game in the 6th. Jim Edmonds was on first when Scott Rolen lofted one to left. Chavez made a spectacular leaping catch. But that wasn't all. He fired the ball to second baseman Jose Valentin, who threw to Carlos Delgado at first, doubling off Edmonds.

By the way, Molina's 9th inning two-run homer off Aaron Heilman won the game and the pennant. St. Louis cares. New York doesn't.

"You'd have good moments and bad moments in your career," said Beltran. "This was a bad moment; one I'll have to live with the rest of my life."

If he only knew....

BILL CHUCK

Please allow me to share an excerpt from Jared Diamond's article "How to Make Babe Ruth Feel Inadequate" from *The Wall Street Journal* of October 9, 2012 (six years after this game):

"Here's the situation: Your favorite baseball team is playing in Game 7 of the World Series. The bases are loaded in the bottom of the ninth, and the team is down three runs. You can choose any hitter from any point in history to come up with a chance to win the game with a grand slam.

Who do you choose? Statistically, your best bet would be St. Louis outfielder Carlos Beltran—the real Mr. October.

After slugging two home runs in Monday's Game 2 of the National League Division Series, Beltran now has a ridiculous 13 home runs in 94 playoff at-bats. That rate of a homer every 7.2 at-bats is the best among all players who have appeared in at least 25 postseason games."

The bottom of the 9th inning was terrific from the Cardinals' perspective, devastating from the Mets' perspective, and incredibly exciting from a baseball fan's perspective.

Jose Valentin and Endy Chavez led off with back-to-back singles off rookie Adam Wainwright. Cliff Floyd took a called third strike, Jose

Reyes lined out to center, and then Paul Lo Duca walked on a 3–1 pitch. I mention that because each of those batters had a chance to tie or win the game for New York. In the *New York Times*, the next day, Ben Shpigel quoted Cards' manager Tony La Russa, "They had all the right guys up, and we got them out."

It then came down to Beltran, who, during the regular season, had homered 41 times and driven home 116. Molina called for a changeup that Beltran took for strike one. He then foul tipped a curve off his foot for strike two.

In this NLCS, Beltran to this point was 8–26 (.308) with three homers. To this point in Beltran's 14-game postseason career against the Cardinals, he was 18–50 (.360) with 20 runs scored, seven homers, nine RBI, and had struck out six times.

As Waino rubbed up a new baseball, Molina signaled by tapping on home plate with his glove. In his column in the *St. Louis Post-Dispatch* on the 10th anniversary of this game, "10 years ago, Wainwright threw the curve that froze New York," Derrick Goold wrote: "Hall of Famer John Smoltz would later call it 'the perfect pitch at the perfect time to the perfect place.'"

Finally, to paraphrase Ernest Thayer,

Oh, somewhere in this favored land, the sun is shining bright,
The band is playing somewhere, and somewhere hearts are light;
And somewhere men are laughing, and somewhere children shout,
But there was no joy in Flushing, the mighty Carlos had struck out.

KING FELIX

SEATTLE 3 BOSTON 0 | FENWAY PARK, BOSTON, MA
TIME: 2:22 • APRIL 11, 2007

BOB RYAN

The pregame buzz was all Japanese. It was Daisuke Matsuzaka's Fenway debut, and the first batter he would face would be Ichiro.

But Mariners' skipper Mike Hargrove foresaw a different storyline. He thought his 21-year-old starting pitcher might just command the most attention. And when the game was over, and Felix Hernandez had hung a complete-game, one-hit shutout on the Red Sox, the ol' Human Rain Delay was saying, "I damn well told ya' so!"

"I was banking on it," he smiled. "I was thinking about it all day long. All that stuff about Ichiro and Matsuzaka, which I understand, but I really wasn't going to be surprised if Felix stole the show."

J.D. Drew's leadoff single in the 8th was all that stood between Hernandez and a no-no. "If he isn't 'on,'" said Dustin Pedroia, "I don't want to see him when he is 'on.'"

"If you're not impressed with him, you're deaf, dumb, and blind," added Hargrove. "His stuff's as good as anyone I've ever seen."

BILL CHUCK

A little history to begin with as to why the Red Sox fans were so excited about the arrival of Daisuke Matsuzaka (and why Mike Hargrove was justifiably enthusiastic about Felix Hernandez).

The Eiji Sawamura Award is given to the top pitcher in Nippon Pro Baseball annually. As explained by Jim Allen in the *Kyodo News*: "The award, voted by a panel of former elite pitchers, honors Nippon Professional Baseball's most impressive starting pitcher, or more specifically, the pitcher who best embodies the spirit of Sawamura, the Yomiuri Giants' Japanese ace from the early days of the nation's first pro league."

Now, Felix Hernandez never won the Sawamura Award. He did win the Cy Young Award in 2010, finished second twice (in 2009 and 2014), and finished in the top eight in voting three other times.

Daisuke Matsuzaka (Dice-K) never won the Cy Young Award, finishing fourth in 2008. He did win the Sawamura Award in 2001 while pitching for the Seibu Lions. The previous winner, in 1999, was Koji Uehara, who became a beloved reliever for Boston from 2013 to 2016. Now I know you want to award me an E-W (Error-Writer) for saying that Koji was the previous winner *two seasons before* Dice-K. Still, another wonderful characteristic of the Sawamura Award is that sometimes the panel feels that no pitcher had been found worthy of winning, which was the case in 2000.

Felix Hernandez was a joy to watch pitch. This was the only one-hitter of his career. However, on August 15, 2012, he pitched a perfect game in a 1–0 win over the Rays. He struck out 12 in that game, one of 35 times he compiled games of 10-plus strikeouts.

Daisuke Matsuzaka was sheer hell to watch pitch. He never pitched a one-hitter or a no-hitter. He did have one complete game in his major league career, which consisted of 132 starts. Matsuzaka could give

Hargrove a run for his money for his "Human Rain Delay" nickname, as Matsuzaka's games seemed endless. He would pick, pick, pick at the edges until fans and players alike drifted into a state of uncomfortable boredom. Dice-K had one good season, and it really was a great season. In 2008, he went 18–3 with a 2.90 ERA. Over the course of the rest of his career in the States, he was a combined 38–40. In 2008, he managed to pitch his way into and out of trouble. He was second in the majors with an average walk rate of 5.05 per nine innings. Felix was 3.59 that season. Dice K led the AL with 94 walks. Felix had 80. But what made Matsuzaka so successful in this one great season was his ability to pitch himself out of trouble. He went to a full count on 109 batters, and even though he walked 44 of them, the remainder only hit .185. But his gift that season was when he loaded the bases. In 2008, he faced 18 batters with the sacks filled. He walked just one. He hit one. Two hit sac flies. The remaining batters were 0–14. In 2007, the year of this game. Matsuzaka faced 32 batters with the sacks filled, third in the majors. He walked three. The remaining batters were 8–29, a .276 BAA.

In Japan, Matsuzaka had a 108–60 record and a 2.95 earned-run average. He also completed 72 games. While Matsuzaka threw just one complete game in the States, he threw many, many pitches. He had 83 games in which he threw over 100 pitches, 15 of which occurred in games in which he threw five innings or less, including four in which he completed no more than 4.2 innings pitched. Dice-K was 38–19 in those games with a 3.29 ERA.

King Felix threw 25 complete games and had 260 games in which he threw over 100 pitches. Hernandez was 121–70 with a 2.73 ERA in those games.

"I hope he arouses the fire that's dormant in the innermost recesses of my soul. I plan to face him with the zeal of a challenger."

—Ichiro Suzuki, prior to facing Dice-K

Ichiro went 0–5 in this game, 0–4 against Dice-K. Ichiro had been 8–34 (.235) in the two years they played against each other in Japan. When their careers were over in the States, Ichiro was 7–27 against Dice-K, a soft .259.

But in the end, Ichiro is on his way to Cooperstown. King Felix did not age gracefully but is beloved by his fans in Seattle, who wore King's Court t-shirts to his game. Dice-K ended up pitching, once again, in Japan… much to the relief of most Red Sox fans.

One more thing…

The ceremonial first pitch for this game was thrown by Yoichi Suzuki, consul general of Japan in Boston.

MOTHER'S DAY MIRACLE

BOSTON 6 BALTIMORE 5 | FENWAY PARK, BOSTON, MA
TIME: 3:10 • MAY 13, 2007

BOB RYAN

Jeremy Guthrie is cruising with a 5–0 lead and one out in the 9th. So, what if catcher Ramon Hernandez drops a Coco Crisp pop-up? The guy's doing fine. He's only thrown 91 pitches.

In what will go down in history as a colossally needless and just plain dumb managerial decision, Oriole skipper Sam Perlozzo yanks his efficient starter. The baseball gods don't hesitate. They punish Perlozzo for his malfeasance.

The Red Sox come up with six runs, the winning tally coming when late-arriving reliever Chris Ray mishandles first baseman's Kevin Millar's toss on a harmless Coco Crisp bouncer, allowing runs five and six to score. Given the day it was, this has officially gone down as the "Mother's Day Miracle."

"It's amazing, here, of all places," said Terry Francona. "A dropped pop-up, and, the next thing you know, a combination of some magic and some really good players that don't quit. You just want a chance to get that tying run to the plate."

BILL CHUCK

This was a 6-5-4-3-2-1 victory. Let me explain as I go granular on Bob's description of the insane 9th inning that created the Mother's Day Miracle.

I never understand a pitcher being removed after an error has been committed behind him, or in this case, in front of him. Julio Lugo had started the 9th with a weak grounder to short, and Jeremy Guthrie had his first out of the inning. Coco Crisp then pops the ball up, and the catcher drops it after stumbling on his own mask. I'm sorry if I sound pedantic here but *let's review:* a weak grounder, then a ball that travels farther up in the air than away from the plate, a pitcher who has a shutout and has thrown 91 pitches and had allowed just three hits and had retired eight straight batters and was two outs shy of a complete game *and you pull him?!?*

In comes Danys Baez. Boom, RBI double off the wall by David Ortiz. Wily Mo Pena, who had replaced Manny Ramirez in the top of the 9th for reasons unknown, certainly not for defensive prowess, singled to put runners on the corners.

Now Perlozzo did what managers do, which is bring in your closer when there is a save situation, which suddenly there was, with the tying run in the on-deck circle. In came Chris Ray, who I would imagine had little time to warm up and even less time to mentally adjust to coming into this contest. Not surprisingly, considering the circumstances, Ray walked J.D. Drew on a full count pitch to load the bases. Then another full count and another walk to Kevin Youkilis made it a 5–2 game, and now the tying run was on first and the winning run at the plate.

With Jason Varitek at the plate and Ray having thrown 13 pitches, nine of which were balls, Tek lines a single to right-center, and two runs score. The slow-footed Varitek reaches second as Nick Markakis briefly bobbles the ball, with the official scorer graciously granting the catcher a double. Let's reset. There's still just one out, the score is now 5–4 O's, and the tying run is on second, and the winning run is on third. Perlozzo then orders an intentional walk to Eric Hinske in the hopes of a ground ball somehow ending this misery.

And that's what he got from Alex Cora (2019 and 2021 Red Sox manager and the infamous Astros coach), who was the next batter. Cora hit a weak ground ball to second base. Brian Roberts throws home and forces Youk. And there's two down.

Up steps Julio Lugo, who started the inning with the weak grounder to short. Ray again goes to a full count before he hits another weak grounder to the right side of the infield that should have been fielded by Roberts but was grabbed by the first baseman Kevin Millar (you know, of 2004 Red Sox fame). This means that Ray needs to quickly get over to first, and Millar needed to make a good throw. Neither happened. Ray is a little late, and the throw doesn't lead Ray and is slightly up the line. The ball clangs off Ray's glove, and not only did Varitek score, but the lumbering Hinske came in from first base on the infield single on the E1.

Let's count it down:

6 Red Sox runs

5 Orioles runs

4 Boston hits

3 walks by Orioles' pitchers

2 Baltimore errors

1 boneheaded move by Sam Perlozzo

Victory!

The miracle of birth has nothing on the Mother's Day Miracle by the Red Sox.

RESPECT FOR DAVID WRIGHT

METS 10 YANKEES 7 | SHEA STADIUM, QUEENS, NY
TIME: 3:36 • MAY 19, 2007

BOB RYAN

Two at-bats were apparently more than enough for Yankee skipper Joe Torre. In his first at-bat, David Wright smashed an estimated 460-footer that cleared the picnic area in distant left field. In his second at-bat, his long fly bounced off center fielder Johnny Damon's glove over the fence for home run number two. And so, Torre walked David Wright intentionally in his next three plate appearances.

"I was a little surprised," admitted Mets' manager Willie Randolph.

"That's a tremendous sign of respect," decided Mets' hurler Tom Glavine. "And it's certainly one we as his teammates are happy to see."

One person who wasn't happy was Johnny Damon. "I got there, timed it perfectly, and the ball hit the wrong part of my glove," he said.

"I felt it pop out. I was just hoping it would stay in. I still can't believe I didn't catch it."

BILL CHUCK

David Wright is one always worthy of baseball respect. He was just one of those players who fans, teammates, and opponents respected for the way he treated the game, whether he was playing or battling back from chronic injuries (three surgical procedures for his neck, back, and shoulder, as well as dealing with the effects of spinal stenosis).

David Wright walked three (or more) times in a game 19 times.

David Wright was intentionally walked two (or more) times in a game four times.

David Wright was intentionally walked three times in a game twice, and this was one of them. The only other time it happened was July 18, 2009, when the Mets were in Atlanta, when Wright came up three times with a runner on second and was walked to set up the force.

In this Subway Series game, Wright came up in the 4th with runners on second and third, and then in the 6th and 8th with a runner on second.

Was this a record for a nine-inning interleague game, you ask? It tied the record set three times by two other players. Who was the player who did it other than Barry Bonds, you ask? Bonds was walked intentionally three times in 1997 against the Angels and in 2002 against these Yankees. In that Yankee game, Barry had five plate appearances, which included three intentional walks, one unintentional pass, and one hit-by-pitch. He was 0–0 with one run scored. The other player who received three IBB was Cliff Floyd in a Marlins/Blue Jays contest in 2001.

Wright was the most recent to be intentionally walked three times and the last to do so with the catcher putting his arm out and the pitcher tossing four wide ones three times, a probable time savings of about two minutes.

One more thing...

Tommy Glavine was the winner in this game, his 645th career game. It was the 295th victory of his career. Glavine would pick up his 300th win on August 5, 2007, pitching for the Mets against the Cubs at Wrigley Field. Glavine finished his career with a record of 244–147 with the Braves and 61–56 with the Mets.

YOUKILIS INSIDE-THE-PARK

BOSTON 5 CLEVELAND 3 | FENWAY PARK, BOSTON, MA
TIME: 3:10 • MAY 28, 2007

BOB RYAN

There's hot, hotter, and you've-got-to-be-kidding-me. That's the only way to describe the roll Kevin Youkilis was on, this being his eighth straight multi-hit game. Spicing the plot was a 7th inning inside-the-park homer.

Youk's shot off Roberto Hernandez went to the 420-foot sign at the famed triangle, bounced off the short Red Sox bullpen wall, and bounded toward left field. It was a no-brainer. He scored, standing up. It was his first career inside-the-parker, and it got him a Standing O curtain call.

The game also marked the Fenway return of Trot Nixon, he of the dirty cap, who batted 5th and went 1-for-3 with a sac fly. He was greeted very warmly by the crowd. "I think I earned the respect of the fans in this city," he said, "even though I didn't put up big numbers."

By the way, Youk finished the game with 17 hits in his last 35 at-bats. That's H-O-T!

BILL CHUCK

The start time weather for this spring day at the Fens was a comfortable 74 degrees, and presumably, without the radiant heat from Kevin Youkilis, it would have been in the low 60s. There is something unbelievably amazing about seeing a batter on a hot streak.

Let me remind you that baseball is a game of failure. This is how Faye Vincent (Major League Baseball's final independent commissioner) put it, "Baseball teaches us, or has taught most of us, how to deal with failure. We learn at a very young age that failure is the norm in baseball and, precisely because we have failed, we hold in high regard those who fail less often—those who hit safely in one out of three chances and become star players. I also find it fascinating that baseball, alone in sport, considers errors to be part of the game, part of its rigorous truth."

So, when a batter like Kevin Youkilis gets hot, we watch with fun and amazement. On May 4, Kevin was hitting .280, almost exactly what we had come to expect from him. Entering the season, in the first 263 games of his career, he was a .275 hitter (he ended up with a lifetime BA of .281 in 1,061 games). But then he got H-O-T, as Bob so aptly described. When this game ended, Youk had hit in 20 straight games and was hitting .354. He was hitting .350 on June 2 because that's what happened when you hit .426 over the course of a 23-game hitting streak.

During the streak, Youkilis hit six homers, and Bob was there for his inside-the-parker, *the only one of his career.*

By the next day, amidst his hitting streak, he also completed a streak in which he had multiple hits in nine straight games, tied for the longest in Red Sox history with Jim Rice in 1978 and Roy Johnson in 1934. To appreciate that, ponder that Ted Williams and Tris Speaker, two of the greatest hitters of all-time, only had streaks of eight games in which they had multiple hits.

Youk finished the season hitting .288. Did you expect a much higher average? That's not how it works in baseball. From June 1 to the end of the season on September 30, Youk hit .248. That is reality. That is baseball.

In closing, we turn to All-Star and philosopher Mark Teixeira, whose Rangers had played the Red Sox the night before: "Baseball is a game of failure. There are plenty of opportunities to be down, or to feel sorry for yourself, or to be upset at somebody or upset at yourself." In other words, it is so much fun to watch a player when he is hot.

BONDS AND GIANTS VISIT

BOSTON 10 SAN FRANCISCO 2 | FENWAY PARK, BOSTON, MA
TIME: 3:09 • JUNE 15, 2007

BOB RYAN

Barry Bonds *almost* homered in his maiden visit to Fenway Park. Greeted in his first at-bat by the predictable "Ster-oids! Ster-oids!" chant from the crowd of 36,508, he whisked one just foul at the right-field Pesky Pole before popping out to second.

Hey, he at least stayed in the game. Big Papi was tossed by plate umpire Tony Randazzo for throwing this bat and helmet after being called out on strikes in the first. A curious aside was ump Randazzo saying Papi had thrown his helmet "too hard." No one knew there was a scale on such matters.

Northern California native and childhood Giants' fan Dustin Pedroia welcomed the visitors to Fenway with his first five-hit game.

"I just put in some pretty good swings all day," he said. "That's pretty much it." He did say it was fun to play against Bonds & Co. "I *was* excited all day playing against the Giants, seeing Barry," he admitted. "It was awesome."

Bonds finished at 1–3 with an intentional walk (of course) and an 8th inning single to right.

"It's a nice ballpark," he declared. "It's really bigger than they say it was. Right field is a long way away."

BILL CHUCK

David Ortiz was indeed ejected in the 1st after arguing with plate umpire Tony Randazzo. It was one of 13 times that Papi got the old heave-ho, most all of them because David was attempting to do the umpire's job as well as his own by commenting on balls and strikes.

Rookie of the Year Dustin Pedroia had his first five-hit game. Pedroia had five five-hit games His homer and double helped him get his first five-RBI game. He had seven of those in his career. Dustin raised his average from .311 to .331 in this game.

Bonds was the freakish curiosity in this game, but it was the Giants' leadoff batter who got the biggest ovation. Now the Giants' center fielder, Dave Roberts, made his first appearance back at Fenway since 2004. Roberts went 2–4 with a double. He singled to lead off the game and scored on a double by Mark Sweeney. A Framingham, Massachusetts, native Sweeney was playing in his first game at Fenway in his 13-year career.

The next day, the Sox won 1–0, Bonds went 0–3 with another IBB (this one was in the 1st with Roberts on second and two outs) and a strikeout. On Sunday, the Sox completed the sweep with a 9–5 victory. Bonds went 2–3 with a walk and a bases-empty homer off Tim Wakefield to lead off the 6th with the Giants trailing 8–3.

One moment of silence…

One of Bob's colleagues at the *Boston Globe*, Larry Whiteside, was remembered before the start of the game with a moment of silence. Sides had died the day before.

One more thing...

In 2018, Dustin Pedroia went 1–11. This meant at the end of the 2018 season, Pedroia had a lifetime BA of .29995, which is listed at .300. In 2019, Pedroia went 2–20, giving him a lifetime BA of .299287, which is listed at .299. He did not play in the COVID 2020 season and his career came to an end at .299.

2007 WORLD SERIES GAME 2

RED SOX LEAD SERIES 2–0
BOSTON 2 COLORADO 1 | FENWAY PARK, BOSTON, MA
TIME: 3:39 • OCTOBER 25, 2007

BOB RYAN

He was on base in the 8th as the potential tying run after his fourth hit of the evening, a two-out shot up the middle, that had nearly taken Jonathan Papelbon out of the game. In fact, Matt Holliday had nearly deprived the Red Sox of *two* key players. Dustin Pedroia needed trainer Paul Lessard's attention after failing to make the play out by second base. Matt Holliday was having himself a sensational evening.

Until he wasn't.

Before ever-dangerous cleanup man Todd Helton had a chance to do any damage, Matt Holliday was slinking back to the Rockies' dugout. The inning was over. The threat was gone. It was a 1–3 in my scorebook. Jonathan Papelbon had picked him off, and it wasn't close. How not close, you say? "He was O-U-T from Fenway to Foxborough. It might be the weakest safe/out call of umpire Mike Everitt's career." Pretty snappy writing, if I do say so myself. In fact, I did write that; check out the *Boston Globe* the next day.

It had been a collaborative effort, the product of inside knowledge and an extraordinary attention to detail. The idea to go for a pickoff had come from first-base coach Brad Mills, who had a color-coded chart of Colorado players on-base tendencies, and it had told him that Holliday likes to steal on the first pitch with two outs. He flashed the sign to Jason Varitek behind the plate, and he relayed his sign to Papelbon. What makes this all the more interesting was that Papelbon *had never before picked anyone off in his major league career.*

"I was going on the pitch, yeah," fessed up Holiday. "I knew he was slow to the plate and I was just trying to be aggressive and get in scoring position."

The Red Sox had won despite leaving 12 men on base thanks to the stellar pitching of Curt Schilling, Hideki Okajima, and Papelbon. Schilling went 5.1 before turning it over to what he called "The Papajima Show." But when it was over, the prime topic of discussion was a killer 1–3 in the scorebook. And little did the 36,730 in attendance know that in addition to the big right-handed reliever, they also owed a big "Thank you" to a first-base coach. This was old-fashioned scouting. The game had yet to get bogged down with, ahem, "analytics."

BILL CHUCK

Hideki Okajima became the first Japanese pitcher to ever appear in a World Series in this game. His performance could have been an ad for a carbonated beverage: seven up/seven down, and that included four whiffs. While that was Okie's first, this game was Schilling's last. In his final big-league appearance, thanks to a Papelbon pickoff, Schilling picked up a win.

2007 WORLD SERIES GAME 4

RED SOX SWEEP
BOSTON 4 COLORADO 3 | COORS FIELD, DENVER, CO
TIME: 3:35 • OCTOBER 29, 2007

BOB RYAN

The baseball phrase is "insurance run," or perhaps "pad run." You always feel you can never have a big enough lead. You just never know what might transpire out there. A two-run lead is better than one, and a three-run lead is better than two, a 24-run lead is better than 23, etc., etc., etc.

But when a spare-part, pinch-hitting outfielder named Bobby Kielty stepped to the plate in the top of the 8th and hit Colorado reliever Brian Fuentes' first pitch over the left-field fence for a leadoff homer to make it 4–1, Sox, I'm not sure I was thinking "game-winner." It was a nice little subplot, I figured. Everything just seemed to be going Boston's way in this Series.

Ha! With one out in the Colorado 8th, Todd Helton singled, and Garrett Atkins took Hideki Okajima deep. The smile was wiped off every Boston fan's face. Now it was 4–3. That Bobby Kielty poke now looked exponentially more important.

Okay, it all worked out. Jonathan Papelbon came on for a five-out save. There was a dramatic moment with one away in the 9th when a Jamey Carroll shot forced left fielder Jacoby Ellsbury into making an acrobatic catch. It might not have been a homer, but at the very least, it would have put the tying run on second base. The moment of crisis passed, Papelbon blew away Seth Smith with a 94-mph fastball to win the game and the Series.

Who was Bobby Kielty, and what happened to him? He was a 30-year-old journeyman playing for his fourth team. As the grandson of a Fitchburg, Massachusetts, mail carrier, he had a bit of a New England connection. As far as the big at-bat was concerned, he said, "I only got one shot in the Series, so there was no way I was going down any way but swinging." It turned out to be his last swing. He never played in the major leagues again.

Further drama was provided by starting pitcher Jon Lester. The 23-year-old southpaw was less than a year away from having had surgery for a blood cancer. He had been nursed along and hadn't even been activated for the Division Series against the Angels.

In the biggest game of his young career, he gave his team 5.2 shutout innings. As the baseball world would learn, this was only the first of many superb postseason outings for Jon Lester.

As for Bobby Kielty, what can you say? Your last career at-bat clinches a World Series. Nope, you surely can't make this stuff up.

BILL CHUCK

With this win, Terry Francona became the first manager to win his first eight World Series games. As for the synchronicity that I so enjoy, the Rockies totaled 29 hits in the Series, and the Sox totaled 29 runs. The Rockies became the third team in Series history (the 1937 Yankees and 1966 Orioles were the others) not to commit an error in a World Series of any length. The only mistake the Coloradans made was playing the Red Sox.

I love the Bobby Kielty story. Here's a guy who played 599 career regular-season games with 1,792 at-bats and hit 53 homers. He played three career League Division games with four at-bats and no homers. He played eight career League Championship games with 10 at-bats and no homers. He played one World Series game, saw one pitch, and hit it for a homer. Now that's a record that can be tied but never broken.

There have been only three pinch-hit home runs hit in a potential World Series–clinching game:

- Chuck Essegian for the Dodgers in 1959, Game 6, won by L.A. 9–3
- Jim Leyritz for the Yankees in 1999, Game 4, won by N.Y. 4–1
- Bobby Kielty for the Red Sox in 2007, Game 4, won by Boston 4–3

There have been 25 pinch-homers hit in the World Series. Yogi Berra hit the first in 1947, while Chuck Essegian is the only player with two (1959).

I can't help but think of Joe Pignatano, the former catcher and long-time coach, who, in his last plate appearance in the majors, hit into a triple play. In contrast, Bobby Kielty's final MLB PA was a home run that clinched the World Series.

PETTITTE'S HORRIBLE ND

NEW YORK 12 KC 11 | YANKEE STADIUM, THE BRONX, NY

TIME: 3:50 • JUNE 7, 2008

BOB RYAN

Andy Pettitte was a lucky man. He matched a career-high by allowing 10 earned runs but escaped without an L. Johnny Damon led a 19-hit assault on seven Kansas City pitchers with a sparkling 6–1–6–4 line, capping his afternoon with a game-winning single in a two-run Yankee 9th.

Damon's stellar performance had come in apparent response to criticism from Boss George Steinbrenner, who didn't appreciate it when Damon disagreed publicly with the idea of sending Joba Chamberlain to the bullpen. "I understand what he said," shrugged Damon. "But I always go out and play. That's what I've always done."

Damon's active afternoon was the seventh five-hit (or more) game of his career and included getting thrown out trying for two on a 6th inning single. "Johnny Damon was really hot," said Royals' skipper Trey Hillman. "And we really weren't sure where to throw him."

There was an 11-minute delay in the 3rd when Joey Gathright's bunt bounced up and hit plate umpire Jerry Layne in the mask, forcing his removal.

Jose Guillen gave it his best shot for Kansas City with two homers, one a grand slam, and seven RBI.

BILL CHUCK

There were just three times in Andy Pettitte's career that he allowed 10 runs; this was the finale. He permitted 10 in 2.2 against Texas on July 30, 1996, and then, while pitching for Houston, he permitted 10 in 4.2 IP against Florida. This time, Andy went 6.2 innings to allow his 10 ER. The biggest difference in this game is that while he took a well-deserved loss in the other two games, and this was the only one in which he got a no-decision.

Allowing at least 10 earned runs with a no-decision is just something we don't see that frequently from a starting pitcher. Since this game that Bob attended, it has only happened twice through the 2021 season. It's only happened 17 times in baseball history and only seven times since 1946.

Just so you know, Mike Moustakas once drove home nine for the Royals, and 13 Royals have had seven ribbies in games, and of those 14 great performances, Jose Guillen, in this game, is the only one who was on the losing game of the scorecard.

Johnny Damon entered this game hitting .308 and left hitting .326. Just so you know, Myril Hoag went 6–6 for the Yankees against the Red Sox in the first game of a double-header (both nine-inning games) on June 6, 1934. Hoag and Damon are the only two Yankees to ever go 6–6 in a nine-inning game for the Yanks. Hoag had six singles and one RBI, and Johnny had a double, a steal, and four RBI. No Yankee ever got more than six hits in a game of any length.

This was a helluva game to keep score.

LACKEY AND RYAN LOSE NO-NO IN 9TH

ANGELS 6 BOSTON 2 | FENWAY PARK, BOSTON, MA
TIME: 2:28 • JULY 29, 2008

BOB RYAN

Was this going to be my long-awaited no-no?

John Lackey was cruising, holding the Red Sox hitless through 8.1 innings at Fenway. But Dustin Pedroia grounded pitch number 103 through the shortstop/third base hole. Adios, no-hitter. And Kevin Youkilis put pitch number 105 over the left-field wall. Adios, shutout. It took Lackey 15 more pitches to salvage his complete game.

The ever-laconic Lackey took it in stride. "I just wanted to win the game," he said. "The no-hitter would have been nice, whatever, but we're about winning games."

BILL CHUCK

John Lackey made one start in which he allowed no hits. Lackey was pitching for the Angels on May 16, 2009, it was his first appearance of the season, following a stint on the Disabled List. In the 1st inning, he was facing Ian Kinsler, who had hit a pair of homers for the Rangers the night before.

Lackey's first pitch sailed behind Kinsler's head. Lackey's next pitch got Kinsler right in the ribs. Kinsler headed to first base, and home plate umpire Bob Davidson headed straight to the mound and ejected Lackey. Lackey was shocked and, needless to say, far from laconic.

So, Lackey had one start, two pitches, one hit batter, no hits, oh and reliever Shane Loux allowed Kinsler to score, and so one run was charged to Lackey, who left with an ERA of infinity.

On July 22, 2010, the Red Sox beat the Mariners, 8–6, in 13 innings. What does this have to do with John Lackey and no-hit bids? Well… Lackey was now pitching for Boston, and despite allowing a 2nd inning run on a walk, a steal, an infield grounder, and a passed ball, Lackey on that day did not allow the Mariners a hit through 7.2, when he permitted back-to-back singles. Meanwhile, the Boston bullpen allowed five runs in the bottom of the 9th, and Lackey missed a win.

In 2015, now pitching for St. Louis, Lackey took a no-hit bid into the 6th in the opening game of the NLDS against Jon Lester and the Cubs, his former "JL" teammate with Boston. Lackey won that matchup, allowing just two hits in 7.1 IP of shutout ball.

Here's an interesting litmus test: It's July 29 of any season, you go to the ballpark, which would you rather see: your team win or your team get no-hit? I say, the greater your love for baseball, the greater your desire to see the no-hitter. It's a great in-between innings discussion.

B2B HBP

CLEVELAND 5 BOSTON 4 | FENWAY PARK, BOSTON, MA
TIME: 3:09 • SEPTEMBER 22, 2008

BOB RYAN

Josh Beckett hit Ryan Garko and Kelly Shoppach back-to-back in the 2nd. Beckett hits Ben Francisco in the 5th. No message, just bad aim.

Now, the weird one: Sox 6th. Jason Bay on second. Jason Varitek on first. Jeff Bailey rifles one down the third-base line for a sure double. What third-base coach DeMarlo Hale doesn't know is that the ball has struck third-base ump Gerry Davis, causing an unusual carom. Before all the craziness has subsided, Bay is out at the plate (in a rundown), and Varitek is out at third. That means 5-2-5 in my scorebook. Hale was very apologetic, not that it was anyone's fault. "I think everyone knows how I felt about it," he said. "I would have preferred it not happen, but occasionally it does."

The loss meant the Red Sox must wait at least one more day to clinch a wild card spot.

BILL CHUCK

This was the first time Beckett ever hit three batters in a game. I believe Bob when he says there was no intent. The only other time he did it came on June 9, 2011, against the Yankees. I would be less sure about his lack of aim in that one.

2008 ALCS GAME 5

RAYS LEAD RED SOX IN ALCS 3–2
BOSTON 8 TAMPA BAY 7 | FENWAY PARK, BOSTON, MA
TIME: 4:08 • OCTOBER 16, 2008

BOB RYAN

They were not just nine outs away from losing this game; they were nine outs away from going home for the winter. The Red Sox were down, 7–0, going to the bottom of the 7th, and no team had erased a comparable postseason gap since the 1929 A's scored 10 in the 7th to erase an 8–0 deficit to the Cubs.

Scott Kazmir was cruising (6.0 IP, two hits, seven K) until he was pulled after 111 pitches. Enter the Rays bullpen, stage right.

- Big Papi's three-run shot highlighted a four-run 7th.
- Coco Crisp culminated a 10-pitch at-bat with a game-tying single in the three-run 8th.

- With two away and bases empty in the 9th, Kevin Youkilis battled Jay Howell through nine pitches before reaching on an infield single to third, to which Evan Longoria affixed a throwing error. Jason Bay was walked intentionally.
- J.D. Drew, who had hit a two-run homer in the 8th, came up. He hit one to right. Let's just say it looked somewhat catchable for Gabe Gross. Okay, here's my *Boston Globe* account: "Gabe Gross appeared to be paralyzed by a screamer hit directly over his head."

Anyway, comeback complete, game over, series extended. Euphoria reigned in Fenway. And then it was off to Florida for what was left of the series.

"I've never seen a group so happy to get on a plane at 1:30 in the morning," said skipper Terry Francona.

BILL CHUCK

The phrase "on the brink" loomed large for both teams. The Red Sox were on the brink of elimination, and the Rays were on the verge of going to their first World Series. But Terry Francona teams don't easily fall into the brink. In 2004, they were on the brink of elimination four straight games in the ALCS against the Yankees and won each time. In 2007, like here in 2008, the Sox were down 3–1 in the ALCS facing elimination to Cleveland, and they won three in a row. Including this win, the Red Sox had won eight straight ALCS elimination games.

Daisuke Matsuzaka had won Game 7 in the 2007 ALCS and was on the mound to save the Sox season on this night. Dice-K was coming off an 18–3 season in which he kept getting out of jams, many of which were of his doing as he led the league with 94 walks (batters were 0–14 against him with the bases loaded that season). In this game, he didn't have the time to walk batters. After the first nine pitches of the game, Tampa Bay was up 2–0 thanks to a Melvin Upton Jr. homer (he would hit four in the ALCS). At the time, he was known as B.J. Upton, and he went 3–4 with four ribbies in this game. In the top of the 3rd, Carlos Pena (who attended Boston's Northeastern University) and Evan

Longoria (his fourth straight game with a homer) went back-to-back to make it 4–0.

The Rays bullpen that imploded in this game during the regular season had led the league in holds and was second in saves and had allowed the smallest percentage of inherited runners to score, but being on the brink can do strange things.

But perhaps it was Joe Maddon's brink decisions that cost the Rays. First, he brought in his closer, Dan Wheeler, in the 7th, and while Wheeler did the job with the one batter he faced that inning, he blew the save in the 8th. That brought in the lefty J.P. Howell in the 9th. With two down, Kevin Youkilis had singled and advanced to second on an Evan Longoria error. Howell could have faced Jason Bay, who had hit .252 against lefties in 2008, and had faced Howell twice that season, striking out in the regular season and striking out in the postseason. But Maddon intentionally walked him to face Drew, who had hit .284 against lefties and was 2–5 against Howell in the 2008 regular and postseason (and 4–7 overall) and who had homered the inning before. And then J.D., who had totaled a mere five 9th inning hits during the regular season, without a walk-off, mind you, hit that screeching liner over Gabe Gross' head for the game winner.

While the Rays had eliminated the "Devil" from their name, when you are on the brink, a good scorecard shows how the devil is in the details.

2008 ALCS GAME 7

TAMPA BAY WINS THE ALCS 4–3
TAMPA BAY 3 BOSTON 1 | TROPICANA FIELD, TAMPA BAY, FL
TIME: 3:31 • OCTOBER 19, 2008

BOB RYAN

Man, were those Joe Maddon managerial wheels turning in the 8th. In baseball postseasons, you gotta do what you gotta do, and if it means five pitchers to get your needed three outs in a Game 7, so be it.

Matt Garza was dealing through seven (two hits, one a solo Dustin Pedroia homer in the 1st inning). But when pinch-hitter Jed Lowrie reached base on an error to start the 8th, Maddon brought in Dan Wheeler. He would be followed by Jay Howell, Chad Bradford, and, finally, rookie southpaw David Price, not long out of Vanderbilt, whose 1–2, 97 mph heater froze J.D. Drew for the final out of the inning. Price survived a leadoff walk to Jason Bay in the 9th, earning his save.

Price was the eighth former number one draft pick employed in this game by Maddon (four were drafted by the Rays). It had been an eventful season for the southpaw. He had started the season in Vero Beach and had made his major league debut a month earlier. (If you can't name the other number one picks, Bill will fill you in)

Tampa Bay Special Adviser Don Zimmer had thrown out the first pitch. Supply your own punch line.

BILL CHUCK

A very brief review here is necessary. The Rays had been up 3–1 in this best-of-seven and had never reached the World Series. The Red Sox seemed to thrive when down 3–1 in a series and were the defending world champs. Sox manager Tito Francona in potential elimination games at this point was 9–1, only losing in the 2005 ALDS to the Pale Hose (he finished with Boston at 9–3). Joe Maddon, on the other hand, was experiencing his first Game 7, his first elimination game as manager (he was Mike Scioscia's bench coach when they won Game 7 of the 2002 World Series).

The Rays had gone from worst-to-first in 2008, compiling a 66–96 record in 2007, good for fifth in the AL East, and a 97–65 record in 2008, finishing first in the AL East. The Rays had never finished above .500 before this season. The only team to have gone from worst to the Series like the Rays had been the 1991 Braves.

Tampa's number ones

1. Boston starter Jon Lester had gone 16–6 for the Sox during the regular season, and **Matt Garza** was in his first season with the Rays, after being a number one pick for the Twins in 2005. He was the ALCS MVP.

2. **Melvin Upton Jr.** (or B.J. Upton as he was known at the time) was Tampa's first-round pick in 2002, and while he went 0–4 in this game, he led both teams with 11 RBI in the ALCS, hitting four homers.

3. **Carlos Pena**, who was the Texas first-round pick in 1998 out of Boston's Northeastern University, was 0–4 in this game, but he hit three homers in the ALCS.

4. Rookie **Evan Longoria**, who was the Rays first-round draft pick in the 2006 draft, doubled in the 4th inning off Lester to drive home the tying run. He hit four homers in this ALCS.

5. The Rays went ahead for good in the 5th inning when **Rocco Baldelli**, the Rays first-round draft pick in the 2000 draft, from Woonsocket, Rhode Island, singled home Willy Aybar. Aybar completed the scoring with a 7th inning leadoff homer off Lester. Baldelli, who battled illness and injuries, played in 2009 for his hometown Red Sox before finishing with 10 games back with the Rays in 2010.

6. **Gabe Gross**, who was acquired in an April 2008 deal with the Milwaukee Brewers, was a first-round pick in 2001 by the Toronto Blue Jays. He was a defensive replacement for Baldelli in the 8th.

7. Amongst the Rays pitchers in the 8th, **J.P. Howell** had been the Royals' first-round draft pick in the 2004 draft.

8. As Bob pointed out, **David Price** (2007 number 1 draft pick for the Rays) did earn the save in this contest. He had pitched in five regular season games, and this was his third of the postseason. Until the 2021 season, it was the only save in Price's regular season or postseason career. Price faced five batters, walking one and whiffing three.

Mike Bianchi, the lead columnist for the *Orlando Sentinel*, wrote the next day about his feeling of amazement with the Rays victory, "I'm World Serious. Let me say it again just so I can believe it myself. The Tampa Bay Rays are going to the World Series. *The World Freaking Series, Nurse Ratched*." His italics, not mine.

But that wasn't even my favorite part of the column. After describing the world crashing down around Joe Maddon and company in Games 5 and 6, Bianchi wrote this: "Even the Boston writers were getting uppity. Wrote Bob Ryan, the venerable columnist of the *Boston Globe*, after the Red Sox pulled off the miracle rally in Game 5, 'The Red Sox are the defending champions. They always come to play nine innings, and if it takes the greatest postseason comeback in 79 years to stay alive, then they will give you the greatest postseason comeback in 79 years. Got that, Rays?'"

Bianchi ended his column quite succinctly, "From worst to World Series. Rays of hope reign supreme. Got that, Red Sox?"

UP BY THE BAY

BOSTON 5 TORONTO 1| FENWAY PARK, BOSTON, MA
TIME: 2:55 • MAY 21, 2009

BOB RYAN

The Red Sox have boasted of many a slugger, beginning with turn-of-the-century bopper Buck Freeman. But if someone asked you, "Which Red Sox player holds the franchise record with 11 consecutive homers with at least one man on?" The chances are remote anyone would say: "Jason Bay."

But it's true. Bay hit a fly toward the Red Sox bullpen with Kevin Youkilis on base in the 1st, and it looked as if right fielder Alex Rios had a chance to get it. Well, he didn't, and Bay had just hit his 11th straight non-solo homer. "I thought he had caught it," Bay admitted. "It was kind of the reaction of the crowd that let me know he didn't."

A record post-WWII Fenway crowd of 38,347 also saw Jacoby Ellsbury extend a hitting streak to 16 games with a 1st inning leadoff double.

BILL CHUCK

In 2001, Barry Bonds (sigh) set the record for the most home runs hit during the Steroid Era with 73. That season, he also set the record for most solo home runs in a season with 46. On this unique list, Mark McGwire (sigh) in 1997 and Sammy Sosa (sigh) in 1998 are next with 37 solo shots. Sosa had two seasons with 36 solos, and Giancarlo Stanton had one. I'm really sorry that I researched this.

The record for homers in a season with men on base is held by McGwire in 1998 with 37, Alex Rodriguez in 2007 with 36, and then Babe Ruth in 1921 with 33. Thank you, George Herman.

Jason Bay, my second favorite Bay after the Bay of Fundy (not to be confused with Dee Fondy), had 1,200 hits in his 11-year career, including 222 homers. Of those 222 homers, he hit 97 homers with runners on, including five grand slams and 125 solo homers, including his solo walk-off. In the 2009 season, he had his career high of 21, including the 11 in a row.

Of the 11 in a row, four were three-run shots, and seven were two-run blasts. I do not have the Statcast numbers, nor do I care that this was before the measurement era. I can share this with you: from April 17 to May 21, 2009, Bay played 32 games and went 33–114, hitting .289, with 11 homers and 37 RBI. He walked 22 times and struck out 31 times. It wasn't a remarkable stretch, but a very successful stretch. Let's just say, fortuitous stretch in which he hit .299 with runners on base and hit 11 home runs that were 26 Boston runs.

Perhaps the best stat that you can pull from this fluky stretch is that his team won in 10 of the games that he homered, and that includes the two-run homer he hit off Mariano Rivera with two outs in the bottom of the 9th on April 24, 2009, in a game that Boston won in 11 on a Kevin Youkilis walk-off blast.

TURNABOUT IS FAIR PLAY

BOSTON 6 ATLANTA 5 | FENWAY PARK, BOSTON, MA
TIME: 2:47 • JUNE 21, 2009

BOB RYAN

Nick Green carved out an eight-year major league career while working for eight teams. He was not a stiff, but he surely was not a star. However, the utility man was on something of a roll entering this game with a .355 average that included two doubles and two homers in his last 10 games. Still, few would have pegged him to settle a game on this overcast, damp afternoon with a walk-off homer off Atlanta's Jeff Bennett. But you never know.

It was hardly a wallop. It was a classic right-field Fenway-only special curling just inside the Pesky Pole at the 302-foot mark. I wrote that "It was 305 feet. 306 max." He himself wasn't sure what he had. "I thought it was going to be an out because the wind (18 mph from the northeast) was so bad," he confessed. "Fortunately, it was blowing to the right. Blew it right where it needed to go."

Now here's the best part: This was his second career walk-off homer. The first? Why, that took place on July 2, 2004. He was playing for the Atlanta Braves, and the opponents were the Boston Red Sox. What can I tell you? You'd can't make this shit up.

BILL CHUCK

C'mon, what are the odds of Nick Green hitting two career walk-off homers, to begin with? The guy hit only 17 homers in his career. And he did it off 17 different pitchers.

He played for a lot of teams, though. Nick played for the Devil Rays, the Marlins, the Braves, the Dodgers, the Yankees, the Mariners, and the Blue Jays. He also signed a minor league deal with the Padres and the Orioles. He was traded to the Rangers but only played in the minors for them too. Nick only played 417 games, but he was fair when it came to that as well: he played 209 at home (wherever he laid his hat was his home) and 208 on the road. He had 127 hits at home and 127 hits on the road (a true Stan Musial wannabe).

He played a lot of positions too. Nick played second, shortstop, third base, first base, left field, right field, DH, PH, PR, and he pitched a game (Bob was there for that too).

Nick had 10 three-hit games in his career, and you'll probably enjoy that on April 24, 2005, playing for Tampa, he had three hits against Boston, and on May 2, 2009, playing for Boston, he had three hits against Tampa. You'll also like that Nick was 5–17 (.417) in Pittsburgh's PNC Park and 5–17 (.417) in Kansas City's Kauffman Stadium.

I don't know him, but I like to think of him as accommodating. Look at his uniform numbers: He wore number 3 with the Marlins. He wore number 17 with the Yankees. He wore number 18 with the Devil Rays. He wore number 20 with the Braves. He wore number 21 with the Dodgers and Blue Jays. He wore number 22 with the Mariners, Red Sox, and Marlins.

So, here's to Nick Green, Mr. Turnabout is Fair Play.

2009 NLDS GAME 1

LOS ANGELES 5 ST. LOUIS 3 | DODGER STADIUM, LOS ANGELES, CA
TIME: 3:54 • OCTOBER 7, 2009

BOB RYAN

Actually, not a whole lot to chew on in this game. That is unless you are a big fan of LOB, of which there were 30. The losing Cards left a man on in every inning but the 6th. The winning Dodgers out-did them, leaving someone stranded on every such opportunity. So, I guess this *is* somewhat historical.

You might also savor this scorecard if you had it in for Chris Carpenter. The Cards' righty had gone 17–4 with a league-leading 2.24 ERA and had been 10–1 following the All-Star Game. His dismal 105-pitch, five-inning stint included nine hits, four earned runs, four walks, and a hit batsman. Well, you can't win 'em all.

Listed attendance: 56,000 even. Really?

BILL CHUCK

The Dodgers did something in this game they never did in the regular season... they beat Chris Carpenter. From 2004 to 2011, in 10 starts, Carpenter went 6–0 against the Dodgers with a 1.52 ERA. In those 10 games, Carpenter totaled nine walks. In the five innings he pitched in this game (the only time he ever faced L.A. in the postseason), he walked four and hit a batter.

Randy Wolf was no bargain for the Dodgers. He threw 3.2 IP and held St. Louis to two runs despite allowing six hits and five walks which sounds, to quote Wallace Shawn in The *Princess Bride*, "Inconceivable!"

Jeff Weaver was awarded the win by the official scorer presumably because he came in the game in the top of the 4th, with the bases loaded, and got Ryan Ludwick on a grounder to the mound. I would have awarded it to Ronald Belisario because, in the top of the 6th, he retired the Cardinals one-two-three, the only pitcher in the game to have a three-up/three-down inning.

Not only were a postseason-record 30 players left on base (16 by the Dodgers and 14 by the Cardinals), but the teams were 5–28 with runners in scoring position (2–15 by the Dodgers and 3–13 by the Cardinals). This begs the question: Were the pitchers good, or were the pitchers bad? I'll let you decide.

The only thing I know for sure is the next day, a 21-year-old pitcher was given his first postseason start by manager Joe Torre. His name was Clayton Kershaw.

BILL CHUCK ON THE 2000s

Champions

2000	New York Yankees (AL)	New York Mets (NL)	4–1
2001	Arizona Diamondbacks (NL)	New York Yankees (AL)	4–3
2002	Anaheim Angels (AL)	San Francisco Giants (NL)	4–3
2003	Florida Marlins (NL)	New York Yankees (AL)	4–2
2004	Boston Red Sox (AL)	St. Louis Cardinals (NL)	4–0
2005	Chicago White Sox (AL)	Houston Astros (NL)	4–0
2006	St. Louis Cardinals (NL)	Detroit Tigers (AL)	4–1
2007	Boston Red Sox (AL)	Colorado Rockies (NL)	4–0
2008	Philadelphia Phillies (NL)	Tampa Bay Rays (AL)	4–1
2009	New York Yankees (AL)	Philadelphia Phillies (NL)	4–2

Batting leaders of the 2000s

- Alex Rodriguez led with 435 home runs, followed by Jim Thome (368) and Albert Pujols (366).
- Alex Rodriguez led with 1,243 RBI, followed by Albert Pujols (1,112) and Manny Ramirez (1,106).
- Ichiro Suzuki led with 2,030 hits, followed by Derek Jeter (1,940) and Miguel Tejada (1,860).
- Adam Dunn led with 1,433 strikeouts (by a batter), followed by Jim Thome (1,431) and Mike Cameron (1,429).
- Juan Pierre led with 459 stolen bases, followed by Carl Crawford (362) and Ichiro Suzuki (341).

Pitching leaders of the 2000s

- Randy Johnson led with 2,182 strikeouts (by a pitcher), followed by Javier Vazquez (2,001) and Johan Santana (1,733).

- Andy Pettitte led with 148 wins, followed by Randy Johnson (143) and Jaime Moyer (140).
- Livan Hernandez led with 124 losses, followed by Javier Vazquez (116) and Jeff Suppan (110).
- Mariano Rivera led with 397 saves, followed by Trevor Hoffman (363) and Jason Isringhausen (284).
- Roy Halladay led with 47 complete games, followed by Livan Hernandez (36) and Randy Johnson (32).
- Roy Halladay led with 14 shutouts, followed by Randy Johnson (12) and Tim Hudson and CC Sabathia (11).

chapter 5

THE
2010s

BOB RYAN

After the Red Sox re-wrote their history in the Aughts, ending an 86-year championship drought in 2004 and then adding another World Series triumph in 2007, they added two more in this decade, in 2013 and 2018. I formally retired from full-time duty at the *Boston Globe* in August of 2012, but I have continued my practice of scoring every game I attend, no matter where. Failing to keep score at a baseball game will always be an unthinkable thought.

10 AND 5

BOSTON 14 SAN DIEGO 5 | FENWAY PARK, BOSTON, MA
TIME: 3:40 • JUNE 20, 2011

BOB RYAN

I'm willing to bet there has never been an inning exactly like the Red Sox 7th. They scored 10 runs on five hits. They had two runs forced home by a hit batsman and one more forced home by a walk. But none of it might have happened had Dustin Pedroia not hustled to beat out a double-play possibility as the second batter of the inning

This was Andrew Miller's Red Sox debut. The Tigers and Marlins discard unveiled a new changeup during his 5.2 innings of work.

It was also the return to Boston of Padres' first-base coach Dave Roberts, who received what the *Globe*'s Michael Vega termed a "hearty ovation."

Said Terry Francona, "If it wasn't for Dave, you'd be talking to somebody else."

BILL CHUCK

May I just take a moment to dip into the history books to bring up Sammy White and Gene Stephens (and very briefly mention Johnny Damon)?

There is a generation of Bostonians who only know the name "Sammy White" in association with his small group (not even a chain) of bowling alleys, which he opened and operated in the vicinity of Fenway Park. Most of the kids who went to birthday parties at the alleys had no idea that Sammy had been a catcher in the majors for 11 seasons, nine with the Red Sox. A lifetime .262 hitter, Sammy did make the All-Star team once, but for the most part he was the kind of player that second-division teams put on the field each day, and in the 1950s, the Sox fit that description.

Also fitting that description is Gene Stephens, a Red Sox outfielder for most of the 1950s before finishing his career with the Orioles, Athletics (of Kansas City), and White Sox (and Chunichi in Japan). He was a lifetime .240 hitter.

I bring Sammy and Gene up here because, on June 18, 1953, they had an inning to remember. The Tigers were facing Boston at Fenway, and the Sox were leading 5–3 entering the 7th inning. When the top of the 8th rolled around, the Tigers were trailing 22–3. The Sox had scored 17 times on 14 hits and left the sacks loaded.

Sammy led off that inning with a single. Gene followed with another single that sent Sammy to third. Stephens then stole second. Tom Umphlett singled them both home. Sammy came up again that inning now with the Sox leading 12–3 and drew a walk. Stephens doubled, driving home two, which included White. The score was 19–3 when White came up again and singled once again, driving home a run to make it 20–3. Stephens again singled to make it 21–3. Umphlett singled (again) to make it 22–3 as White came around to score.

If you are keeping track, White tied the MLB record, scoring three times in an inning, and Stephens set the modern MLB record with three hits in an inning. FYI: Umphlett had two hits and a walk in the inning.

The brief mention of Johnny Damon

On June 27, 2003, the Sox defeated the Marlins, 25–8, and scored 14 times in the 1st inning. Damon fell a homer shy of the cycle *in the 1*st *inning* as he tied Stephens' record.

In Bob's bizarre inning, Jacoby Ellsbury walked and singled, Adrian Gonzalez doubled and singled and had three RBI. Jason Varitek (he had three career HBP with the bases filled) was hit in back-to-back PA with the sacks full, and each got a bruise and an RBI, and Dustin Pedroia drew a bases-loaded walk (he had 10 of those in his career).

Dave Roberts

The last time these two teams met at Fenway Park, the Sox were still cursed, as they played their games of June 8–10, 2004. Dave Roberts was still playing for the Dodgers. After retiring as a player, Roberts worked in the Padres front office, and 2011 was his first season back in uniform coaching for the Padres. Roberts' relationship with the Padres began in December, following his heroics with the 2004 Sox when he was traded by Boston and played with them for two seasons before signing with San Francisco. Bob was at the game at Fenway when he returned with the Giants (see June 15, 2007).

ELLSBURY WALK-OFF

BOSTON 4 CLEVELAND 3 | FENWAY PARK, BOSTON, MA
TIME: 3:01 • AUGUST 3, 2011

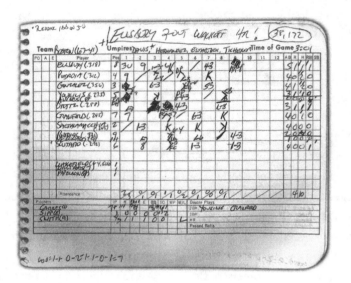

BOB RYAN

Jacoby Ellsbury hadn't done much. He came to the plate in the 9th with two away in a 3–3 game as an 0-for-4 man with only one ball out of the infield. But now you could make it two, as his long fly ball landed in the center-field bleachers for a walk-off home run.

Tim Wakefield was in pursuit of his 200th career win, but he had to settle for a no-decision. He did pitch into the 7th and succeeded in placing three of the four Ks suffered by Carlos Santana in his golden sombrero night.

And do let the record show that Jason Kipnis' solo homer was his third in three games at Fenway.

BILL CHUCK

Jacoby Ellsbury hit 104 homers in his career (which appears to be over at the time of this writing following the 2021 season). On the subject of writing, Jacoby should write a thank you note to Bob acknowledging Mr. Ryan's presence at the occasion of the only walk-off homer in Mr. Ellsbury's career.

As for milestones, this was the second of eight Tim Wakefield starts in his effort to pick up win number 200. Wake finally got it on September 13 and then ended his career with two starts and two losses to finish 200–180. In Tim's 627 career games, which included 463 starts, he had a 2.55 ERA in his 200 wins, a 7.10 ERA in his 180 losses, and a 4.46 ERA in his 225 no-decisions.

As for milestones, to date, this was the first of two golden sombreros earned by Carlos Santana. The second one came on July 15, 2016, against the Twins. At least in the latter, he went 1–5. Santana is adept at drawing walks and has had four games with four walks.

And if you are curious, Jason Kipnis' streak of a homer a game at Fenway ended at three. Since Kipnis came into the majors in 2011, only Sal Perez of the Royals had a longer streak. In four games at Fenway, from August 22, 2015, to July 28, 2017, Perez hit five homers.

WHAT DIDN'T HAPPEN?

BOSTON 7 HOUSTON 3 | FENWAY PARK, BOSTON, MA
TIME: 3:49 • APRIL 26, 2013

BOB RYAN

The crowd of 29,312 got their money's worth. They saw the first four Red Sox hits constitute a cycle. They saw the forgotten Pedro Ciriaco hit a triple. They saw the first-ever All-Canadian starting pitching matchup. They saw David Ross hit two homers and go 4-for-4 to raise his batting average 121 points. They saw the Astros' 4-5-6 men need 11 plate appearances before one of them put the ball in play. As a bonus, they got to see the Astros cleanup man Brandon Laird go for the golden sombrero. It took a lengthy 3:49, but it was worth it.

The Canadian pitching matchup was Boston's right-hander Ryan Dempster vs. Baltimore's southpaw Erik Bedard. Dempster prevailed with six solid innings.

David Ortiz entered the game with an OPS of 1.421, and he padded it with a homer. He also dispensed a pregame batting tip to Ross.

"He said, 'See the ball. Hit the ball. Don't make it too complicated,'" explained the backup catcher. Two homers, two singles, and three runs scored later, Ross had soared from .120 to .241. Big Papi knows.

BILL CHUCK

Oh, my

As Dick Enberg was fond of saying. Just so that you can appreciate how perceptive Bob Ryan is, let me elaborate on the cycle:

- Bottom of the 1st—leadoff single by Jacoby Ellsbury
- Bottom of the 1st—one-out double by Dustin Pedroia
- Bottom of the 2nd—two-out homer by David Ross
- Bottom of the 2nd—two-out triple by Pedro Ciriaco

Who even notices things like that?

Oh, brother

Brandon Laird is Gerald Laird's brother. Brandon played 53 MLB games; his better-known brother played 799 games. This was the only golden sombrero for either brother.

Oh, Canada

- Ryan Dempster was born in Sechelt, British Columbia.
- Erik Bedard was born in Navan, Ontario.
- Reggie Cleveland, who Bob and I love to write about, was the first Canadian pitcher to start a World Series game. The native of Swift River, Saskatchewan, started Game 5 of the 1975 World Series on October 16, 1975, for the Red Sox against the Reds.

Oh, David

This was the only four-hit game of David Ross's career, and he can thank David O.

Oh, one more thing...

Pedro Ciriaco defines a utility player. In 2012 and 2013, Ciriaco played 77 games in the field for Boston:

- One game at first base
- 19 games at second base
- 45 games at third base
- 20 games at shortstop
- Two games in left field
- Three games in center field
- Two games in right field
- 15 games as a DH
- He was also a pinch-hitter five times and a pinch-runner seven times

20 HITS-NO HR

BOSTON 11 COLORADO 4 | FENWAY PARK, BOSTON, MA
TIME: 3:40 • JUNE 25, 2013

BOB RYAN

They all had their hitting shoes on, but you'd think that among 20 hits in Fenway Park, at least one would hit the ball where no one could catch it. But that wasn't the case here, as all nine starters had at least one hit, but no one hit a home run. They *almost* had one, but J.D. Drew's blast to the TV cameras in dead center was downgraded to a triple upon video review.

They truly abused Rockies' starter Juan Nicasio, who faced 21 men and only retired seven.

Seven Red Sox batters had a multiple-hit game, led by shortstop Jose Iglesias. Not many number nine hitters enter a game hitting .426 before putting up a 5–2–3–1 line.

The one shining moment for Colorado came when Wilin Rosario got all of a Dempster offering in the second. "I didn't see it," joked Dempster. "I think it hit a car on the (Mass) Turnpike."

BILL CHUCK

- Since 1901, the Red Sox have had 29 games in which they had 20-plus hits and zero homers.
- Since 1901, the Red Sox have had 15 home games in which they had 20-plus hits and zero homers.
- Since 1912, the Red Sox have had 12 home games at Fenway Park in which they had 20-plus hits and zero homers.
- Since 1920, the end of the dead-ball era, the Red Sox have had 10 home games at Fenway Park in which they had 20-plus hits and zero homers.
- Since 1947, the start of the integration era, the Red Sox have had five home games at Fenway Park in which they had 20-plus hits and zero homers.
- Since 1961, the start of the expansion era, the Red Sox have had four home games at Fenway Park in which they had 20-plus hits and zero homers.
- Since 1969, the start of the divisional era, the Red Sox have had four home games at Fenway Park in which they had 20-plus hits and zero homers.
- Since 1995, the start of the wild card era, the Red Sox have played one game anywhere in which they had 20-plus hits and zero homers… and this was it.
- This was the most recent one by the Sox and the most recent allowed by the Rockies, who have permitted four such games in their history.

And…

Jose Iglesias finished the game hitting .434.

Juan Nicasio allowed 12 hits in 2.1 IP, the most hits he allowed in a game in his career.

GOMES WALK-OFF

BOSTON 2 SAN DIEGO 1 | FENWAY PARK, BOSTON, MA
TIME: 3:05 • JULY 3, 2013

BOB RYAN

Few things make a manager look smarter than a pinch-hitter delivering the goods. Skipper John Farrell sent Jonny Gomes up to hit for Brandon Snyder to lead off the 9th inning of a 1–1 game, and soon everyone in the Red Sox dugout was pounding backs and high fiving. Gomes had hit a Luke Gregerson pitch over the left-field wall (barely), and that was that.

Oh, it was a real wallop, all right. But that wall *is* 37-feet tall, and the fact is The Wall taketh much more often than it giveth. "I knew I hit it far enough, but that green wall can be tricky sometimes," said Gomes. "I just hoped I had enough air under it to get out."

Jon Lester followed a 32-pitch 1st inning with a five-pitch 2nd as he went seven strong innings to get the win.

BILL CHUCK

Jonny Gomes hit four walk-off homers in his career and 10 pinch-hit homers in his career, including four in the 2013 season alone. The Sox in 2013 had 11 walk-off wins.

This was the only pinch-walk-off homer Jonny Gomes hit in his career.

This was the only pinch-walk-off homer Luke Gregerson allowed in his career.

This is how a team wins a world championship.

JOHN HENRY NIGHT

BOSTON 13 BALTIMORE 2 | FENWAY PARK, BOSTON, MA
TIME: 2:59 • AUGUST 27, 2013

BOB RYAN

My wife and I enjoyed this game from an unusual vantage point. We were the guests of Red Sox owner John Henry in his upstairs box.

And he couldn't have been in a better mood after watching his club pound five Orioles pitchers for 14 hits and three home runs. The Big Bopper was Shane Victorino, who submitted a startling 3–4–3–7 line that included two homers, a double, a walk, and a hit-by-pitch.

It was Victorino's second career two-homer game and they happened to be career homers number 100 and 101. Unfortunately, the Hawaiian was a in a party pooper mood. "Tonight, I was the hero and had a good game," he shrugged, "but tomorrow, who knows?"

BILL CHUCK

Shane Victorino was born in Wailuku, Hawaii, and as a result was blessed with the great nickname "The Flyin' Hawaiian" and even appeared in a 2012 episode of *Hawaii Five-0*. In Shane's 1,299 games in the bigs, this was his only game with over five RBI.

The Sox 1-2-3 hitters went 9–13 and the 9-1-2-3 hitters went 11–17, which is some sweet hitting.

Finally, in answer to Victorino's question, he went 1–4 in his next game.

Mr. Henry

I need to speak about John Henry for a moment. Clearly, if Mr. Henry was kind enough to invite Bob and Elaine to his box for a game, he must be a nice man. He also seemed very nice when my wife and I met him, despite my making a fool of myself. Yes, I will explain.

Max and I were walking on Beacon Street in Boston when I saw Mr. Henry approaching us. Now, it's important to point out that I'm never good with names. And while I have met many important people, sometimes I get a little nervous. In this case, I choked because as I introduced Max to Mr. Henry, I blurted out, "And this is Tom Werner, owner of the Red Sox." He was very kind as he corrected me, but I never got an invite to his box.

2013 ALCS GAME 1

TIGERS LEAD RED SOX 1–0 IN ALCS
DETROIT 1 BOSTON 0 | FENWAY PARK, BOSTON, MA
TIME: 3:56 • OCTOBER 12, 2013

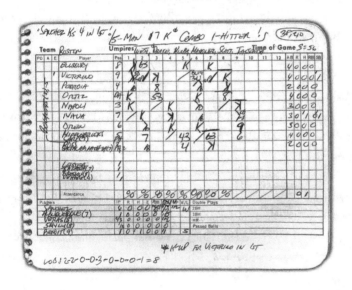

BOB RYAN

Now *here's* a one-off, as the Brits say, at least in my experience. One-hitter? Sure, I've seen those. But a playoff five-pitcher one-hitter? Ah, no. That's something new.

Five Detroit pitchers combined on a 17K one-hitter. As an added bonus, one-time Red Sox property Anibal Sanchez struck out four men in the 1st inning, his swinging third strike to Shane Victorino eluding catcher Alex Avila.

The no-hit drama went right into the 9th, when Daniel Nava spoiled the no-no with a one-out single to center off closer Joaquin Benoit. It had been a true pitchers' duel, the only run off Sox starter Jon Lester coming on a bloop RBI single by Jhonny Peralta in the 6th.

Boston's batters bitched and moaned about the ball-and-strike judgments of plate ump Joe West all night. But skipper John Farrell took the high road. "There might have been a couple of pitches that were pitcher's pitches that went against us," he pointed out. "But to say the umpiring was the reason why we didn't get a hit until the 9th inning, that would be a little shortsighted on my part."

Tigers' manager Jim Leyland was sanguine about the near no-no. "I wasn't really worried about a no-hitter," he said. "It would have been nice. But it worked out for us."

BILL CHUCK

Anibal Sanchez tossed six no-hit innings, striking out 12 and walking six. He threw 116 pitches. Earlier in the season, Sanchez threw a complete-game one-hitter shutting out the Twins on 130 pitches, also striking out 12 but walking just three.

There have only been four postseason games in which a pitcher left with 6.0-plus innings of no-hit ball, most famously Don Larsen's perfect game in the 1956 World Series. Roy Halladay threw a no-hitter in the 2010 NLDS. And then the only other performance that preceded this was in the 1999 ALDS, when Pedro Martinez threw six no-hit innings or the Red Sox *in relief*.

The Tigers pitchers struck out 17 batters, an LCS record for a nine-inning game that is still intact. In 2020, the Rays struck out 18 Yankees in the ALDS.

There is but one other pitcher who recorded at least six walks and 12 strikeouts in a postseason game: Walter Johnson. In the opener of the 1924 World Series, Johnson threw, and lost, a 12-inning complete game to the New York Giants, 4–3, in which he too walked six and whiffed 12. While Sanchez allowed no hits, Johnson permitted 14, but we know that is not the only difference between Sanchez and The Big Train.

One of my favorite baseball names is Orval Overall, who pitched in the early 20th century for the Cubs and the Reds. Orval was better in the postseason than in the regular season. In four Series, he compiled a 3–1 record with a 1.58 ERA in 51.1 IP. Overall won back-to-back championships with the Cubs in 1907 and 1908, defeating the Tigers in each case. In the clinching Game 5 in 1908, Orval struck out 10, including Charley O'Leary, Ty Cobb, Claude Rossman, and Germany Schaefer in the 1st, the only other hurler besides Anibal Sanchez to whiff four in an inning in the postseason.

2013 ALCS GAME 2

ALCS TIED 1–1
BOSTON 6 DETROIT 5 | FENWAY PARK, BOSTON, MA
TIME: 3:28 • OCTOBER 13, 2013

BOB RYAN

Dave Roberts threw out the first pitch. So how were the Red Sox going to lose? By getting down 5–1 entering the 8th, that's how.

Max Scherzer had held them to two hits and one run through seven. Manager Jim Leyland thought 108 pitches was enough, and so the fun started, until Joaquin Benoit, his fourth pitcher of the inning, was facing Big Papi with the bases loaded and two out. He started off with a changeup. Bad idea. Papi put on a good swing. The ball landed in the Red Sox bullpen for a game-tying grand slam.

Globe photographer Stan Grossfeld was able to capture the moment with a shot that caught Tigers' right fielder Torii Hunter tumbling into the pen headfirst with his legs spread as nearby bullpen Boston policeman Steve Horgan was throwing up both arms to form a combined "W." It is one of the iconic photos in Boston sports history.

"That pitch was hittable," said David Ortiz. "I know he's not gonna throw me a fastball there. He's got a good split, but that pitch was hittable, and I got a good swing on it."

And was he thinking about tying the game? Nope. "My idea wasn't going to go out there and hit a grand slam," Papi said. "If I were telling you about thinking about hitting a grand slam, I'd be lying to you now."

The Red Six still needed a run to win, and they got it in the 9th. Jonny Gomes had an infield hit to short, and Jose Iglesias made it worse with a throwing error, sending Gomes to second. He moved to third on a wild pitch and scored on a Jarrod Saltalamacchia single to center. He should be hailed in Boston forever. Sadly, for him, all anyone remembers about this game are Big Papi, Torii Hunter, and Steve Horgan.

BILL CHUCK

The final score of this game is no reflection of the dueling of pitchers that had begun in Game 1. The Tigers had won the opener, 1–0. In that game, the Sox did not get their lone hit of the game until one down in the 9th versus five Tigers pitchers. In this game, against Max Scherzer, the Sox did not get their first hit until two down in the 6th, when Shane Victorino singled, and then Dustin Pedroia followed with a run-scoring double to make the score, Detroit 5, Boston 1.

Those were the only two hits Scherzer allowed in 7.0 IP, and after 13 strikeouts and 108 pitches, the Tigers went to their bullpen in the bottom of the 8th with a 5–1 lead. And Bob told you what happened next.

A few flourishes to add:

- In Game 1, David Ortiz was 0–4 with two whiffs, and in this game, before the slam, Papi was 0–2 with a walk and two whiffs.
- The losing pitcher, Rick Porcello, was a Cy Young Award winner in 2016 for the Red Sox.
- Jose Iglesias, who was traded to the Tigers by the Red Sox on July 30, 2013, came into the game for defensive purposes in the 8th, only to make the critical error in the 9th.

- The Tigers' GM was Dave Dombrowski, who became president of baseball operations for the Red Sox in August 2015.

Finally, I would like to draw your attention to the regular season game of July 8, 2014, when the Reds defeated the Cubs, 6–5. It was in the second game of a double-header, and six Cubs pitchers each allowed a run. Now, feel free to look at this game, again 6–5, the only other game in baseball history in which six pitchers each allowed one run and no more than one run.

2013 WORLD SERIES GAME 6 CLINCHER

BOSTON 6 ST. LOUIS 1 | FENWAY PARK, BOSTON, MA
TIME: 3:15 • OCTOBER 30, 2013

BOB RYAN

Last to first. That was the chief subplot as the Red Sox won their third World Series of the 21st century. And it was redemption for winning pitcher John Lackey, who had been a local pariah in 2011, but who walked off the mound in the 7th inning to a thunderous ovation. "I think it's almost fitting that he's on the mound to finish it out tonight," observed Sox manager John Farrell. "I think people have seen the turn-around in him; they've seen the turnaround in us."

With this win, Lackey became the first person to win clinching World Series games for two different teams. He had previously done it as a rookie with the 2002 Angels.

The Series also ended with David Ortiz walking in the 1st and then being laughably waved to first base three subsequent times by Cardinals manager Mike Matheny. And why not? The Cardinals couldn't get him out. No kidding. Big Papi finished the series having reached base 19 times in 25 plate appearances, compiling a surreal 1.948 OPS.

Shane Victorino, one of general manager Ben Cherington's many sage off-season pick-ups, concluded his season with a four RBI night. And speaking of sage acquisitions, the honor of receiving the post-game handshakes was given to closer Koji Uehara, whose 1-2-3 9th, capped by striking out Matt Carpenter, concluded a glorious season in which his 21 saves featured a you-gotta-be-kidding-me 0.565 WHIP.

This was the unforgettable season punctuated by the shocking Patriots Day Marathon bombing, which took place a few blocks from Fenway Park. It turned out to be a record-breaking 108-win campaign, culminated by a romp through the postseason. It may have been the greatest Red Sox season of all. Without doubt, it was the most emotional.

BILL CHUCK

With this win, the Red Sox clinched their first World Series championship at home since 1918 (Bob did not attend the 1918 event). Since the team swept in 2004 and 2007, the Game 4s were in St. Louis and Denver, respectively.

In this game, David Ortiz became the seventh of the seven players who have drawn a record four walks in a World Series game and the fourth to do it in a nine-inning game. He also became the fourth player to get three intentional passes in a game. The first was Boston's Rudy York in 1946, who also did it against the Cardinals. The second should be no surprise: Barry Bonds in 2002. The third really shouldn't be a surprise either: In 2011, Game 5, the Texas Rangers walked the Cardinals' Albert Pujols in their 4–2 win. Papi was the only one to draw four walks and the only one to score twice.

Papi finished with a .688 BA in the six games, the highest average for a six-game Series. Ortiz went 11–16 with a pair of homers and six RBI. He walked eight times and whiffed just once. He scored seven times. He was awesome.

MOOKIE'S FIRST

CHICAGO 16 BOSTON 9 | FENWAY PARK, BOSTON, MA
TIME: 4:19 • JULY 2, 2014

BOB RYAN

Of course, this was the Cubs' night, with 19 hits and 16 runs. Every Cubs' starter had a hit and scored a run and everyone except Anthony Rizzo had an RBI.

Buried therein was a milestone moment for Red Sox rookie Mookie Betts, who followed an A.J. Pierzynski 5th-inning walk with a shot into the Monster Seats for his first career homer. His Pete Rose–like sprint around the bases almost caught the lumbering catcher.

"I don't think I'm a home run hitter," explained Betts, "so any time I hit one I take off sprinting."

BILL CHUCK

This game completed a three-game sweep by the Cubs at Fenway. The Cubs were not a great team, compiling a record of 37–46 following the sweep. The Sox were equally bad at 38–47 (actually one percentage point better than the Cubs). The Sox left 14 on base that night in what proved to be their longest nine-inning game of the season. The *Boston Globe*'s Nick Cafardo led his column the next day, perfectly and succinctly: "Welcome to rock bottom."

A.J. Pierzynski's walk was his ninth of the season in 263 PA. Jackie Bradley Jr., and his .208 BA, was on the bench, perhaps sitting next to Stephen Drew, who was hitting .136. Mookie's 2–5 night boosted his season average to an even .200. His teammate and fellow rookie, Xander Bogaerts, went 0–4 and was hitless in his last 23 AB.

It may have been rock bottom, but Mookie hit his first.

LADDER BALL

BOSTON 5 KC 4 | FENWAY PARK, BOSTON, MA
TIME: 3:31 • JULY 18, 2014

BOB RYAN

Displaying the wisdom of a veteran, Jonny Gomes thought he might pinch-hit, and he thought he might end up facing Kelly Downs. So, when he batted for Jackie Bradley Jr. in the 6th and hit a game-deciding three-run homer off, yup, Kelly Downs, he thought that was just the way things were meant to be.

"That at-bat technically started at two o'clock," he declared.

As Fenway fans know, there is an honest-to-God ladder on the left-field wall, a remnant of the pre-Monster Seat days. Every once in a while, someone will hit a ball off the ladder, which is exactly what Omar Infante did to get himself a double in the 1st inning.

409

An "oops" moment in the 4th: Eric Hosmer was awarded a ground-rule double when the ball girl mistakenly fielded his shot down the right-field line.

BILL CHUCK

"Wrigley Rooftops is a name for the 16 rooftops of residential buildings which have bleachers or seating on them to view baseball games or other major events at Wrigley Field. Since 1914, Wrigley roofs have dotted the neighborhood of Wrigleyville around Wrigley Field, where the Chicago Cubs play Major League Baseball. Venues on Waveland Avenue overlook left field, while those along Sheffield Avenue have a view over right field."

Why, you ask, would I possibly include a Wikipedia quote about Wrigley Field in a game that took place at Fenway Park? Excellent question, but there is a method to my madness, and it has to do with Red Sox owner John I. Taylor.

Taylor was the Sox owner in 1910, and he wanted to build a new ballpark for his team since the Huntington Avenue Grounds was becoming increasingly unplayable. Looking around Boston, Taylor chose Boston's Fenway neighborhood for the new location of his team. In building the new facility, Taylor was more prescient than the group that built Weeghman Park, Wrigley's original name, in that he saw that there were a few buildings on Lansdowne Street that were tall enough to allow fans to watch a game from their window or rooftop.

The solution was a 25-foot-high wooden fence from just beyond the left-field foul pole to the center-field flagpole to keep curious eyes from seeing the game for free. Hence, the birth of the Green Monster. Well, sort of. A fire destroyed the park in January 1934, and when the park opened anew in April, The Wall as we know it became part of the firmament.

It was around this time that a 23-foot-tall net was added above and beyond the top of the 37-foot wall. There are two theories as to why the net was installed: 1) to keep home runs from damaging businesses on Lansdowne, and 2) so that the balls could be re-used. The likelihood is that both reasons are true. No matter what you believe, the baseballs that landed in the nets ultimately had to be retrieved. Consequently, a metal ladder to the top was attached to the wall. And when the nets came down in 2003 and were replaced by seats, Sox owner John Henry was savvy enough to keep the ladder, and occasionally a fan is lucky enough to attend a game where a ball takes a weird carom after hitting the ladder. And that lucky fan (drumroll please) was Bob Ryan.

Fenway Park ground rule:
Fair ball striking the ladder below the top of the left-field wall and bounding out of the park: two bases.

Fenway Park ground-rule urban myth:
Fair ball striking the ladder below the top of left-field wall and becoming embedded: three bases.

Sorry folks, it's just not true. For a while, credible sources made the claim that a ball striking the ladder or becoming embedded behind the ladder was officially a ground-rule triple. It's a double or in play, and the batter and the outfielder must do their best.

JETER'S FAREWELL

NEW YORK 9 BOSTON 5 | FENWAY PARK, BOSTON, MA
TIME: 3:14 • SEPTEMBER 28, 2014

BOB RYAN

Ted Williams had a hit in his last career at-bat. Fifty-four years to the day later, in the same ballpark, fellow Hall of Famer Derek Jeter also had a hit in his last career at-bat.

Okay, The Thumper's was a homer. Jeter's was somewhat less dramatic, but still appropriately Jeter-like. With a man on third in the 3rd inning and less than two out, he got the professional job done, knocking in the run with a little chopper off home plate. Hey, it was hit number 3,465 and it looks like a line drive in the metaphorical box score, right? He was removed for pinch runner Brian McCann, and he was done.

"I knew that was my last at-bat," he said. "I was just trying to get a hit. I gave everything I had physically and everything I had mentally. Now it's time to step back."

It wasn't exactly a pretty season-ender for the Sox, who put out a lineup including just Daniel Nava from the one seen in the home opener and who fanned 15 times against four Yankee hurlers.

One improvement: Ted Williams' last game was played on a gloomy, dank September weekday afternoon. Jeter's last game was played on a gorgeous 80-degree Sunday afternoon.

BILL CHUCK

You may have heard of this Jeter kid. He played 20 seasons, all for the Yankees, and then six years after that he was inducted into the Hall of Fame.

He became a Yankee in 1995 and retired in 2014. Amidst that, from 1995 to 2007, Jeter and the Yankees went to the postseason every season and won the World Series four times. Jeter and the boys won a fifth together in 2009.

In his last game at Yankee Stadium, on September 25, in Jeter's last at-bat, in the 9th inning, Derek Jeter singled home the winning run, enabling the Yankees to beat Baltimore, 6–5.

Now many people forget that when Teddy Ballgame homered in that last at-bat at Fenway Park on September 28, 1960, against the Orioles (if you want some more symmetry) it *did not have to be his last game*. After the Sox won that game, 5–4, on a walk-off error, there were three more Sox games to be played. And, if you want another dose of symmetry, they were against the Yankees in New York. It was only after that game that Boston manager Mike Higgins announced that Ted would not go to New York with the club for the final three games. Ted wanted to bow out on top. One final bit of Ted symmetry (simply because I can't help myself): in this final season, in which he turned 42 on August 30, in Ted's first at-bat of the season, he homered as well. Impressive bookends if you ask me.

But the Yankee captain wanted to play until the end and so he joined his teammates and headed to Fenway Park. He took Friday night off and returned to action on Saturday as the DH and struck out in his first time up, hitting a weak infield single his second and last time up. Now Jeter could have called it a career right then. I mean, after all, a weak single and a line-drive single look the same in the box score. But Jeter came back on Sunday, for his team's final game of the season and the final game of his career. Both Bob and I were there (nowhere near each other) scoring that game.

In his first AB against Clay Buchholz, Jeter lined to short. Okay, he got his barrel, so this day was fine already. In the top of the 3rd, Ichiro (speaking of Hall of Famers) hit a one-out, two-run triple and that brought up Derek Jeter. And the great Fenway fans cheered mightily and gave him a standing ovation as he approached the plate. The Red Sox wanted to use the late Bob Sheppard's introduction of Jeter as an homage to both Jeter and the Voice of God, but Jeter said please don't, Fenway was the last place he wanted to hear the Yankee Stadium pronouncement of his name.

The infield was in against Jeter. He took a called strike on his first pitch, as the Yankees all stood anxiously at the dugout railing. No one knew when Jeter's final at-bat would be; manager Joe Girardi said they would take it at-bat by at-bat. The second pitch was just outside. The count was now 1–1. Jeter fouled off the next pitch as Dustin Pedroia and David Ortiz stood side by side watching from the Sox dugout. It was now 1–2 and Jeter chopped the ball towards third, and as high as Boston's third sacker Garin Cecchini could leap, the ball still bounced off his outstretched bare hand for a base hit. Jeter's 149th hit of the season, his 3,465th of his career. It was his 50th RBI of the season, the 1,311th of his career. Cut to Derek's parents lovingly watching from the stands as their son safely reached first base.

And then we saw a true baseball rarity. You won't see it in Bob's scorebook or in any box score. As Jeter walked backed to first, Girardi looked toward Jeter with palms upraised asking what Derek wanted to do. And then Girardi checked the answer by slicing his hand under his chin and when he got the nod, he called for a pinch-runner. Fans standing, players standing, Jeter was given hugs by everyone he came near, including opposing pitcher Clay Buchholz, as he ran across the diamond. The Sox dugout was standing and clapping, and the Yankees dugout was doing the same as they waited to greet their captain. Every player, every coach said some words to Jeter and hugged him. Fenway broke out into a rhythmic shout of "Der-ek Jet-er" warmly imitating their colleagues in New York. Time stood still as love poured out through signs, cheers, and salutes. And then, Derek took his helmet off and waved his appreciation to the fans.

For Jeter it was always about winning, excellence, and the fans. In Jeter's Hall of Fame induction speech, he was greeted by the fans, still limited in their attendance by the pandemic, break into the chant of "Der-ek Jet-er" as he approached the podium. "I forgot how good that feels," Jeter said.

Derek ended his speech by telling the generation ahead of him and reminding us all, "The one common thread with all of us on this stage, is we understand there's no one individual bigger than the game. The game goes on because of the great fans we have. So, take care of it, protect it, respect it, and don't take the time you have playing the game for granted. It's more than just a game."

MOOKIE'S SPECTACULAR OPENER

BOSTON 9 WASHINGTON 4 | FENWAY PARK, BOSTON, MA
TIME: 3:01 • APRIL 13, 2015

BOB RYAN

Tom Brady took a few pregame batting cage cuts against Pedro Martinez and then threw out the first pitch. He settled back with the other 37,202 in attendance for the Red Sox home opener, unaware of the amazing show he was about to see.

How's this? A homer, a single, a walk, two stolen bases and a spectacular homer-saving catch. That was Mookie Betts *in the first three innings!* And the stolen bases were bang-bang. Mookie stole second with the Nats in a shift, realized third base was unoccupied, and kept right on going for stolen base number two.

Rick Porcello was the winner in his Boston home debut, but the only name on peoples' lips afterward was Mookie's. "It's the Mookie show," proclaimed Hanley Ramirez.

"It's a no-doubter he's going to be a superstar," one-upped Big Papi.

BILL CHUCK

Mookie finished the 2014 season hitting .291 in 52 games. Mookie finished the 2015 season hitting .291 in 145 games. By the end of 2021, in 971 games, Mookie was a .296 hitter. This was his first home opener, having joined the Sox in June of 2014. As Nick Cafardo wrote the next day in the *Boston Globe*, "Nobody ever would have expected the name Mookie would be popular in Boston one day. Not after Mookie Wilson dribbled that ball through Bill Buckner's legs in Game 6 of the 1986 World Series. But maybe the Baseball Gods have a way of evening things up."

There have only been 17 games in baseball history that a leadoff batter has homered, driven in at least four, and stolen at least two bases. No other Red Sox leadoff batter has ever had a game like that. Interestingly, Davey Lopes in 1983 had a similar game leading off for the Dodgers in the Opening Game of their season.

The best robs the best

That spectacular homer-saving grab in the 1st inning by Betts was a ball hit off the bat of Bryce Harper.

(ANOTHER) MOOKIE 3-HR GAME

BOSTON 16 ARIZONA 2 | FENWAY PARK, BOSTON, MA
TIME: 2:49 • AUGUST 14, 2016

BOB RYAN

Mookie Betts made outs his last two times up. But that was okay, since in his first four at-bats he had hit three homers and a single while driving in eight runs and scoring four.

It was part of a 19-hit bombardment that began with a severe trouncing of Zack Greinke, who couldn't get out of the second. The *Globe*'s Nick Cafardo wrote, "The right-hander allowed 10 hits and nine runs and threw 43 of the worst pitches of his career."

Leadoff man Dustin Pedroia checked in with a 6–3–5–2 line. Former leadoff man Mookie liked his new spot in the order. "There are more RBI opportunities," he reasoned. "Dustin gets on base so much. It's fun being able to drive him in."

x

x

The happy beneficiary of this offense was starter Rick Porcello, who was cruising to his 16th win in what would be a Cy Young Award season.

BILL CHUCK

In the words of the *Boston Globe*'s Dan Shaughnessy, "Boston batters put a Western Kentucky area code (270) on the Monster's manually operated scoreboard in the first three innings."

Mookie hit three homers for the second time in his career and Dustin Pedroia had five hits for the fifth and final time in his career. The five five-hit days are the most in Red Sox history.

Rick Porcello advanced to 16–3 and finished 22–4 on the year as he edged out Justin Verlander for the Cy Young Award despite Porcello's 4.7 WAR compared to Verlander's 7.4.

And David Ortiz continued his farewell tour.

BIG PAPI'S BIG FINALE

TORONTO 2 BOSTON 1
FENWAY PARK (BY THE DAVID ORTIZ BRIDGE) BOSTON, MA
TIME: 3:14 • OCTOBER 2, 2016

BOB RYAN

The day was all about the pregame.

This was the culmination of a season-long Farewell Tour for David Ortiz. It would have been nice to go out with a Ted Williams–like bang, but this wasn't Big Papi's day: 0-for-4, two Ks, a fly to center, and a final dribbler in front of the plate.

There was a lengthy pregame ceremony attended by all sorts of people, including many ex-teammates. "I saw some of my teammates that I didn't even remember I played with," he said. "It took me a minute. I was like, 'Wow!'"

Papi was blown away by the news that a bridge on adjacent Brookline Avenue would be named after him. Mary J. Blige was imported to sing the anthem.

It was more than I expected," he said. "It was something I'll never forget."

BILL CHUCK

David Ortiz played 14 seasons with the Boston Red Sox, from 2003 to 2016.

- During that time, Big Papi hit .290, with an OBP of .386, and a slugging pct. of .570, resulting in an OPS of .956.
- He hit 483 homers, second during that time to Albert Pujols' 520.
- He had 1,530 RBI, third during that time Pujols' 1,560 and Miguel Cabrera's 1,553.
- He slammed 524 doubles, leading the league in his final season with 48. He led the majors in doubles during that period, one more than Cabrera.
- He had 2,079 hits, eighth during that period.
- He had 1,133 walks, second to Adam Dunn's 1,151.
- He struck out 1,411 times, the 12th most of any batter during that stretch.
- His 4,084 total bases from 2003 to 2016 ranked third behind Pujols (4,541) and Cabrera (4,414).
- He scored 1,204 times, fourth during that time.
- He only appeared in the field in 146 games as a first baseman, the rest of his games were as a DH.
- The Red Sox retired Ortiz's uniform number, 34, on June 23, 2017.

TWO-OUT DAMAGE

BOSTON 8 TAMPA BAY 7 | FENWAY PARK, BOSTON, MA
TIME: 3:50 • APRIL 8, 2018

BOB RYAN

It was the first of many memorable nights in a magical season, a reward for 31,974 fans shivering on a 38-degree afternoon. Trailing 7–2 in the 8th with two outs and no runs in, the Red Sox came up with six two-out runs to win the game. Three of their seven hits were with two strikes.

A somewhat panicked Tampa Bay skipper Kevin Cash went to closer Alex Colome, and that was fine with Alex Cora. "We pushed him to bring him in early," Cora said. "After that, it was good at-bat after good at-bat. It was fun to watch."

Highlighting the outburst was a wall-job RBI double by the slow-starting Mitch Moreland, a hit that made it 7–3. It was his first hit of the young season.

It takes 27 outs to beat us," reminded Cora.

BILL CHUCK

The Rays were nine games into the season and 1–8 after this loss. Alex Colome already had two blown saves, and he took his first loss in this game. By the end of May, the Rays dealt him and Denard Span to Minnesota for two players who never played a game for them.

Despite this start, Kevin Cash and the Rays finished the season 90–72, in third place in the AL East. Tribute to this great organization who understands this game (and business) as well as any. I'm sure they used Colome's $5.3 million salary savings to their advantage.

WALK-OFF GRANNY

BOSTON 6 TORONTO 2 | FENWAY PARK, BOSTON, MA
TIME: 3:32 • JULY 14, 2018

BOB RYAN

I guess you could call it overkill when all you need is a fairly routine fly ball, and you wind up with a 10th inning walk-off grand slam. But Xander Bogaerts was happy to take it.

The bases were loaded with one out in a 2–2 game when Bogaerts stepped in against Chris Rowley. "I hit it real good, but I didn't expect it to go out," Bogaerts explained. "But I knew I hit it good, and I knew it was at least a sacrifice fly, and we would win it."

Brock Holt was on second base. "As soon as he hit it, it was like, 'We won the game,'" he said.

Until the game-winning blast to dead center, the key moment in the game had come in the 6th, when starter Eduardo Rodriguez, sailing along nicely, had to leave the game following a bizarre collision at first base with Toronto's second baseman Lourdes Gurriel Jr.

Bill CHUCK

I have to admit, I love walk-off homers and have a fondness for grand slams. I particularly like these events when there are outs already recorded. In 2018, there were nine walk-off grand slams. Four were hit with one out and five were hit with two outs. But rather than give you all the broad facts of these homers, I will rank them in order from the least exciting to the one that got my heart racing.

9. On September 14, 2018, the Royals' Salvador Perez slammed the Twins, with one out in the bottom of the 9th and the score tied, 4–4.

8. On July 14, 2018, we have Bob's game in which the Red Sox' Xander Bogaerts slammed the Blue Jays, with one out in the bottom of the 10th. This is up a slot because it was in extra innings, and the score was tied, 2–2.

7. The very next day, on July 15, 2018, the Twins' Brian Dozier slammed the Rays, with one out in the bottom of the 10th, and the score tied, 7–7. These first three homers are what I call "Men at Work Slams." If you haven't figured out why, Bob gave you a clue; the answer will be at the bottom.

6. On September 16, 2018, the Padres' Francisco Mejia slammed the Rangers, with two out in the bottom of the 9th and the score tied, 3–3. Note this one was a two-out blast

5. On July 6, 2018, the Mets' Jose Bautista slammed the Rays, with two out in the bottom of the 9th, and the score tied, 1–1. I gave the edge to this homer because it broke up a pitcher's duel.

4. On September 19, 2018, Cleveland's Jason Kipnis slammed the White Sox, with one out in the bottom of the 9th and his team *trailing*, 1–0.

3. On June 6, 2018, the Cubs' Jason Heyward slammed the Phillies, with *two out* in the bottom of the 9th and his team *trailing by two*, 5–3.

2. On July 22, 2018, the Rays' Daniel Robertson slammed the Marlins, with *two out* in the bottom of the 9th and his team *trailing by two*,

4–2. This gets the number two slot because the Rays scored five times in the bottom of the 9th to win 6–4.

1. THE ULTIMATE GRAND SLAM: That's what it's called when a player hits a grand slam when his team is trailing by three runs in the bottom of the 9th to win the game. And that's what David Bote of the Cubs did on August 12, 2018, against Ryan Madson of the Nationals.

The score was 3–0 Nationals when Bote came up to pinch-hit for Justin Wilson. Cole Hamels had started this game for the Cubs and was brilliant, allowing one run on one hit and one walk and striking out nine in 7.0 innings. Max Scherzer was slightly more brilliant, even though he allowed three hits in his seven shutout innings while striking out 11.

Madson entered the 9th looking for the save, up by three. Ben Zobrist led off grounding out to first. Jason Heyward singled. Albert Almora then is hit by a pitch. With a chance to tie the game, Kyle Schwarber hits a foul pop to third. With a chance to tie the game on a 2–2 pitch, Willson Contreras gets hit by a pitch to load the bases.

Up steps Bote, and on another 2–2 pitch, with the fans standing and screaming, Bote hits a blast to dead-center field. Like a rocket, it lands on the batter's eye in the Wrigley bleachers, and like an airplane, Bote circles the bases.

There have only been 31 ultimate grand slams in baseball history, the most recent, Dan Vogelbach's blast on September 5, 2021, against the Cardinals. The first one was hit by Roger Connor in 1881. The first one in the modern era was hit by Babe Ruth in 1925. The coolest one was hit by Roberto Clemente because his was an inside-the-park ultimate grand slam. Thirty-one slams by 31 different batters, eight by pinch-hitters, and three in extra innings.

Now wasn't that fun?

One more thing…

In 1983, Colin Hay and his Australian mates had an international hit with the song "Overkill." The group's name was "Men at Work."

CHRIS DAVIS NOW 0–54

BOSTON 6 BALTIMORE 4 | FENWAY PARK, BOSTON, MA
TIME: 2:55 • APRIL 12, 2019

BOB RYAN

Baltimore's Chris Davis pinch-hit in the 9th. He hit a soft liner to second. So what?

Well, it meant that a man who had once hit 53 homers had now gone 54 at-bats into the 2019 season without a hit.

The big plus for Boston was the pitching of Eduardo Rodriguez, who had induced 21 swing-and-misses during his 6.2 innings of work. The breakdown: 10 fastballs, 10 change-tips, and one cutter.

0–54. Wow.

BILL CHUCK

This was the 14th game of the season, and at its completion, each team was an unimpressive 5–9. Yet even 5–9 seems impressive compared to the performance of Chris Davis.

The Davis travails (note-to-self: "The Davis Travails" great movie title) began during September of the 2018 season, which I feel obliged to recount.

- From September 8 to September 12, Davis went hitless in four games, going 0–15.
- September 13, the O's won as Davis sat.
- On September 14, in the bottom of the 2nd, Davis doubled off James Shields of the White Sox.
- Davis went 0–3 in his next three at-bats.
- From September 15 to September 22 (Davis' season-ending game), he went hitless in five games, going 0–18.
- So, Davis ended 2018 going 0–21 and 1–37.
- He ended the season hitting .168, dropping his career batting average to .238.

Let's bring you up to date on his seasons:
- Following the 2013 season, when he finished third in the AL MVP voting, Davis had a .266 lifetime BA after hitting .286 with 53 homers. That season, he struck out 199 times.
- In 2014, he played in only 127 games and hit .196, a foreshadowing of the years to come.
- In 2015, he was back on top of the home run leaderboard with 47 in 160 games. He hit .262 but struck out a league-leading 208 times.
- In 2016, his batting average dropped 41 points to .221. He hit 38 homers but struck out 219 times to lead everyone. He had become the all-or-nothing poster child.
- The decline got worse in 2017, as his average dropped to .215. In 128 games, he hit 26 homers but struck out 195 times.
- We are now back to 2018, when, once again, he played in 128 games, and his average dropped another 43 points from the prior year, and his home run total was now down to 16. He still managed to strike out 192 times.

2019

- The 2019 season began with Davis carrying a 0–21 burden.
- In his first four games, he went 0–3 in each. He was now 0–33.
- 0–2, 0–3, 0–2 brought him to 0–40 through seven games.
- He was no longer an automatic in the Orioles' lineup, but he was still an automatic out. He went 0–4, 0–5, and on April 10, he went 0–1, and he was now 0-for-the-2019 season, 0–29 at the plate, and 0–50 going back to last season.
- On April 9, he had set the major league record with his 0–5, which had brought him to 0–49.
- On April 10, his pinch-hit flyout made it 57 plate appearances without a hit, tying him with Tony Bernazard, who suffered through his own hell for Cleveland in 1984.
- Each day, Davis was out early taking extra batting practice, only proving that sometimes practice makes perfectly awful.
- On April 11, Davis went 0–3 with a walk. He was at 53 at-bats and 61 plate appearances without a hit. He was 0–32 in 2019. Davis also set the record for most consecutive hitless at-bats at home, topping Eugenio Velez, who ended his MLB career in 2010–11 by going 0-for-46 playing for the Giants and the Dodgers at home. Davis was a broken record, breaking records.
- In that April 11 game, the homophonic A's DH, Kris Davis, for the second straight day, hit two homers and had nine on the season.
- On April 12, Davis lined into the shift with two down in the 9th, right into the waiting glove of Eduardo Nunez.

(Cue the music: "Tomorrow" show tune from the musical *Annie*, with music by Charles Strouse and lyrics by Martin Charnin, published in 1977.)

A Khris Davis moment

- In 2015, Khris Davis hit .247.
- In 2016, Khris Davis hit .247.
- In 2017, Khris Davis hit .247.
- In 2018, Khris Davis hit .247.

A Chris Davis/Khris Davis moment

- From July 29, 2015, to July 27, 2016—Chris Davis had 143 hits, 45 homers, and 111 RBI.
- From July 29, 2015, to July 27, 2016—Khris Davis had 143 hits, 45 homers, and 111 RBI.
- From 2012 to 2015, Chris Davis led the majors with 159 homers.
- From 2016 to 2019, Khris Davis hit 156 homers and led the majors for a good portion of that time.

COLORADO WHIFFS 24 TIMES

COLORADO 5 BOSTON 4 (11 INNINGS)
FENWAY PARK, BOSTON, MA
TIME: 3:42 • MAY 14, 2019

BOB RYAN

A gaudy K total doesn't mean necessarily mean you're going to win. A messy day whiffing—in this case, 24 times—doesn't necessarily mean you're going to lose. This game is Exhibit A of both premises.

Chris Sale fanned a career-high 17 while walking nobody in 7.0 innings. He got a no-decision. Brandon Workman and Matt Barnes tacked on seven more Ks. Didn't matter. The Rockies fashioned a run off Ryan Brasier in the 11th to win the game.

The Rockies had hung in there thanks to a pair of two-run homers. Nolan Arenado hit one off Sale in the 7th, and Charlie Blackmon hit one off Brandon Workman in the 8th. The first three Red Sox runs had come on solo homers by Michael Chavis, J.D. Martinez, and Rafael Devers. It was a bracing 42 degrees at game time, and the fans were forced to shiver for three hours and 42 minutes.

Alex Cora had sympathy for his starter. "It sucks because of the way he pitched, but it is what it is," he said.

BILL CHUCK

Eleven different Rockies came to the plate in the game, and 11 different Rockies struck out at least once. Five different Rockies struck out three times apiece. Perhaps the funniest thing is that the only golden sombrero was recorded by Boston's leadoff batter, Andrew Benintendi, who went 0–6. Mookie Betts was hitting second and went 0–5.

There have only been eight occasions in big-league history when a pitcher has struck out at least 17 batters and come away with a no-decision. Not surprisingly, Randy Johnson and Nolan Ryan each have two of the games. The other three were by Vida Blue, Chris Short, and Jack Coombs. No pitcher had this strange honor by pitching fewer innings than 7.0 pitched by Sale in this contest.

I love Sale's final inning (the 7th) because it just shows his focus in this game. Trevor Story led off the 7th with a single, and Nolan Arenado followed with a homer. Nothing to be ashamed of allowing hits and runs to those great hitters. Sale rebounded by striking out the next three batters to end his workday and left the game winning 3–2.

This represented Chris Sale's career-high for most strikeouts in a game. Sale has had 10 games with at least 14 strikeouts; his record in those games is a rather pedestrian four wins, two losses, and four no-decisions. I guess it indeed is what it is.

MOOKIE BACK-TO-BACK TRIPLES

TORONTO 13 BOSTON 7 | FENWAY PARK, BOSTON, MA
TIME: 3:43 • JULY 13, 2018

BOB RYAN

In case anyone was asking, "What can Mookie do next?" Mr. Betts provided an answer when he tripled and scored in the 1st and tripled and scored in the 2nd.

Yup, back-to-back triples. It's too bad it happened to take place in a game in which Rick Porcello just didn't have it (eight runs in two innings-plus), and the Red Sox had a 10-game winning streak snapped.

But Mookie had given the crowd of 37,018 something to cling to.

BILL CHUCK

Nobody has ever hit three triples in a game at Fenway Park. Since the Titanic has sunk, there have been only 74 occasions in which a player has hit two triples in a game at Fenway. Harry Hooper had four games with two triples, but the last one was over 100 years ago, and you get the sense that the ball and everything were different in those days.

There are eight players with two two-triple games. Amongst visitors to the Fens, Amos Strunk hit his two for Philadelphia when Babe Ruth was still with the Sox. Jerry Priddy did it once in 1946 when he played for the Senators and once in 1952 when he played for the Tigers.

Carl Reynolds played for the Sox in 1934, and he did it twice that season. Dom DiMaggio, "the Little Professor," did it twice for the Sox in 1950. Just to let you know, Joe DiMaggio had three career games with two triples and one game with three triples, none at Fenway, but that's pretty cool.

George "Boomer" Scott" had two triples in two games at Fenway. The Babe had a two-triple game at Fenway, so did Jim Ed Rice and David Ortiz. Three guys who probably needed oxygen upon their arrival at third.

The Red Sox only hit two 1st inning triples in 2018 (Betts and Xander Bogaerts) and four 2nd inning triples (Betts hit two and J.D. Martinez and Andrew Benintendi each hit one).

One more thing...

On Mookie's second triple, the ball hit very close to the line in center field, which indicates a homer. The Sox appealed, but the call of a triple on the field was upheld, and Bob and I had something to write about.

(YET ANOTHER) MOOKIE 3 HR GAME

BOSTON 10 NEW YORK 5 | FENWAY PARK, BOSTON, MA
TIME: 3:16 • JULY 26, 2019

BOB RYAN

Mookie Betts was in control from his first plate appearance when he hit James Paxton's eighth pitch out for a home run. He hit another home run in the 3rd off Paxton and, yes one more off Paxton in the 4th. It was his fifth career three-homer game.

"He was working the count and using the strike zone to his advantage," analyzed Alex Cora. "From there he just took off."

Mookie added a double off David Hale in the 6th. For those of you scoring at home, that's 14 total bases.

The winning pitcher was newly acquired Andrew Cashner, who went 6.2 innings while allowing 10 hits and striking out six in only his

435

second Red Sox Fenway start. "It was awesome," he said. "The fans are locked in on every pitch."

BILL CHUCK

We recognize a future Hall of Famer, and Bob pretty much was there at Mookie Betts' beginnings.

At the time of this writing (following the 2021 season), Mookie Betts had six three-homer games, five for Boston and one for the Dodgers, for whom I suspect there will be more to come (perhaps when you are reading this, they have landed already).

Betts is one of those players who can do it all, as exhibited by his five All-Star appearances (through 2021). He is an outstanding fielder as exhibited through his five Gold Gloves (midway through 2021). He owns a batting title. He has been an MVP. He is a great baserunner. His .346 batting average in 2018 was the second-best ever by a player in a 30/30 season, topped only by Hall of Famer Larry Walker's .366 for the Rockies in 1997. He is a two-time World Series champion. And he is a great bowler competing in a number of PBA events and bowling a perfect 300 game in the World Series of Bowling.

Mookie Betts is indeed one of the greats in the game and we have loved watching him play.

BILL CHUCK ON THE 2010s

Teams W-L records 2010–2019

Team	W	L	W-L%
Yankees	921	699	.569
Dodgers	919	701	.567
Cardinals	899	721	.555
Nationals	879	740	.543
Red Sox	872	748	.538
Rays	860	761	.531
Cleveland	855	763	.528
Braves	843	776	.521
Rangers	843	778	.520
A's	839	781	.518
Brewers	824	797	.508
Angels	822	798	.507
Giants	821	799	.507
Cubs	817	803	.504
Blue Jays	794	826	.490
Diamondbacks	793	827	.490
Mets	793	827	.490
Pirates	792	826	.489
Astros	789	831	.487
Phillies	787	833	.486
Tigers	782	835	.484
Reds	775	845	.478
Twins	765	855	.472
F Marlins	152	172	.469
Mariners	758	862	.468
Royals	758	862	.468

Orioles	755	865	.466
Rockies	752	869	.464
White Sox	743	876	.459
Padres	739	881	.456
M Marlins	555	739	.429

Teams Postseason W-L records 2010–2019

Team	W	L	
ARI	3	6	
ATL	5	13	
BAL	6	8	
BOS	23	14	
CHC	19	18	
CIN	2	7	
CLE	12	12	
COL	1	4	
DET	17	21	
HOU	28	22	
KCR	22	9	(.710, best record in the majors)
LAA	0	3	
LAD	33	33	
MIL	11	11	
MIN	0	7	
NYM	8	7	
NYY	24	27	
OAK	4	9	
PHI	7	7	
PIT	3	5	
SFG	36	17	
STL	1	3	
STL	35	35	
TBR	8	12	
TEX	20	22	
TOR	10	10	
WSN	19	17	

And a last one for the road…

OUT OF POSITION

BOSTON 11 CHICAGO 4 | FENWAY PARK, BOSTON, MA
TIME: 3:15 • APRIL 19, 2021

BOB RYAN

The Red Sox didn't seem to mind the traditional Patriots Day 11:00 AM start. Kiké Hernandez began with a leadoff homer, and the next five men in the order followed with base hits, each coming around to score. Number nine man Bobby Dalbec worked his way to a 14-pitch base on balls against Lucas Giolito before their inning ended.

ChiSox skipper Tony La Russa waved the white flag in the 7th by turning to a pair of position players to pitch. DH Yermin Mercedes gave up a run on three hits and a pair of walks, but infielder Danny Mendick, who had some pitching experience, gained bragging rights with Franchy Cordero by fanning him on a 61-mph curveball before embarrassing Hernandez with a 39 mph eephus pitch that resulted in an inning-ending 6-4 force-out.

BILL CHUCK

For me, the only thing that is important about this game is that Bob was in the ballpark in scoring position.

It was 2021, and there were only 4,738 in attendance, including Bob.

Fenway was not always a magnet for fans. I looked for a game that had about the same attendance as Bob's game, and it didn't take a long time to find a 10-inning walk-off win as the Sox defeated the Washington Senators on August 24, 1961. Yaz, hitting all of .254, was in that Boston lineup, along with Pumpsie Green (first Black player for the Sox), Pete Runnels (the defending AL batting champion), and a whole lot of players whose baseball cards' value was that they could be used for flipping and pitching. So, while the baseball world was watching Mantle (46 homers) and Maris (50 homers), nobody really gave a damn about watching two teams with a combined record of 110–143.

But 2021 was different. The fans who survived the COVID-19 pandemic and were smart enough to get the vaccine were now allowed back in the ballpark.

And Bob was one of them.

And there was this…

In the long history of the White Sox, only five times have there been a game in which they used two position players on the mound. And it's really fewer than that.

- On June 11, 1901: Zaza Harvey started against the Senators. Zaza, in 1901, played 12 games in the outfield and pitched 16 times. He was followed on the mound by Jimmy Callahan, who was on the mound that season 27 times and in the field eight times. I don't regard them as pure positional players, so I'm eliminating that game.
- On July 24, 1901: Callahan started and moved to 7-0, and Harvey relieved as the Sox defeated the Senators. Same status as the other game—doesn't count.
- On September 28, 1902, Frank Isbell started for the White Sox and then moved behind the plate and was relieved by his catcher, Sam

Mertes, who went 7.2 IP and picked up the win against the Browns. It was Isbell's only pitching appearance of the season, although he did make 13 appearances, including nine starts, in 1898. As for Mertes, it was the only mound visit of his career. This definitely feels like it is out of the Tampa Bay Rays playbook.

- On September 15, 2015, the Sox lost to Oakland, 17–6. Infielder Leury Garcia made his second MLB pitching appearance, and infielder Alexei Ramirez made his first and only.
- And on April 19, 2021, there were Yermin Mercedes, Danny Mendick, and, of course, Bob Ryan there to see it and, as always, record the moment, in scoring position.

ACKNOWLEDGMENTS

This book was Bill Chuck's. We were chatting on the phone in an early-COVID afternoon when the subject of my scorebooks came up. He said he thought there was a book in them, and I should run the idea by people. I did, and I got a positive response. I then contacted my agent, Andrew Blauner, who was likewise enthused, and he went to work. This led us to Triumph and Jesse Jordan, who has been on our wavelength from the start.

My love of baseball came from my father Bill Ryan. I can also thank my hometown of Trenton, N.J., which was a vibrant baseball town while I was growing up in the 1950s. A succession of *Boston Globe* sports editors indulged my passion for the game. So, a hearty thanks to the late Ernie Roberts, as well as Dave Smith, Vince Doria, Don Skwar, and Joe Sullivan.

And how many writers are fortunate enough to have a wife who thinks it's a lovely idea to spend a week or two traveling to see baseball games, including such vacation hot spots as Batavia, New York, Peoria, Illinois, and Appleton, Wisconsin? That would be the great Elaine Ryan. (But then again, we have been to Paris 20 times).

—Bob Ryan

My thanks begin and end with my wonderful wife, Max, without whom this book does not happen. Each day, Max and Casey and I would walk and talk about the book. She not only supported and encouraged me, but she guided me through the process, read chapters, and showed me why she was both a great and beloved developmental editor for so many years.

Speaking of editors, my thanks and gratitude to Jesse Jordan at Triumph Books. He shepherded us through this book, and his support and encouragement throughout were invaluable. Thank you to the team at Triumph; it is an honor to work with you. Thanks to our "scan man" Adam Senott, without whom, you would not get to see Bob's scorecards. And thanks to our agent Andrew Blauner, whom I promise to give more work.

Every baseball book, every baseball podcast, every baseball article, broadcast, and telecast should thank the team at Baseball-Reference.com. Sean Foreman has created the second-best website ever, trailing only Google. I look forward to Sean being honored at Cooperstown.

Long before Cooperstown officially brought you in, Jayson Stark, you have been in my personal Hall of Fame. It is an honor to know you and a thrill to have you join us. Thank you, Jayson.

Thank you, Todd Radom. Fortunately, we *do* judge books by their cover, and you are both a great designer and an excellent source of baseball knowledge. I know of you because of Buster Olney, a great baseball writer and my daily must-listen-to podcaster.

In my research for this book, I repeatedly was proud to be a SABR and a Hall of Fame member, reading bios of some of the players mentioned was of great assistance. Likewise, *The Boston Globe* has had some of the greatest baseball writers in their pages. It is no coincidence that Red Sox Nation is filled with savvy fans. Using the invaluable Newspapers.com treasure trove, I was able to read accounts of games and players written by Ray Fitzgerald, Gordon Edes, Larry Whiteside, Leigh Montville, Peter Gammons (G.O.A.T), our buddy, Dan Shaughnessy, and the wonderful Nick Cafardo, who made all these relationships possible for me. I wish he were here to enjoy this book. But there were so many more baseball reporters who educated me through their writing in publications like *The New York Daily News, Lowell Sun, Sports Illustrated, The Brooklyn Eagle,* Baseball-Almanac.com, retrosheet.com, *Chicago Tribune,* MLB.com, *Arizona Republic, Los Angeles Times, San Francisco Examiner, Montreal Gazette, USA Today* (Bob Nightengale), *Seattle Times,* and Buster

Olney (of the *Baltimore Sun* and *New York Times*), Ken Rosenthal (of the *Baltimore Sun*), and Jayson Stark (of the *Philadelphia Inquirer*). Thank you, Rafe Anderson, TruMedia means true friendship. Thank you to all those incredibly talented people.

While I'm at it…

My Playground 10 gang, including Peter Meisel (who read some drafts), Mitch Orfuss, and Mark Bittman, who have been there for me for close to 60 years, not just talking baseball but providing me with their love and support. Their humor has been life-sustaining. Speaking of which, my current wonderful neighbors in Sleepy Hollow kept me alive (Heidi, Brendon, and so many others) when I had COVID. Thanking Mitch and Marc (et al) and the doggies at the Dog Park, who are always there for me, and Casey (who is always there for me). And thanks to my neighborhood baseball buddy Scott Kaplan who is no rube when it comes to baseball knowledge.

My Boston Baseball Gang of Alex Bok, John McSheffrey, and Steve Markos are loving friends who are extraordinary baseball fans. Their feedback and encouragement were essential to my wanting to write quality material.

Thank you to my dad, Henry Chuck, and my father-in-law, Jack Effenson. They both loved baseball and shared old baseball stories that molded my thinking about the game. They would have loved this book and loved my writing partner.

Thank you, Max and Ebie and Jen, you are so loving and so talented and so wonderful.

It has frequently been said how painful and agonizing it is to write a book. I beg to differ. Working with Bob Ryan is such a great joy. I'm so appreciative to him for letting me share his baseball experiences and write his baseball memoir with him. He is genuinely one of the great sportswriters of our time, and I want to be judged by the company I keep.

—Bill Chuck